CUB1163427

For the Love *of* My Sister

Paula Gallant's Legacy

Lynn Gallant Blackburn

For the Love of My Sister
Copyright © 2024 by Lynn Gallant Blackburn & Cora Cole

All rights reserved. No part of this publication may be reproduced, distributed, or transmitted in any form or by any means, including photocopying, recording, or other electronic or mechanical methods, without the prior written permission of the author, except in the case of brief quotations embodied in critical reviews and certain other non-commercial uses permitted by copyright law.

tellwell

Tellwell Talent
www.tellwell.ca

ISBN
978-1-7-7-962070-5 (Hardcover)
978-1-7-7-962069-9 (Paperback)
978-1-7-7-962071-2 (eBook)

Table of Contents

Dedication v
Foreword vii
Acknowledgements ix
Introduction xiii
Chapter 1 A Foundation of Love 1
Chapter 2 Love and Grief 14
Chapter 3 Love Shall Carry Us Through 23
Chapter 4 Our Love Grows 36
Chapter 5 Christmas Love and Joy 47
Chapter 6 Love and Death 56
Chapter 7 Love Will Find a Way 68
Chapter 8 A Survivor Made by Love 85
Chapter 9 Love Leads to Advocacy 100
Chapter 10 Love Gets a Conviction 111
Chapter 11 With Love the Truth Speaks 132
Chapter 12 Lessons Because of Love 187
Chapter 13 The Greatest of These Is Love 199
Afterwards - Love Brings Peace 241
About the Author 245

Dedication

To my baby sister, the late Paula Anne Gallant. You have left a legacy that is immeasurable, and you continue to make a difference in all the lives your story touches. I will never stop missing you with my whole being and am so very thankful you live on in Anna.

To my middle sister, Lana Christine (Gallant) Kenny. I could never have travelled my lifelong journey without you. Thank you for your unconditional love, and for supporting me through both the good times and the challenging ones. Together with your late husband Paul, you brought Anna home, and that is bigger than life itself.

To my parents, Paul and Dianne Gallant. I am who I am because of you and I am forever grateful God picked you both for me.

Foreword

This is a story of betrayal, grief, perseverance, and patience—but above all else, it is a story of love, truth, and faith in the goodness of caring people.

In 2009, I was assigned as the Detective Sergeant-In-Charge of the Halifax Regional Police and Royal Canadian Mounted Police (RCMP) Integrated Major Crime Section. This included responsibility for the homicide investigation of Paula Gallant, as well as most other serious crimes committed in the Halifax Region of Nova Scotia.

For over four years, Paula's sisters Lynn Gallant Blackburn and Lana Kenny, along with their families, kept Paula's case in the public eye while holding public officials, including the police, accountable. Their diligent and unrelenting search for justice for Paula led directly to our meeting at the Tantallon detachment of the RCMP in 2009. To be candid, there was considerable apprehension about the family's expectations of the police and the risks of sharing too much information about the investigation. Could we deliver justice in such a tragic case?

As a Detective, my basic rule of thumb was what would I want and expect to be done if something so tragic befell my family, and what would I be prepared to do? By the end of the meeting, I realized we were all on the same page and had reached a level of trust and respect. Lynn and Lana always respected the integrity of our investigation while demonstrating unwavering love for Paula and her daughter, Anna. Their family bond was and continues to be palpable to everyone and a model for all families.

I believe Lynn and Lana's tenacity empowered investigators to perform at their highest level. We often conducted investigations where the victims and the public had little interest in cooperating with police. In contrast, Lynn and Lana were ready and willing to do whatever was required to bring justice for Paula.

Throughout 2009 and 2010, we conducted a thorough investigative review, which led to the approval of an in-depth operational plan, including an undercover investigation of Paula Gallants' homicide. On August 17th, 2010, a man was arrested for Paula's murder. Upon sentencing, Justice Kevin Coady stated: "The reality is he is a very dangerous person–the potential for violence is real."

Since the investigation, I have formed a strong friendship with Lynn and Lana's families and have never ceased to be amazed with the breadth of their positive influence in our community. To this day, Lynn remains a dedicated advocate for victims of family violence in Nova Scotia. It was a true privilege and honour when Lynn asked me to write the foreword to this book.

This is a book written from the depth of her heart in a way only Lynn can express. *For the Love of My Sister* promises to be an uplifting and inspiring experience for all. Lynn's love for her sister, which she shares with you, will never end.

Frank Chambers, Detective Sergeant (ret'd)
Halifax Regional Police

Acknowledgements

How do you even begin to acknowledge the people who have travelled your life journey with you, especially a life filled with incredible joy and immense grief? The abundance of joy that filled my soul with happiness and love started on Coady Street, the first place I called home. It is the beginning of the story of three sisters who lived at 7 Coady with parents who gave each of us the absolute best part of themselves.

To my husband Alain, who is the rock in our family and is the doer of everything for us and anyone in need!! His strength, his love for his family, his generous soul, his sense of humour, and positive outlook on life is truly our blessing.

To my two sons, Tim and Connor, I know the course of your life was altered forever in the most horrific and senseless way. My hope is that Paula's spiritual presence and the memories you shared with her help you live a fulfilled and meaningful life. May you forever cherish the love and laughter she filled your soul with. I am so very proud of you both.

To my brother-in-law, the late Paul Kenny. You loved Paula like a sister. You created the most beautiful website in Paula's memory that will forever be forged in the hearts and minds of all who had the opportunity to experience its love and beauty.

My nephew Dylan, and nieces Emily and Anna, you are amazing, beautiful and perfect in every way. Thank you for colouring my world with the most vibrant energy and love.

Many thanks to my dearest family, especially my Gallant aunts and uncles and the entire Gillis clan from Lingan. I hope my cousins know how very proud and grateful my dad and mom would be for the love and support you have extended to me and our family over the years. To the Blackburn family—my thanks to each of you. I am forever grateful for your presence and acceptance.

I don't know who I would be without our Coady Street family, including 23 Hillside Avenue, who have loved me and supported me through my life. You all continue to be a huge part of my life, thank you.

To retired Detective Sergeant Frank Chambers, you have made an impact on my heart and life that I hold onto daily. Thank you for your dedication in seeking justice for Paula. I know Lana's your favourite but that's okay, as she is always everyone's favourite!

To the dedicated HRP and RCMP resources involved in working on Paula's case. There were so many of you, most I likely never met, but please know our family is forever grateful for your commitment to Paula.

To Denise Smith and Christine Driscoll, NS Public Prosecution Services, you carried the torch of justice on Paula's behalf and treated our family with compassion, dignity, and respect. You balanced the scale of justice!

To Susanne Litke, your dedication to women and children, your experience in Child Protection Law, the extensive work in the area of violence against women you do, and your dedication to justice brought Anna home to our family. Thank you. Please know you gave Paula the ability to finally rest in peace.

To the media, including the RCMP Media Relations resources, through your continued reporting and commitment to the truth for Paula, you kept her voice alive and her story at the forefront for over five years. She became a household name thanks to your coverage. There were some incredibly special media personnel we worked with throughout the years who left an indelible imprint on our hearts. Thank you for your compassion and professionalism.

Paula's most cherished place to be was in her classroom, with her students. To Miss Gallant's Grade 3 class of 2005, to all the students whose lives she impacted, the BLT school administration, the teachers, and all the support resources, thank you for making a difference in her life and for keeping her memory alive.

To the Beechville-Lakeside-Timberlea community. Paula certainly picked the right place to live, teach, and start her family. She met so many wonderful families in this community. After she died, you stood shoulder to shoulder with our family in the building of her art room, forever known as Paula's Place. You came to every walk and function at BLT to celebrate her birthday. There were days you fuelled me to keep going. On the tough days, I knew I had a whole community supporting our fight for justice.

To Father Jim Richards, your source of faith, hope, and belief that justice would prevail helped me through the days I questioned "WHY." During one Mass in the early days following Paula's death, as I held Anna tightly and continued to question God, your sermon talked about Kairos, which in the New Testament means "the appointed time in the purpose of God," essentially the time when God acts. I carry that with me always and have come to trust in Kairos.

To my dear friend Lynne and my mom's best friend, Pat. You kept believing in me and knew my true purpose in all of this was to one day tell Paula's story. Thank you for not ever letting me forget I could do it and that it deserved to be shared as a story based on love, strength and courage.

To the Naughty Nines: Lana, Andre, Tish, Theresa, Patti, Jerri, Delores, and Nancy. We have shared so much through the years and every time we are together and toast sweet Paula, her light and love shines through in each of you.

To the Smith and Mason family for the dove release, to the pipers, choirs, and singers for sharing the gift of your music, to Carol for her sunflower creations, and to everyone who contributed in some way as we **P**ersevered for **P**rosecution so we would one day feel **P**eace. I will never forget how each of you lifted the heaviness in my soul through this journey with your generosity and support.

And to my village, and it is a big one, I am not sure how I would have survived without each and every one of you. I have been blessed by the presence of so many wonderful people throughout my journey. Please know that I carry your love in my heart, and always will. I am forever grateful.

Cora Cole, every time I try to find the words to express how profoundly grateful I am to have "randomly" met you at the International Women's Day Conference on that rainy day in March 2024, I cry. I cry, because you helped me write the story I have been carrying in every fibre of my being since my sister was murdered almost twenty years ago. They are tears of joy that I cannot express with words, only feel deep inside my soul. Thank you for being with me every step of the way on this journey. I think our grandmothers and Paula were waiting for the perfect time for us to meet. Thank you, my co-author and friend. I would encourage each of you to read Cora's book, *Lessons From My Grandmother: About Love, Life and the Art of Forgiveness*, as it is truly a story we can take lessons from and feel joy, comfort, and love.

Special thanks to "Connect," the Provincial Association of Women's Centres and each of the nine Women's Centres. A woman in need can walk in your doors for any reason, or for no reason, and find support and safety—and that's amazing! The work you do is needed and important; please don't ever stop. Your support for the writing and publishing of this book was incredibly generous, and made the path to sharing Paula's legacy so much easier.

Introduction

"A garden of love grows in a grandmother's heart." —Unknown

    I have sat face-to-face with this blank page for years. In my mind, I have filled this page and written this book many times over, with thousands of words belying countless, confounding layers of emotion. So, why start today? One could ask, what's different about today than yesterday? Than a year ago? Ten years ago? What about the time I was riding the bus to work in a snowstorm, and in the time capsule of gridlocked streets, I typed a version of this same introduction, and that's as far as I got? Why now?

    Today, January 26th, 2024, is my Grammie Gallant's birthday. She would have been 110. And today, I am ready. At long last, bolstered by her memory, I feel strong enough to embark upon the telling of my sister's story with clarity and purpose. I loved Grammie, and I deeply admired her, and I believe, in my heart, it was her death that ultimately contributed to bringing closure to my sister's ongoing murder investigation. After my sister's murder, every time someone we loved died, I would say that the recently departed would "stir the pot", equipping the police with what they needed to finally make an arrest. Yes—I have come to believe

Grammie Gallant at Peggy's Cove, NS

in my heart that when someone leaves behind unfinished business, they will help provide closure. That's my belief, based not on scientific evidence but a strong need for hope.

Grammie died the way I'd like to go myself. With a full belly, following a true Gallant-style breakfast. No suffering, no burdensome prolonged stays in hospitals or nursing homes. She died knowing who she was, along with the names of her children, her grandchildren, and likely all her great-grandchildren. Grammie and Grandad raised eleven children, including my dad, their oldest boy. I would say they were poor, but they always put food on the table and clothes on backs, so some may disagree with me. Grammie probably played 45s or crib the night before, and that morning, she might have even recorded the weather in her notebook in the kitchen drawer, the way she often did. If she ever forgot a date, an event, or family fact, she would simply say "Get me my book," where she would inevitably find it. An author in her own right, as Grammie was always writing us long handwritten letters to ask about our lives and catch us up on the news around the farm.

The last conversation I had with Grammie was in that same kitchen, on her farm in Prince Edward Island. She was sitting in her rocking chair beside her wood-burning kitchen stove and I knelt down beside her. She took my hands and looked at me with her beautiful blue eyes, and she asked, "Did he do it?"

It was the first time she'd ever asked the question out loud.

I said, "Yes, Grammie, he did."

"That bastard."

I'd never heard her swear—other than the odd "damn" when she was playing cards—but this two-word response was filled with hurt, anger, and the realization of truth. It confirmed for me that Grammie also had likely known the truth in her heart all along. She closed her eyes and continued to rock, and I saw a tear trickle down her cheek. I wrapped my arms around her and kissed her face. In turn, she patted my head and told me it would be okay.

The day before I got the news that Grammie died I found a letter from her in my mailbox, written in her own hand. She'd stopped writing letters in her final years, as it had grown too hard on her overworked farmer's hands, so I immediately thought she was writing to tell me bad news. I was so afraid, in fact, that I called a friend and told her about the letter, saying I was too scared to open it. I didn't think I could bear any more bad news. My dear friend told me to go make myself a cup of tea, find a quiet place to sit, and read what Grammie had to say. So that's what I did. And to my surprise and awe, it was simply a tender note filled with ramblings about the spring and her difficult winter. In true Grammie fashion, there was no white space left on the writing paper; she even wrote down the margins. In short, it was simply a note filled with love, from the Grammie I loved with my whole heart. It must have been her way of saying goodbye, as if she knew her day was coming.

For some time now I have strongly felt Grammie's presence. I have seen those soft blue eyes looking at me with compassion and love. I have felt her strong hands around me, giving me the courage and the confidence to tell this story. Paula's story. My story. Our story. The story I need to write. Even if it's never published or read by another person, it's my story, my version, my perspective. I write it now with Grammie beside me, telling me I can do it and that it's too important not to share.

I know most people would agree that murder is ugly and its impacts are profound. But I am living proof that one could never imagine how horrific it really is, the sense of helplessness you feel, the chaos you live in, the overwhelming sadness, the isolation, the unbearable pain, and how it changes you forever.

There was a time I thought I would never have a story worthy of a book. I thought my life was too ordinary. Now, I desperately wish it had stayed ordinary. Many would say my father bestowed upon me his gift for talking, but the writing part? Well, that's a different thing altogether. How does one even begin to take all of their complex thoughts and assemble them into a story that is logical and flows easily enough for others to want to read? Especially a story as important as this one. My brain is like a multiplex movie theatre, with about twelve different movies playing all at once. Which story will I start with? Which one will I end with? What about the parts of this story that I will never be able to share? So, where to start?

My dad always said, "Life experience contributes greatly to who we become." I take that to mean where you came from shapes who you are and what you become. To honour my dad and Grammie, I will start this story talking about where I am from and finish with how murder changed the course of my life and ultimately, who I became.

Chapter 1

A Foundation of Love

> "To understand the ending you sometimes have to go back to the beginning." —Unknown

Some say Disney World is the happiest place on earth, but I bet the eighteen kids who lived on Coady Street in Cape Breton, Nova Scotia, during the 1970s and early 1980s would vehemently disagree. Abounding with the kind of innocence and whimsy that is usually reserved for staged Hollywood sitcoms, our street radiated love, laughter, and joy. Endless days were filled with games of Red-Light-Green-Light and hopscotch in the middle of the road. Nobody locked their doors. Looking back, it almost feels like a dream.

How did such an oasis come to be? In 1968 my father, Paul Gallant, went to a meeting led by Father Donnie Angus MacDonald, to hear about a cooperative opportunity for young families wanting to build a home in Glace Bay. This initiative was one of many provided through the Coady Institute, which still exists to this day. Five men, including my dad, agreed to have Father MacDonald apply on their behalf, and thus, the Breezeway Coop was formed. Members were allowed to borrow between eight to twelve thousand dollars to build homes for their growing families. They shared tools, pooled building skills, and bought building material with their "bulk" discounts. At the end of the day, they shared in both the rewards and the risks.

We moved into our partially finished home in the fall of 1969. I was seven. My middle sister, Lana, was two. And Paula, my youngest sister, was born just a few weeks later in December. Eventually there were eighteen kids in six homes on our small street and everyone

Coady Street

looked out for one another. At times we seemed to operate like one large family and every parent on the street had free rein to encourage or discipline us, whether we liked it or not. Our community was built on respect and love.

To this day, we refer to each other's families in reference to our house numbers: 1 Coady, 3 Coady, or 4 Coady. We lived at 7 Coady, so we were—and will always be—7 Coady. To this day, the girls from number 1, 4, and 7 refer to each other as "the Coady Street Sisters."

Ours was a childhood full of energy and action. In the winter, we played all-ages coed hockey on the frozen bog behind our house. The frozen bulrushes made the best defencemen and we had nothing but rocks for nets. We even had our own version of the Stanley Cup to win. During the summer, we never wished for a perfectly manicured ball field with real bases; it was much more fun to gather in the roughly mowed field behind 4 Coady for endless innings. Most of the dads formed their own ball team, and win or lose, whenever they got home from a game, we'd all have a little post-game social in one of the backyards. On hot sunny days, Dad and Barry from 4 Coady would load up the truck with as many of us kids who could fit on the flatbed and head to Dominion Beach. No seatbelts, no matter.

It seemed everyone brought their own strengths and skills to the street. At the end of the day, all the parents on Coady Street worked hard to carve out good lives. We had a nurse, a banker, an airline ramp worker, Devco workers who were associated with the coal-mine, a crosswalk guard, a principal, and a few stay-at-home moms.

My mom stayed home for most of my life while my dad was the mechanic Bay Chev Olds, at a local garage where he serviced our street and what felt like the whole town of Glace Bay. No one was cash rich, but boy did we have the stuff dreams were made of.

Sometimes for vacations, we would go camping in one of those old pop-up canvas trailers where you couldn't touch the walls or you would start a leak! Other times, we would just go clam digging. Often, we would visit our grandparents on Prince Edward Island (PEI) where my dad grew up. It was a place that felt like an extension of the oasis we had at home because we were surrounded by our family's love. My grandparents' yard was always filled with kids laughing while they tried to outrun Jurassic-sized mosquitoes. We had too many first cousins to keep track of—upwards of 37, at last count—and in Grammie's famous kitchen there was always a game of 45s taking place that you could join in.

Gallant Family Fun

My dad was originally from a small farm on Lot 11 in PEI. As the eldest boy of eleven children, he possessed a farmer's commitment to hard work and a sense of responsibility to care for his family. When he was just sixteen he joined the air force in Regina, Saskatchewan. After three years of service, he went back home and worked on the farm. Then, in the spring of 1957, he left PEI to go to Toronto with his brothers to look for work.

My maternal grandmother was one of eighteen children, part of the Gillis clan in Lingan, Cape Breton. She had my mother out of wedlock in an era when many families would have shunned her, but not the Gillis clan. Everyone in her large extended family helped take care of my mother—which I credit, at least in part, for her enduring sense of optimism and patience. When Mom was only three years old, her mother died from tuberculosis, which led to her being raised by her aunt Tina and throughout our life Tina was lovingly referred to as Nan. Together, Mom and Tina moved to Toronto Later in life, my mom talked about how much she disliked living in Toronto and often expressed her wish to come home, until she met the love of her life.

Mom and Dad met at a dance when she was just sixteen and he was twenty-two. It was love at first sight—a connection so deep, I like to believe they were kindred spirits. Because Mom wasn't of age, she needed special permission to marry Dad, and they celebrated their love with a double wedding ceremony in the early morning, alongside Mom's best friend Terry. From that day until the very end of their time together, their love flowed effortlessly. As many have remarked over the years, they truly were meant to be.

Mr. & Mrs. Gallant 1960

I was born two years after my parents married. People have said that Paul Gallant lives on in me, and I'm honoured to think it's true. My dad was my hero and my biggest supporter. I loved and admired everything about him. I would wash cars at the garage where he worked just so I could hang out with him. I would bike all over town to watch him play softball. Dad's hands were always calloused and stained with grease. My son Connor is a roofer, and I often find myself looking at his equally calloused hands and saying, "You have your grandfather's hands and are so much like him."

My dad filled our home with humour. He was a fighter for the underdog and believed in justice. For a man who had very little education, he was one of the smartest people I've known. During our supper-table spelling contests Dad would intentionally misspell words so we could correct him, and feel like we were smarter. He always had a mischievous twinkle in his eyes and was the best April Fool's joker. He got us—and almost everyone on the street—every year!

I came home in Grade 8 and told Dad I wanted to join the school's basketball team. I was five feet tall and had never played a day in my life. Dad encouraged me to go for it and taught me to play like I was a towering giant. He studied the game so he could eventually coach my sisters, when they too decided to play. I always believed I could do anything with him by my side. When I played basketball for Cape Breton University, Dad was my biggest and most steadfast fan. No matter where the game was, I could always look in the stands and see Dad and Mom there. While I'll never know for sure where my basketball nickname "Gunner" came from, I'm guessing Dad and his good buddy Alan MacEachern had something to do with it.

When I think about my mom, my heart swells with deep love for her. She was quiet, kind, gentle, and ever-so giving. A tiny woman who hardly had to stoop to pick the blueberries that grew in the fields in Lingan where she was born. I remember her so clearly, washing out milk bags and hanging them on the clothesline to dry. Mom found the good in every single person; I never heard her say a bad word about anyone, except maybe during a rowdy game of cards. My son Timothy is like her in that way, and for that I am so grateful.

I always felt lucky and proud that my mom was one of the Coady Street women who didn't work outside the home. As such, she was one of the main keepers of the neighbourhood kids. Everyone counted on her. If any of us—her own children or others—had to come home from school early due to a belly or earache, Mom was there. Although Mom was a good cook, she particularly loved baking and could tell how good something would taste just by reading a recipe. Other moms were happy to prepare entrees for any gathering we were having as long as she would bring some of her baked goods. I can still smell her tea biscuits and cinnamon rolls. On occasion I try to bake them myself, but they never taste like hers.

In addition to her pregnancies, Mom miscarried several times and had an ectopic pregnancy. To the best of my knowledge those lost babies were all boys. There was a time when women thought they could influence the sex of their children, perhaps by eating certain foods; salty foods for boys and more dairy for girls. Science aside, Mom always felt she'd somehow disappointed my father because *she* couldn't give him a son. No father loved having a houseful of girls more than ours, and I know in my heart that Dad never felt this way, but certainly it bothered Mom.

When Mom came home with her third baby girl I was delighted. I was thrilled to have a baby sister as it felt like I had my own living doll. Paula Anne Gallant got the best of Mom and Dad—both in her name and her personality. Husbands didn't go into the hospital like they do now, so shortly after Paula's birth, the doctor called Dad to head in. The doctor grew concerned that Mom might continue trying for a son despite her history of increasingly dangerous and unsuccessful pregnancies. Fearing for her health, the doctor felt compelled to ask Dad for permission to perform a hysterectomy, as it was the only way to protect her from further risk. Not wanting to risk the love of his life, Dad agreed, and Mom had no say at all. It was a different time back then, and eventually, I think Mom agreed it was the best decision that could be made in a tough situation.

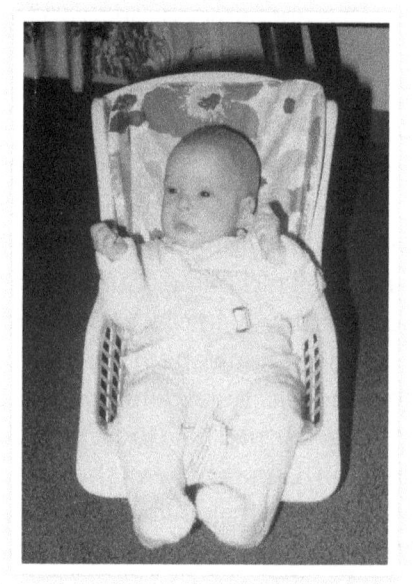

My Baby-Doll Sister -Paula Anne

These heart-breaking pregnancy losses explain why there is a five- and seven-year age gap between Lana, Paula, and me respectively. In my mind, it always seemed Lana and Paula were closer as sisters than I was. Their similar ages allowed them to play more easily together and share similar interests. Without a doubt, seven years creates a canyon of differences between a seventeen-year-old's interests and a ten-year-old's. Yet our parents helped create deep and meaningful ties among us, and the three of us formed the 7 Coady Street triumvirate.

I am sure, behind closed doors, our parents had disagreements. I'm sure they stressed about money and bills, us kids driving them crazy–normal household stuff, yet I never heard my parents speak an unkind word to each other or raise their voices. If we pestered Mom enough, she would threaten to take off her knitted slipper and smack us across the butt, a joke that usually led to laughter. If we did something Dad didn't approve of, the look of disappointment was enough of a reprimand. Together, they taught us lessons through stories and subtle actions. They set a steady example of self-regulation. They allowed my sisters and me to flourish, each in our own unique way, grounded in our individual interests and abilities. If I was the closest thing my father had to a boy—a comparison I never really minded—Lana and Paula both inherited Mom's gentle and loving nature.

Mom and Dad, True Kindred Spirits

Twelve girls and six boys grew up on Coady Street. The youngest was sixteen years younger than me—Sheri, from 1 Coady—with the rest of the kids falling somewhere in the middle. I took the role of second-eldest kid on Coady Street very seriously and loved every minute of it. I coordinated concerts for the kids to perform, with nothing but a white sheet on the clothesline as the stage backdrop. I organized games on front lawns. For every major and minor holiday—and

One of many, Coady St. Birthday Parties

sometimes for no reason at all—I would marshal all the children down the street in a parade. I would regularly get calls from parents asking me to organize someone's birthday party. I have no idea why or how I was given so much responsibility at such a young age, but I relished it at the time. Now, I realize it was just the universe preparing me for what life was going to throw my way later on.

One night, I was "sassy" and talked back to my parents, for which I was grounded and told I couldn't go to the school dance. So, I opened my bedroom window and stepped onto the picnic table where, just hours before, my family had gathered for a barbeque. Thinking I had made the great escape—and somehow beaten my parents at their own game—I gleefully made my way to the dance and had the best rebellion-fuelled time. When I came home, I was relieved to find all the lights off, suggesting that everyone was in bed and none the wiser. I quietly approached the back door but to my utter shock and horror it was locked. Never in my life had I seen a locked door on Coady Street. I tiptoed around the house and found the front door also locked, with a note taped to the glass in my father's manly, pencilled script: *"You can come in the same way you went out."*

Since my age set me apart from the rest of the Coady Street pack, it was quite helpful to all the parents when my dad came home with a car for me—a manual Chevrolet Vega. He only paid fifty dollars for it, which was likely twenty-five dollars too much. It was supposedly "Nevada Silver" in colour, but all the dull, dark bodywork repair patches obscured the shine it may once have had. The passenger side didn't even have a floor! I was a precocious, spoiled teenager, so I refused to drive it for weeks, especially as I didn't know how to drive a manual.

Eventually, the taste of freedom was too much to resist. I spent time with Dad learning to rivet the floor myself. And one long hot summer day, with him sitting beside me as teacher, I learned to drive. I stalled the car on the first slight incline I encountered. I was frustrated. I told him it was a dumb car. Dad simply looked out the window and said he could sit there all day, that there was no rush, and with patience, he knew I could learn. And I did. Then one day, I came home from school to find the Vega gone. I asked Mom where *my* car was and she told me very calmly that Dad had sold it. I was astounded and angry; it was my first car, and I felt some weird sort of attachment to it. I was mid-rant when Dad pulled into the driveway with a beautiful cobalt blue Pontiac Beaumont, its chrome so shiny I could apply lipstick by looking at the bumper. In Dad's eyes, I had proven I was responsible enough and appreciative enough with the rust-bucket Vega, so he upgraded me. The Beaumont upped my street cred instantaneously.

My hip Beaumont became a place to hang out. One very cold winter night, I was the designated driver at a community dance when seven or eight "cool" kids climbed in to listen to some music and have a few drinks before heading inside. What I didn't know was that they decided to use the car throughout the night as well. By the time the dance was over, the interior smelled like a bathroom bar. I was still asleep the next morning when my dad came into my room with an old grey bucket, rags, and a brush—and the largest bottle of Pine Sol cleaning liquid I had ever seen. Someone had left a couple of bottles of beer under the seat and when the temperature dropped overnight, they exploded. Our parents never yelled at us but their messages were always very clear. That was how they raised us, and it worked well.

For example, once Dad was building a garage just behind our house. It was a big deal to have a garage back then, as it was a serious financial commitment and took a lot of Dad's time. Meanwhile, Lana genuinely needed new jeans, and she wanted them before a certain social event. I can't remember if the pair she wanted was at Toby's, Ein's, or Marshalls, but I do remember they were expensive at forty dollars. Not wanting to dip into her own babysitting money, Lana begged and cajoled for my parents to pay for them. Dad was up on the roof of the garage shed, laying shingles with Alan MacEachern, while Lana pleaded her case over and over from the ground. Without saying a word, Dad shimmied down from the ladder and handed Lana twenty bucks. When she begged for more, Dad simply said twenty dollars was the price for jeans our family bought and if she wanted the forty-dollar jeans she could use her own money. No other words were exchanged as he climbed the ladder and went back to laying shingles.

Paula, Lynn & Lana at Christmas

Then there was the day when Paula was still young, but old enough to not like being told no, so she decided to run away from home. She packed a little blue suitcase that usually held Barbie clothes and she stormed across a grassy meadow straight through to a neighbouring street. Mom watched through the kitchen window as she trekked across the field to the McCormack house, where Suzanne, one of Paula's best childhood friends, lived. While they didn't have a Coady Street address (they lived at 23 Hillside) they were part of our community and shared many great times with our family. Joe and Pat were special friends of our parents and the stories of their adventures together are endless. When Paula arrived at the McCormacks', our wall-mounted rotary phone rang and Mom answered it. She was told in those hushed tones that only moms can hear that Paula arrived safely and it was okay that she cooled her temper there. Paula likely spent the entire day feeling quite righteous, until suppertime. When Paula learned what was being served at 23 Hillside she quickly decided to come home. After another hushed-toned phone call from Pat, our kind and gentle mother watched Paula drag her little blue suitcase through the field once more and waited for her at our back door with one of her favourite meals on the table.

There was the time I was helping my dad paint the garage—or maybe it was the foundation of the house? I really can't remember, but it was a hot, perfectly sunny summer day and there I was working with my dad. My friends walked by and said they were going to hang out by the brook that ran behind Coady Street over to Alexander Street, where we liked to go. They asked if I was coming. My immediate response was, "Yep—be there in a minute." Without thinking, I started to squeeze the excess paint off my brush against the rim of the can, trying hard not to let it drip down the side. Finally, my dad caught my eye and asked one question that had me yelling down the street to my friends that I wouldn't make it after all. He didn't say I couldn't go, he didn't lay on the guilt, and he didn't bribe me to stay. He simply asked, "If you go, who's going to help me finish this?"

In hindsight, it was a beautiful way to be parented, because values were communicated and lessons taught without anger or articulating disappointment. I have always hoped I brought some of that to my own parenting style. Another thing I have come to appreciate is that my parents never harped to me about school. They knew, and I knew, what had to be done and when. This trust they placed in me—to bring my books home, to study for a test, to complete my homework on time—gave me a sense of autonomy, which grew into leadership and management skills. Especially when it came to making decisions about life after high school.

Upon graduation, one of my best friends, Bernita, and I decided to enroll in the brand-new Bachelor of Arts in Community Studies program at the nearby University College of Cape Breton. I made the women's basketball team and received a scholarship, despite my height challenges. It was there that I earned the nickname "Ankle-Biter." I loved playing small college–level basketball. In truth, basketball was probably the foremost reason I went to university. I loved that my dad and mom were in the stands for every home game, and often travelled to see me play against the Nova Scotia Teachers College, the Agricultural College, and Mount St. Vincent University on the mainland.

As part of our curriculum we volunteered at Bridgeport School, which at the time offered non-inclusive education to students with a variety of disabilities and different levels of needs. Based on our major, we were assigned to what was then called the "Special Needs" classroom. As it turned out, that one day I spent at Bridgeport changed the course of my career as I was so deeply moved by the students and the teachers. I still cannot articulate the myriad of emotions that I experienced that day: so much love, so much worry, so much joy, and so many struggles. I was completely overcome at the end of the day when a male student who had spent his entire life in a wheelchair asked me to dance. It broke my heart a little, which led to a kind of awakening for me. I knew then that a career in this field wasn't for me. I knew I didn't have the internal grace to do this kind of work. I made the decision on the way home not to continue with my program. Like many student athletes, I was more worried about telling my basketball coach than my parents that I was quitting. As fate would have it, Coach wouldn't let me quit—likely because with only eight other players that season, it would mean we wouldn't have enough players to keep the team on the court. Which, if I'm honest, is probably the main reason I made the team in the first place. Coach went so far as to help me switch majors. I ended up enrolling in the Bachelor of Business Administration program, and I got to continue playing basketball. My parents were supportive, right up until I told them that I would have to go to Saint Mary's University in Halifax to finish my degree. Eventually, Dad came around, and I knew I would be fine because he believed in me.

At the end of the day, I couldn't have dreamed up a better childhood, a better extended family or neighbourhood. My sisters and I were so blessed to have the parents we did, and together we dreamed of them growing old together. Mom used to say, "No matter what happens, I'll be okay because your dad will be by my side forever." We all believed that. Maybe we were all naïve. Maybe we didn't see the hardships ours and other families endured. All we saw was acceptance and deep friendships in our little village of love. If it sounds like I'm bragging a bit, it's because I am. I cannot think of one bad thing about my youth or childhood. My life, at that point, was idyllic. We had everything.

Mom and her three girls at the Homestead in Lingan, Cape Breton

Chapter 2

Love and Grief

"If you look deeply into the palm of your hand, you will see your parents and all generations of your ancestors. All of them are alive in this moment. Each is present in your body. You are the continuation of each of these people." —Thich Nhat Hanh

It was in 1976 that the first tragedy burst our seemingly utopian bubble. Ray Ferguson of 3 Coady was only thirty-eight when he had a heart attack and died on the way to the hospital. He was there one minute and gone the next. At the time it was unfathomable. The profound suddenness of it, the utter shock that one of our parents could disappear from our lives, on our very special street, was earth-shattering. I was in Grade 8 and I remember the loss vividly. The Fergusons had four children, aged fourteen, twelve, eight, and two, and Tillie Ferguson was a stay-at-home mom. It was natural to wonder how she would be able to raise her young family and maintain her home on her own. What would have to change in their lives in dear Ray's absence to do this?

The answer was nothing–simply because they lived on Coady Street, and we took care of each other. The other dads and moms stepped up to do whatever Tillie and her family needed to get through their loss. Tillie became even more of an anchor on our street and in our community. Everyone loved her. She and my mom were wonderful friends and my dad loved to torment her—she fell for his pranks hook, line, and sinker!

In the spring of 1984 I moved to Halifax, Nova Scotia, to finish my business degree at St. Mary's University. The day I left home, it was my birthday weekend, and while my mom and sisters cried, my dad was so quiet it broke my heart. I knew they were proud of me, but leaving Coady Street, my neighbourhood, family, and my home was something I never thought I'd do. I never have imagined living anywhere else and that day, I truly believed the move was a temporary one, and I'd be back.

My bike and I moved into residence. I remember that summer well as the Tall Ships were in Halifax, so I used to bike down to the waterfront and watch people watching the ships. While my heart was never far from Coady Street, it was a whole new world for me: student life in the "big city." The sights! The sounds! The shops! The new food and all the people!

When I graduated, I moved into a house on Clyde Street with four other girls, and life was fun-filled with the innocent kind of chaos that can only be experienced at the time in life between your parents' home and an eventual home of your own. I had a retail job at The Bay and was trying to make ends meet. Other than work and Peddlers Pub on Saturday afternoons, I had no real responsibilities, until I got a call from a former classmate from back at home.

She had, impressively, secured a "real" job at the Maritime Telegraph and Telephone Company, aka MT&T, the only telephone company in Nova Scotia at the time. In those days, unless you knew someone working there it was hard to secure a coveted job with MT&T. She knew a bunch of us were living on Clyde Street and was calling to ask if anyone in the house wanted a job. Thankfully, I was the one who answered the phone! I was looking for a way to make better use of my degree, so of course I said yes. That one phone call opened the door to an unexpected and very successful thirty-five-year career.

Since there was a formal hiring freeze, I began as a temporary worker and was paid from petty cash—something that would never happen now. I loved the work. I had an amazing manager, who gave me every opportunity to learn and grow by assigning me to a variety of projects and teams. One day I was counting phone lines in federal government buildings; the next, I was working on a project with the data team. I was cross-training before I even knew what that term meant. I was thrilled to be hired permanently at the beginning of April 1985. I will never forget how proud my mom and dad were. A job with the phone company was a big deal! I remember thinking *Wow, I am in the big leagues now . . . how did this happen? How lucky am I?*

Later that month, on April 23rd, 1985, I received another phone call that would also change my life forever. It was the worst news I'd ever received and could ever have imagined, and I thought it would be the most tragic call of my life. "Aunt" Marge, my mom's first cousin, called to tell me that at the age of forty-eight, my dad had suffered a brain aneurysm. I didn't even understand what that meant. I had never heard of an aneurysm, and certainly didn't have Google, Siri, or an iPhone to do any quick research. All I knew was that it was serious, and I had to get home quickly. On the short flight home, I recall thinking my dad was in great shape. He lifted weights, coached basketball, played softball, and was in the prime of his life. *He'll be fine*, I told myself, *he'll beat whatever this brain thing is.*

Dad and Paula with her Holly Hobby Doll

I couldn't have been more wrong. When I got to the hospital, I found nearly every member of my Coady Street family and my community there praying for Dad and supporting my mom and my family.

After three brain surgeries, my dad ended up in a coma. Our days were spent sitting at his hospital bedside, filled with so many conflicting emotions: hope, sadness, frustration, and faith. Our neighbours sat with us. Cards were delivered and food was prepared. Even the basketball team at Glace Bay Junior High where Dad coached sent their love and prayers. We survived only through the love of others.

Lana and Paula tried to focus on school and their activities, although I know their hearts were not in it. After a couple of months of being home, I spoke to Mom about not going back to Halifax. I told her I didn't want to go back, that I couldn't leave and go back to my "normal" life there. Mom assured me she would be okay as she had my two sisters, Nan, my grandparents, and our Coady Street family. Then, she said that Dad would be disappointed if I didn't go back, and that we had to keep looking forward. It was the first time my mom opposed a decision I wanted to make. It was also the first time I ever thought my dad could be disappointed in me, and I couldn't take that risk. So, I returned to Halifax.

When I returned to work, I was buoyed by a different kind of love. My roommates had paid my share of bills and hadn't given my room away. On my first day back to work, my senior boss took me down to the food court at the Maritime Centre, the building that housed our offices. He slid an envelope across the table. Inside was all my back pay in the form of paycheques. "Kid, don't think you owe us for holding your job," he said. "It was the right thing to do. Just work hard going forward, and do your best." Beyond a great financial relief, it was also a great personal comfort. It was precisely the kind of thing that my dad would have done.

In June, I went back to Cape Breton for my university graduation ceremony and Lana's high school graduation. Our milestones were celebrated with our Coady Street family propping us up while Dad lay in a coma. I went home so many times that year that my car likely could have driven the route on its own. I would get a call that Dad was going to die, and I would rush back to Cape Breton as soon as I could, grateful that Dad would live another day. In September, Lana moved to Halifax and in with me to go to school, and she was a great travelling companion. Miraculously, we only got stopped for speeding once, and the officer let me go with just a warning. We celebrated Dad's 49th birthday at his hospital bedside, as well as Mom and Dad's 25th wedding anniversary, with Mom always holding his hand and telling him how much we loved him. She read him the newspaper every day and talked to him endlessly. We were hoping beyond hope that he'd wake up.

On December 1st, 1985, just five days before Paula's sweet sixteen birthday, after being in a coma for seven months, our dad died at the age of forty-nine. I will never get the image out of my head of my grandad crying at our kitchen table. He sat half mumbling, half praying that no dad should ever have to watch his son die. It was the first time I ever saw my grandad cry.

The day Dad died, my heart was shattered, my innocence was lost, and I was forever changed. Mom's beautiful brown eyes, which had always shone bright and were filled with hope, dimmed with her endless flowing tears. Lana and Paula hung on to each other, emotionally numb. It didn't feel real.

At the age of twenty-three I felt I had to somehow hold all the pieces of Mom's brokenness, my sisters' brokenness, my own brokenness—our collective brokenness—in my hands. No one ever made me feel responsible. I just felt like I was the one who could do it, and that it was what my dad would have expected of me. I barely remember the wake or the funeral service. As a fair and honest mechanic, my dad knew a lot of people and it felt like every one of Glace Bay's 28,000 residents came to pay him their respects. That day, the grief was a physical heaviness that surrounded me. I remember holding Paula in my arms throughout the service, and the sound of her heart-wrenching cries. I thought there could and never would be a worse time in my life. My dad was too young to die, and we needed him still.

In its unimaginable, unknowable way that it tends to, life carried on. The Coady Street community supported Mom as they had Tillie years earlier. Everyone watched out for her, rallying when a faucet or roof leaked. Mom would go out somewhere, come home, and find her lawn mowed. The community of love on Coady Street kept us afloat.

Lana and I went home as often as we could. As Paula was still in high school she and Mom became inseparable, best friends, really. On many days, they would share a clubhouse sandwich from Mike's Lunch—one of Dad's favourite places. During this time, Mom took courses that allowed her, for the first time, to work outside the home. She went to the occasional social event and was going through the motions of living, and rather convincingly. Yet I couldn't help but notice the light in my mother's eyes hadn't returned. I could see the loneliness and ache she felt in her subtle, quiet motions.

Soon it was the fall of 1988, and it was time for Paula to fulfill her lifelong dream of becoming a teacher. This meant leaving home to go to the Nova Scotia Teachers' College in Truro, Nova Scotia. Naturally, Paula resisted going and leaving Mom alone, but with our encouragement and support, she packed up and moved. By that spring my own life had taken on a new, somewhat happy, yet tenuous rhythm. I had met and fallen in love with Alain Blackburn, a colleague at MT&T, and we purchased our first home. I remember Mom saying, "Now you have a home for your sisters." I quickly and adamantly told her that "7 Coady Street will always be our home." She just smiled, in her quiet gentle manner that didn't at all seem like the foreshadowing it turned out to be. We were getting ready to celebrate Lana's birthday, and I was excited to host it in my own place, only to be interrupted by another life-altering phone call. Grandad Gallant had died. Mom took the shuttle up from Cape Breton, Paula took the train from Truro, and we all went to PEI for Granddad's funeral instead of christening my new home with birthday cake and champagne.

Mom, Paula, Lynn, Lana at Paula's High School Graduation

Soon Paula finished her first year of teachers' college and she loved it. She couldn't wait to have a classroom of her own—she had so much energy and so many ideas that she was excited to implement. Paula decided to stay in Halifax with Alain and I that summer. She landed a great temp job at MT&T and could commute to work with Alain and I; it was all good. One beautiful, sunny weekend day in June, Alain had gone to his sister's. I was painting–a passionate hobby of mine at the time–and Paula was reading in her room when the phone rang. Paula answered the call. Once again, it was Aunt Marge. She asked to speak with me. "Lynn," she said, "you need to get home as quickly as possible. Your mom has suffered a brain aneurysm."

It was a catastrophic, devastating moment of déjà vu. In shock, I hung up on her. She immediately called back and I picked it up without speaking. "I'm so sorry," was all Aunt Marge could say. To this day, it still feels like the worst kind of irony that I worked for a company that supplied the technology that delivered all my life's worst news. In utter disbelief, I insisted on speaking with the doctor, as I didn't understand how this same condition that claimed my father could have affected my mother. He came to the phone and said it broke his heart to share the news about Mom.

We caught a flight that night and when we walked into the hospital, our family and friends once again lined the walls. Love and concern shone from each person's eyes as we walked past them to our mom's room. It was a miracle, but Mom waited until we got there to take her last breath and gave us a chance to say our goodbyes. Mom was only forty-six years old.

The days that followed are still a blur. As I write this, my sobs are as deep and as painful as they were that day in June 1989. After Mom died, doctors came into the room to talk with us—they wanted to know how we felt about organ donation. All of Mom's organs, other than her brain, which had been affected by the aneurysm, were healthy. Somehow, we saw through our deepest pain, knowing that Mom would have wanted to help others, and we said yes. Mom's organs helped several people, including an eight-and-a-half-year-old girl and a fifty-six-year-old man from Ontario who received her liver and heart respectively. Two men, one from Nova Scotia and one from Newfoundland, received her kidneys; and two others had their sight restored with the gift of her corneas. Helping others was foundational to living on Coady Street, so looking back on it now, this was an exceedingly easy decision.

Somehow we planned the service, held her wake and funeral. All day, I kept hearing Mom's words from a few months earlier echoing in my mind: *"Now you have a home for your sisters."* Just like with Dad, it felt like everyone in town came. Yet this time, there was an impenetrable silence that filled the air around us. It was as if everyone was holding their breath, afraid to muffle the sound of the sobbing emanating from my sisters and me. This time, the added cruelty of coincidence, or fate—depending on who and what you believe in—became the horrible elephant in the room. How could they both have had an aneurysm? I know that at some point in every person's life, they lose their parents. We all become orphans. I knew this would happen one day, but I never imagined I would lose both my parents, so young, from the same relatively rare condition. It's unexplainable why they both lost their lives this way. My parents, doctor, a local judge's wife, and our insurance agent all died from brain aneurysms at similarly young ages. I have wracked my brain for answers. I and others have wondered about the environmental impacts of the heavy water plants, coal mines, and steel plants that surrounded our communities.

After our parents died, Paula sent out a request to friends and family asking them to share some memories. People wrote about my parents' deep kind of love, how my dad was a prankster, and Mom naïve to fall for his pranks every time. These tributes validated the relationship I know they shared. Paula captured those stories in a scrapbook and gave one to Lana and me. There are still no words to describe how much this gift from Paula meant.

But tragedy was not done with the Coady Street families. As the years passed, our little street of just six homes lost many more. A book could be written about each home and the untimely, tragic losses suffered. At the time of writing, 4 Coady is the only neighbourhood family with a set of parents still living together. Numbers 5 and 6 Coady still have their mothers, but for the rest of us, all that remains are memories. I have to admit, I sometimes wondered if, despite our best intentions, our little Coady Street development somehow disturbed an ancient burial site or disrupted a deep energy vortex. How else can you rationalize the extremes we've been dealt: the idyllic beginning with such genuine love, paired with all the tragedy that has followed? What are the chances? To this day, I sometimes feel like we are being punished for all the joy we once had.

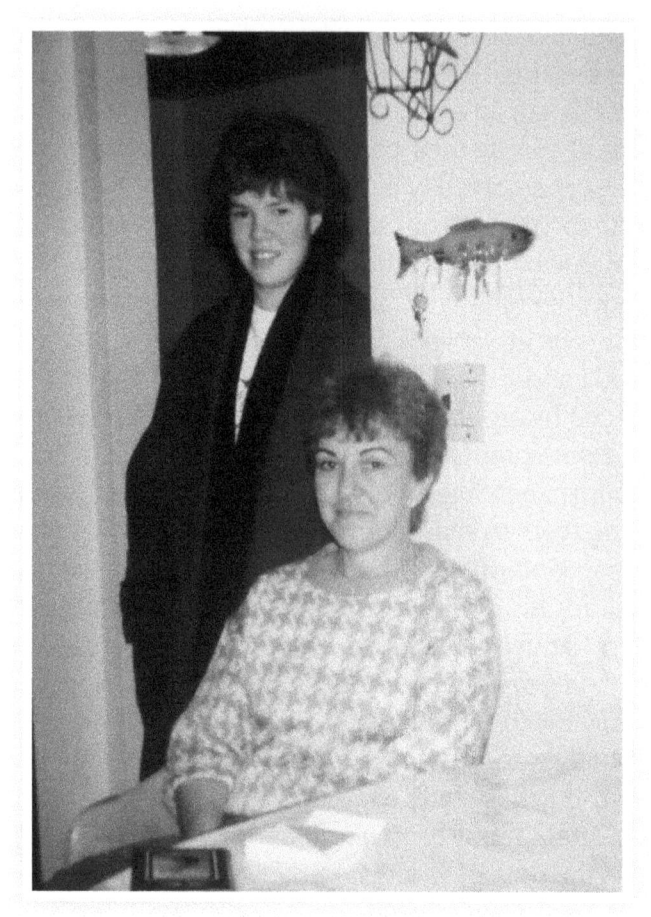

Paula and Mom

Chapter 3

Love Shall Carry Us Through

"The strongest hearts have the most scars."
—Unknown

In hindsight, it's helpful to think that Dad knew, whether subconsciously or not, that his and Mom's lives would be short. So, on some level, he was preparing me to take charge sooner than any of us wanted. The extraordinary sense of responsibility bestowed upon me was fun in my youth for the levity and freedom it afforded. As an adult, in the wake of both my parents' passing, it has been a blessing and a curse. Just a couple of years ago my Aunt Florence said that Dad's family never understood why I was given so much responsibility at such a young age, and why I was always included in adult conversations and activities. I didn't really understand why at the time, but I do now. After my mom died, I had no time to wallow in self-pity. I leveraged the skills I needed to support my sisters, to shepherd us forward, so we could honour our parents by creating lives that were fulfilling and reflective of all the love they gave us. I sometimes feel desperate to believe my parents knew that one day I would require the intangible skill to rally others, to problem-solve, to ask questions and to persevere. It helps to think of things this way, to create some sort of sense out of the path my life has taken.

In 1968 we were one of the first families to sign up for the dream that became Coady Street. And twenty years later, we were the first family to officially leave. Our parents were gone, and all three of us girls lived away from Cape Breton. We were busy, establishing our careers and families, and it no longer made much sense to keep the Glace Bay house that had raised us. In the summer of 1989, we sold 7 Coady Street. To this day I still feel guilty about breaking up our village.

We were intentional in who we sold it to. We wanted it to go to a family that would carry on our legacy of love and laughter and would hopefully keep plenty of baked goods on hand. In the end, I know our mom and dad would be happy with our choice: a single mom and her two children filled our empty home with noise and energy. It genuinely was not about the price they could pay. It was about giving another family an opportunity to be part of our Coady Street family. We wanted to ensure someone else could raise kids on the best street in the world. It was about passing on the love and grace growing up on Coady Street instilled in each of us during our childhoods and after the death of our parents.

Even though we didn't prioritize sale price when we sold the house, people we knew speculated about what we would do with "all" the money. We received a lot of advice—some solicited, most unsolicited—about what to do with our comparatively small inheritance. For all the ways in which our bigger "family" was always so supportive, there was no talk about mental health in those days, and few questions about how we were coping. I believe most people were at a loss for words, looking on with broken hearts, hoping we would make wise choices going forward. In any case, I did my best to guide the three of us toward the choices that I hope would have made Mom and Dad smile.

We knew we wanted to spend some of the money on something our parents would have enjoyed themselves and something that would create memories to last us our lifetime. So, we went to the happiest place on earth to bring some light and levity back into our hearts. In Disney World, we did indeed create memories that we carry to this day, and I thank Mom and Dad for that.

For better or worse, our lives resumed. Lana and Paula returned to jobs for which they had to travel by public transit, often in the dark. Paula was still at teachers' college in Truro, and taking the train back and forth to Halifax. Lana was working night shifts in the security department at The Bay.

One night, Lana was followed by two men from the bus stop all the way to her apartment in Fairview. There is no way on God's green earth that our mechanic father would have allowed his daughters to be dependent on public transportation for such late-night travels. I know he would have bought second-hand cars for each of my sisters, just as he had for me. Chances are I would have been right next to him picking them out, or at least helping him clean them before they were given as gifts. So, I strongly encouraged Lana and Paula to each buy a car for their safety, to "allow" Dad to do what he would have done, if he were still here with us.

Growing up, the only thing all us kids thought was missing from Coady Street was a pool. Dad, being the jokester that he was, used to tease and tell us that they'd put a pool in the empty field next to our house the next year . . . then it was the next year, and the one after that. They were never actually going to put it in a pool. It was probably some form of bribery to get us kids to fall in line, but it became one of our urban myths. As sisters, we decided to use the rest of our inheritance to make that dream come true—sort of. We put in a pool at the house I shared with Alain, and it became another reason for us to gather. Mom and Dad would have been overjoyed to see their grandchildren and neighbourhood kids congregating at our house to swim in the pool. It was like a piece of the Coady Street dream got fulfilled after all.

The years that followed Mom's death and selling our family home in Glace Bay were a time of immense change for us sisters. We had no mom or dad to call for advice on any of the challenges you face in young adulthood. There were no trips home for long weekends to recharge our batteries. We just had each other. We grew so close, many people said we could finish each other's sentences. While we approached our lives differently, one thing that was not different was the grief we carried and the need to support each other. We did nothing and everything together. I remember telling my sisters what doctor, dentist, hairdresser I had so they could get their services where I did. Sometimes they followed my suggestions and sometimes they didn't. Naturally, our lives evolved and grew into something new, yet familiar, because we were so close, our daily lives were deeply entwined. People used to say, "When you are a friend to one sister, you are a friend to all three sisters!"

As the eldest, I was already "the bossy one" and with both of our parents gone it felt natural for me to take on a pseudo-parental role. With a five-year age gap between me and Lana—and seven years between me and Paula—I gave into the urge to care for, protect, and keep them safe whole-heartedly. I didn't want them to feel any pain ever again. Although I know they never saw it that way, I loved them as if they were *my* children. It wasn't until I had my own children that I could articulate how deeply, and how maternally, I love them both. I am sure there were times they whispered about my controlling nature but everything I said or did, I did out of pure love for them. They had both suffered so much at such a young age and my heart broke for them. At this time in my life, my focus and energy was on my career, my partner Alain, and my sisters. Looking back, I was just trying to get through each day as I pushed my grief aside. I never really took the time to feel the pain—I don't think any of us did.

In comparison to me, Lana, the quintessential middle sister, was so easily loved by all. As a Pisces born in a centennial year, we knew Lana would be special right off the bat. Given our age gap, I had the distinct privilege of watching her grow from a timid, blond-haired, blue-eyed little girl into a strong, confident, and gifted woman. Understandably, Lana was favoured by many of the aunts and uncles—most notably by Uncle Leonard, who was never shy about letting it be known that she was his favourite. Lana has an inner strength and beauty that I, like so many others, am inexplicably drawn to. With her fun and easygoing nature, she has no shortage of friends who share special memories and experiences with her.

Lana is so much like Mom. Kind, gentle, radiating a type of calmness that makes people want to be close. A deep thinker, she never rushes into anything and many seek her compassionate advice. Lana would give you the shirt off her back and she is dryly funny and sarcastic. Some would call it Cape Breton humour, and Lana often doesn't realize how much she makes people laugh.

When Lana moved to Halifax she went to Mrs. Murphy's Business School. At first she wanted to go into dental hygiene, but it was no surprise to me that she excelled in business. Nor was it a surprise that Lana earned the highest grade in typing in her graduating class, considering that as a little girl she wanted to be a cash register. Not a cashier . . . a cash register! I often teased Lana that it was her childhood love for any kind of keyboard and buttons, and the endless hours of ringing mock groceries through on her bejewelled calculator, that prepared her for a world of information processing. This was a character trait that served her well in her chosen career. When Lana secured her job it felt a little bit like déjà vu. I received yet another phone call, from another girl I went to school with in Glace Bay, who called to say Lana's resume had come across her desk for a job opening at the insurance company she worked for. She knew that Lana and I were sisters, asked if Lana was still looking for work, and I said yes. Lana went for an interview and got the job. She advanced from receptionist to a commercial underwriter very quickly and was named Insurance Woman of the Year in 2015. She stayed with the insurance company until she retired after a thirty-eight-year career.

And Paula—well, she was my princess, my sweet baby sister. Like me, I'm not sure if she ever imagined she'd live anywhere but Glace Bay, but we both did. Armed with remarkable wit and the most beautiful smile, Paula loved to surprise people and make them happy.

Paula always wanted to be a teacher. As a young girl, she would gather some of the younger Coady kids to play "school." Heather, one of our Coady sisters, recalls Paula playing the role of teacher so well, complete with a chalkboard, desks, and school supplies. Years later, when Heather applied to teachers' college herself, she stayed with Paula in her Truro apartment. Paula helped her prepare for the interview and they spent the night hanging out and reminiscing. Heather plays a critical role with the Halifax Regional Centre for Education to this day. While still in college in Truro, Paula formed lifelong friendships with people from the Pictou County area, who remain a very special part of our family. Paula was all about building lasting relationships.

When Paula graduated from teachers' college and moved to Halifax, she came to stay with me and Alain for a while. Like all new teachers Paula bounced around between schools to do her practice teaching and work as a substitute teacher before securing a permanent position. I loved being her home base and I loved watching her fulfill her dream. I took full advantage of this opportunity for maximum maternalism, once telling Paula in no uncertain terms that she was not allowed to move to Texas to teach, because they had killer bees.

Paula was inclusive before inclusivity was even part of our common language. She brought people and her students together. Whenever she went to visit anyone with children, Paula would first kneel down and chat with the kids about their day, their favourite subjects, and sports, before engaging in conversation with anyone else. A parent of one of Paula's students said to me that Paula had a gift for getting people to do something before they even realized they'd signed up.

Throughout life, Lana and Paula were best friends and confidants. When we were kids this felt very convenient for me. Since they had each other to play with it meant that, as the older sibling, I was free to go out with my friends. They were always close, and when Paula came to Halifax with us, their bond strengthened even more. This offered me a great deal of comfort as I had Alain and was getting ready to start my own branch of our family tree. By the time Paula landed her dream job, teaching at her beloved Beechville-Lakeside-Timberlea school (BLT), she and Lana were ready to stop paying rent. So they bought a house together in Timberlea. It was only fifteen minutes from me, close to Paula's school, and on route to Lana's job. Their house became a stopover for friends and family from home who visited Halifax, a gathering place for card games, karaoke dinners, and full-on parties. Together, they brought laughter, joy, and likely hangovers to their treasured guests. In 1994, Paula adopted a Pomeranian-Retriever mix from Bide Awhile shelter in Dartmouth even though this shelter didn't often have dogs back. The strange combo of a puppy was just what Paula was looking for. This little rescue dog was Paula's

Paula's Fur-baby- Coady Street Glace Bay Gallant

first baby and her first true love. She called the puppy "Coady Street Glace Bay Gallant." Coady, for short, had the personality and heart of a Retriever packed into the size of a Pomeranian. Paula broke a few rules with her fur baby and often brought the dog into her classroom or other places dogs weren't expected or welcomed.

In many ways, this became a great time in our lives. My sisters and I had all secured careers we were passionate about, and we had a wonderful circle of friends that were like family. If you didn't know the hardships we'd endured at such a young age, we probably looked like we were just three sisters starting our lives with good jobs, homes of our own, extended family nearby in PEI, and our wonderful Coady Street community from childhood who were always behind us. Everybody that was part of our history was proud of us, and that somehow made me feel lighter.

However, below the surface, Paula was struggling with guilt. She blamed herself for leaving Mom alone to go to Truro for school. Lana and I regularly reminded her that we had to practically pry her out of Glace Bay to go to college, and like Dad, nothing could have prevented Mom's death. Dad always said to take your beginnings and allow them to fill you with meaning and purpose, and let them keep you moving forward; take the foundation of love you have, throw in some perseverance, and you can overcome anything. At this moment in our lives, I believed him. It seemed like a recipe for how our dad lived his life.

Mom had her own set of recipes to offer nourishment and comfort to anyone who entered our home. Like Mom, Paula was a great cook and baker. She often baked oatcakes, muffins, or other treats from Mom's recipe books to share with those she felt could use a "little happy" in their day. The following is a selection of cherished recipes from our Mom, Grammie Gallant, and Paula—lovingly compiled by Lana, just in case you need a little "happy" in your day.

> "Sometimes the best menu is simply a family recipe passed down with love and seasoned with laughter."
> —Unknown

Our Mom's Lemon Squares
1 cup cracker crumbs
¾ cup flour
1 tsp baking powder
½ cup sugar
½ cup coconut
½ cup margarine
1 package lemon filling

Preheat oven to 350°F. Mix first six ingredients together and place ¾ of mixture in bottom of lightly buttered 9x9 pan. Cook 1 package lemon filling according to directions. Pour over bottom layer. Top with reserve crumbs. Bake at 350°F for 12 minutes.

Mexican Hash Casserole - A main staple when Paula, Lana, and Paul lived together.
1 tbsp oil
1 lb ground beef
1 med onion chopped
½ tsp salt
½ tsp pepper
½ tsp cumin
1 tsp garlic
1 – 500ml jar taco sauce
12 taco shells, broken
¼ lb grated cheddar cheese

Preheat oven to 350°F. In a skillet, heat oil and brown meat. Add onion and fry until softened. Add spices and taco sauce, cook for 20-30 min. In a greased 9x9 pan, arrange alternate layers of tacos, meat and cheese. Bake at 350°F for 30-40 minutes. Top with sour cream if desired.

Fettuccine with Chicken - Paula introduced Lana to this one when they lived together. It reminds Lana of Paula every time she makes it, which is frequently.

Cooked and cut-up chicken
2 tbsp + 2 tsp margarine
4 garlic cloves chopped
2 tbsp flour
2 cups milk
½ cup Parmesan cheese
¼ tsp each of nutmeg, salt, pepper
3 cups cooked fettuccine
2 cups broccoli

Cook chicken and keep warm. Melt butter and add garlic; add flour and stir constantly with whisk for about 1 min. Continue to stir, slowly add milk, stirring constantly until bubbly and thick (3 min).

Add cheese, salt, pepper, and nutmeg until cheese melts. Add fettuccine, broccoli, and chicken, reduce heat to low and put in all ingredients.

Paula's Oatcakes - This recipe has been shared with many families and friends; Paula was famous for these. Nothing better than an oatcake and a cup of tea!

½ cup margarine
½ cup shortening
¾ cup white sugar (I use less)
1 ½ cup flour
1 tsp salt
2 cups rolled oats
½ tsp baking soda
2 tbsp. hot water (tap)

Preheat oven to 350° F. Mix everything together with fingers, then roll out on large cookie sheet until flat. Cut in squares, sprinkle with sugar on top and cook for 15-20 min. at 350°. Cut out again when removed from the oven.

Banana Chocolate Chip Muffins - Paula would frequently make these for friends who needed a little "HAPPY" that day! They are still baked, and shared, by Lana and me.
1 ½ cups flour
¾ cup sugar
1 egg
½ cup melted butter
1 tsp baking powder
1 cup of chocolate chips
1 tsp baking soda
1 tsp salt
3-4 ripe bananas

Preheat oven to 350ºF. Mix dry ingredients together. In a separate bowl, mash bananas. Melt butter and add to banana mixture. Mix in with dry ingredients. Add chocolate chips and walnuts if preferred. Bake at 350°F approximately 12-18 minutes.

Foo Yong Supreme Salad- Paula got this recipe from her Fab 5 friend group and made it often with supper.
Romaine lettuce
Bacon strips, crumbled
Bean sprouts
2 hard boiled eggs
Dressing:
¼ cup oil
¼ cup sugar
2 tbsp vinegar
3 tbsp ketchup
1 tbsp grated onion
1 tsp worcestershire sauce

Chocolate Chip Cookies - This was Paula's nephew Tim's favourite recipe.
  1 cup margarine
  ½ cup white sugar
  1 cup brown sugar
  2 eggs
  2 tsp vanilla
  2 cups flour
  ¼ tsp salt
  1 tsp baking soda
  1 bag chocolate chips

Preheat oven to 375 ° F. Mix margarine and eggs, then add white and brown sugar and vanilla. Mix together, then add flour, salt, baking soda, and chocolate chips. Bake at 375 ° for 8 minutes.

Fruit Pizza - One of the neighbourhood kids, Holly Chisholm, remembers this summer favourite of Paula's.
  Crust:
  ½ cup margarine
  ¾ cup sugar
  1 egg
  Mix well.
  Add:
  1 tbsp milk
  1 tsp vanilla
  1 ¼ cups flour
  ¼ tsp baking powder
  ¼ tsp salt

Spread dough over greased pizza pan, leaving a rim around the edge. Flour hands well to avoid sticky dough. Prick with fork. Bake 8-10 minutes at 375° until lightly brown and let cool.

Filling:
8 oz cream cheese
1/3 cup white sugar
1 ½ tsp vanilla
Cream together and spread over crust

Fruit:
Arrange at least 3 different types of fruit over crust in pizza fashion. Paula was very generous with her fruit with an artistic flair, adding banana, pineapple, strawberries, blueberries, raspberries, and blackberries. When asked what kind of fruit to use, Paula would say, Whatever you like!

Glaze:
½ cup white sugar
Dash salt
2 tbsp cornstarch
½ cup orange juice
¼ cup lemon juice
½ cup water

Mix well in saucepan. Bring to a boil, stirring constantly until thick. Pour over fruit. Chill and serve. If you have a plentiful amount of fruit you may want to go one and a half times the glaze or even double to ensure all the fruit is covered.

Mom's Tea Biscuits - Neither Mom nor Paula ever used this recipe, as they baked them so often, they knew it by heart. Mom cut out her tea biscuits with an empty baby food can and it had a dent where her thumb would fit!

2 cups flour
½ tsp salt
4 tsp baking powder
1 tsp sugar
½ cup shortening
1 cup of milk (maybe a bit more)

Preheat oven to 425°F. Mix dry ingredients in a bowl. Cut in shortening with a pastry blender, two forks or your fingers until mealy. Add milk and mix with a fork, working quickly, and then knead lightly until dough forms a ball and put on a floured counter. With a floured rolling pin, roll out lightly until about an inch thick and cut with a biscuit cutter (it must have a sharp edge, not a glass).

Bake at 425°F, approx. 15-18 min.

Grammie Gallant's Cinnamon Rolls - These rolls of deliciousness used to be hidden in her pantry, but we all knew where to find them. They are still a household favourite!

3 cups flour
6 tsp baking powder
¼ cup white sugar
¼ c brown sugar
1 tsp salt

Preheat the oven to 400°F. Mix the dry ingredients in a bowl.

Cut in ½ cup shortening with a pastry blender, two forks, or your fingers until oatmeal texture.

Add 2 beaten eggs in a 1-cup capacity measuring cup and top with milk (may need a little more).

Knead into a ball, gently. Use a floured rolling pin and roll out and spread with butter. Add brown sugar and then cover with cinnamon. Pick up edges and roll tight and cut ¾ to 1 inch with a sharp knife. Place on a cookie sheet.

Bake at 400°F, approx. 15-20 min.

Chapter 4

Our Love Grows

"Our family is a circle of strength and love; with every birth and every union, the circle will grow. Every joy shared adds more love; every crisis faced together makes the circle stronger." —Unknown

Alain and I were married on December 29th, 1990, in Cape Breton Nova Scotia. Though I was surrounded by the love of family and friends, it once again felt like there was an elephant in the room. It was the first major life event without my parents, and their absence deepened the canyon of loss in my heart. Our wedding had a quiet undertone of sadness kept at bay only by the love Alain and I shared. My sweet, beautiful Grammie Gallant walked me down the aisle. Even now, if I close my eyes, I can still feel Grammie's love and strength pass from her to me like a warm wind as we walked, arm-in-arm, slowly down the aisle.

Lynn's wedding with Lana (left) and Paula (right)

It wasn't until I had my own children that I realized how hard that day must have been for Grammie, knowing her oldest son died too young to walk me down the aisle himself. Her heart must have been breaking with each step, yet she offered *me* comfort and support. My wedding day was just one of the ways that Grammie helped us move forward. Since we rarely went "home" to Cape Breton, Grammie kept us from feeling like orphans through constant

Grammie walking Lynn down the aisle

contact and endless invited (insisted) trips "home" to PEI on holidays. Grammie and all my Gallant aunts and uncles kept our connection to Dad alive and ensured we always felt we were still part of the Gallant family. Through her trademark strength, Grammie continued the life lessons Dad had started, affirmations about the importance of family, and upholding good human values. I like to think these were character traits that Grammie, Dad, and I all shared. Grammie kept Dad alive for us because she brought us to the Gallant family, and being around that extended family was so nurturing and healing that it was like Mom and Dad were sending their love from beyond. When I felt like I couldn't breathe, Grammie would be the space where I could go and do so.

The same is true whenever we are with people from "down home," Cape Breton, especially Coady Street and 23 Hillside families. They were all such a big part of our life when our parents were alive that just being with them created a familiar connection to our parents.

I know now that when Dad gave me responsibilities that were above my age and often my skill set, he set me up to be an employee who showed initiative, loyalty, leadership, and knew how to create a workplace community. My bosses also always gave me projects that would allow me to grow and learn new things and punch above my weight or reach above my height, so to speak, just like Dad did. As a result, I was often assigned to clients and situations that needed a "fixer." I handled disgruntled clients and supported my peers to do the same. Once, I was assigned to alleviate the dissatisfaction of an important customer, a CIO, facing a major customer service problem. In the first meeting, the CIO asked why he should trust me.

I said, "You shouldn't, yet. But I trust *myself* to make this right."

In the end, this client stayed with us, and we had a great working relationship for many years. I was fortunate to work with wonderful people throughout my career. In fact, when my son opened his own roofing company, my very first boss and mentor from decades before was one of *his* first clients. Moments like that assured me that the Coady Street sense of community was alive and well within us, instilled deeply by the relationships our parents taught us how to make.

I was the first of the sisters to get pregnant. I believe that your labor and delivery experience provides insights into the kind of personality your child will have. I was sent home three times over that long weekend in May, and the doctors and nurses simply said "This baby was in no hurry to come out." I was so embarrassed after the second time that I refused to go back in until I was absolutely certain the baby was coming. It was sixty-three long, painful hours from my first contraction until Tim was born, and I wanted my mom for every minute. When Tim finally made his grand entrance, he looked a little like a Conehead character from a Saturday Night Live skit. Lana and Paula were big fans of SNL, so they had a lot of fun with this. And to this day, Tim is rarely in a hurry.

When Tim was born, I wanted nothing more than to show my mom that we finally had a baby boy in the family. On one hand, I felt fortunate to have this healthy boy; on the other hand, I felt a deep sadness that Mom wasn't there to share in the joy. I remember sitting on the hospital bed, looking up to the sky and saying, "It's all good, Mom. We finally got our boy." It was a layer of emotion I wasn't prepared for. On some level, I think it would have been emotionally easier if I had a girl. I think my mom's absence, in particular, was heightened because the first grandchild was a boy. I guess in some weird twist of tradition it was fitting that as Dad's tomboy baby girl I had a son. I remember thinking I had no idea what to do with a baby boy, but I had Alain to help with that, of course.

Once the wave of pain that my parents wouldn't be able to hold their grandson subsided, I felt an inexplicable sense of maternal accomplishment. Again, science aside, I felt that I made this beautiful boy and I wouldn't trade him for anything on earth. Mom would have loved Tim as they have similar personalities. Like Mom, Tim is gentle and full of wisdom, and he even resembles her! Paula looked like Mom as well and when she took Tim out, people often thought he was her son. Even now, watching Tim gives me a feeling of deep connection to my mother, for which I am ever-so grateful.

Throughout my second pregnancy I felt like I was carrying a boy, as the pregnancy "felt" similar to the first one. Alain, however, was adamant it was a girl. He was so confident we were having a girl that he came home from a golfing trip with a little pink dress and he brought it to the hospital when I was in labour. When our son Connor was born, I remember my doctor saying, "This little boy's gonna look so cute in that pink dress." Alain still didn't believe that we had another son until the doctor said, "Trust me. This baby may want a dress someday, but right now it's got all the parts to be a boy." Thirty years later, much to Connor's embarrassment, that pink dress still hangs in a closet.

As if to further prove my point, Connor's labor also reflects his personality. Connor was born ready to run; he hardly waited for help to make his way into this world. To this day, Connor is always in go-mode. If Tim is a reflection of my mother, then Connor evokes a connection to my dad, right down to the tar stains on his hands and nails. I hope these similarities offered comfort to Lana and Paula.

During the summer of 1996 Lana, Paula, and another friend from Cape Breton were staying at Hubbard's Campground and joined an epic party at the (in)famous Shore Club. I can never do justice to telling the story of that weekend like Lana can, as that was the weekend she met her forever love, Paul Kenny. Lana was incredibly happy. In 1997, Paul moved in with Lana and Paula and their shared home became a parody of the TV show *Three's Company*, full of laughter, gags, and love. They quickly became a family: three adults and two fur babies, Coady and Kaylee, Paul's singing husky mix.

Eventually Lana and Paul bought their own home in Hammonds Plains, and Paula opted to stay in Timberlea. If you looked on a map, our houses formed a perfect triangle—a symbol of strength and stability. It reminded me of the triangle pinky ring Mom had made for us out of Dad's wedding band. We lived about 15 minutes away from each other, which was just far enough and just close enough for us to drop in as needed.

In June of 1998, one of our family's happiest celebrations took place at the very same Shore Club. Lana and Paul were married, and my charismatic middle sister beamed the brightest I had ever seen her. I know it was not an easy-breezy day for her, just as my wedding day had been difficult for me. Lana simply glowed, surrounded by the love of our family and friends and completely embraced by her new family: the Kenny and McQuaid clans.

Lana's Wedding

Two years later, Lana and Paul had their first child. A boy! Paul was a diehard Bob Dylan fan, so they named their sweet baby Dylan James, after Paul's dad. Dylan has grown into an amazing young man with his father's very dry sense of humour. Four years later, they welcomed a baby girl. Lana and Paul named their blue-eyed, blond, curly-haired, bundle of infectious energy Emily Dianne. Emily has been a breath of positivity and a ray of light since the day she was born. The Kenny family had indeed blossomed.

While Lana and I were starting our families, Paula was working hard to establish herself in her teaching profession. Her love of teaching was evident in all she did, both in and out of the classroom. She was fulfilling a lifelong dream. All that seemed to be missing was someone special to share her hopes and passions with.

Paula spent a lot of time with family and was always ready to step in to babysit or take one or all of "the kids" on an excursion for some

Auntie time. Some of Paula's best friends lived in Pictou County and she would often take trips out of the city to spend time with them. She graciously watched each of them fall in love, get married, and start to have their own families, and she really couldn't wait for that to happen for her as well. It seemed she was always the bridesmaid, and never the bride.

In 2001, as a congratulations for securing a permanent teaching position, Alain and I gifted Paula with a ticket to British Columbia. She would go visit one of her best friends stationed there as an RCMP officer. The trip was scheduled over March break, so I had the flexibility to pick Paula up at the airport and was very much looking forward to it. When I offered to pick her up, Paula said, a little sheepishly, that her friend Jason would be giving her a ride. It became clear they were dating and Paula had been keeping him a secret, which was incredibly strange. Things this important just didn't go unsaid among us sisters–or so I thought. I donned my pseudo-mother hat and began the inquisition. Who was this Jason? Where had she met him? Where was he from? And, in true Cape Breton tradition, I asked who his father was.

What I learned was, his name was Jason MacRae and they had met at a party. For some reason, Paula drove him home after the party and he apparently left something with her and then tracked her down to get it back. That's how their relationship started. Satisfied I was caught up on her new "friend," I told Paula I was going to drop off a pot of soup at her place, so she'd have something to eat when she got home from B.C. She told me Jason was vegetarian. "Fine," I said. "I'll make sure it's vegetable soup."

I had let myself into my sister's home countless times in the past. Normally I would just use my key, as we all had keys to each other's homes, but some instinct made me suspect that Jason was at Paula's that day. I politely but begrudgingly knocked and it felt strange, as this place was basically an extension of my own home. Indeed, Jason was there, and opened the door like he owned the house and I was selling vacuums. All I could smell was marijuana, and all I could see was this slightly dishevelled guy blocking my way into my home-away-from-home. How dare he? Didn't he know we were a triumvirate?

All the hairs on the back of my neck stood up. I introduced myself and mentioned that Paula must have told him I was stopping by. Jason didn't move to let me in. It felt like a strange standoff between Paula's old life and her new one, and for the first time, I was part of the old. At first, I leaned in to pass him the soup pot. Then I summoned my courage like a mama bear and I thought, *this is my family,* and pushed right past him.

"I'll just put it on the stove," I said. I remember that short walk from the semi's split-entry to the kitchen, thinking the place was too messy for Paula's taste. She was always the neat and tidy one of the three of us. There was a shift in energy in the house that I couldn't name and it made me feel disoriented. The sensation of being uncomfortable in my sister's home made me want to get the hell out of there and I retreated quickly. I could only get out the words, "Don't forget to pick up Paula," before I closed the door behind me, maybe just a little too firmly.

About two weeks later, over Easter weekend, I was formally introduced to Jason as Paula's boyfriend. That was the year I'd gone on a cooking strike, saying I refused to spend days prepping for a multi-course meal only to have it consumed in under thirty minutes. Given that neither of my sisters had ever cooked a turkey, we made reservations at a restaurant in Black Point. "Jason is a vegetarian," Paula reminded us, in a way that felt a little needling at the time. But we loved Paula, so I called the restaurant and confirmed that they would indeed have some vegetarian options available.

For big family meals, Alain and I always invited our neighbour, a senior who lived alone and served as a surrogate grandfather to our kids. His real name was Murray but we all called him Poppy. So, for this Easter dinner Alain and I, our two boys, Lana, Paul, and baby Dylan waited for Paula, Jason, and Poppy to come. I heard Paula's car pull up, so I started to get Tim and Connor ready to go.

Paula came into the house first and she was laughing. She had this really beautiful, wonderful laugh that made you feel good whenever you heard it.

"What are you laughing at?" I asked her.

"When Jason and I were getting out of the car, Poppy was coming down the lane. He took Jason's hands, folded them in his, looked

Jason in the eye, and said, 'If you ever hurt her I'll break both your legs.'"

When Poppy came in, I told him he couldn't say those things. He looked at me with this *fait accompli* look and said, "Oh yes, I can. I love you three girls like my own."

Murray left us in October 2002 and Jason stayed.

Soon after that, Jason officially moved into the home that Paula and Lana had shared. With time, we got to know him, and it did seem he and Paula were well matched. Paula was a very health-conscious person, and collecting and cooking vegetarian recipes didn't faze her a bit. They had a wide circle of friends and enjoyed socializing. As you do when new people come into to your life, we adapted our ways to make sure Jason felt welcome in our family. With his parents and family living far away, Jason adopted Alain and me as his pseudo-parents, just as Paula had. And, with time, Jason became the "cool" uncle to the kids–the one with the energy to play football on the beach while the rest of us parents lounged about. He found time to play mini-golf and regularly attended their sporting events.

One night in 2002, Jason showed up unexpectedly at our door to ask me and Alain if he could propose to Paula. He promised to love her, take care of her, and be a wonderful husband forever. He said he was the luckiest man alive to have her in his life. Naturally, we said yes.

Paula appeared happy, and it seemed that Jason was well liked by everyone in our circle. Still, it felt like the pseudo-parent thing to do, so one day leading up to the wedding, I sat Paula down, looked her in the eye, and asked if she was sure this was the man for her. I remember experiencing a very acute, mom-like moment, almost like a physical hot-flash sensation, when I asked her. Paula told me she was sure. It was one of those times when you realize your "kids" are grown and you can no longer really influence their big decisions; you have no choice but to be supportive. So, that's what I did.

In 2003 on a hot, humid day, I walked my beautiful sister down the aisle and gave her my love and blessings. I welcomed Jason MacRae and his family into our close-knit, trusting, and accepting circle. In the guest book at the Kenny cottage in PEI where they celebrated their honeymoon, Paula wrote: *I am truly blessed to have married my best friend.*

In 2005, Paula experienced the ultimate joy as she celebrated her daughter's birth. On January 6th, I held my sister's hand and whispered encouraging words of support and comfort during the labour and delivery of her baby.

Paula's wedding with Lynn and Lana

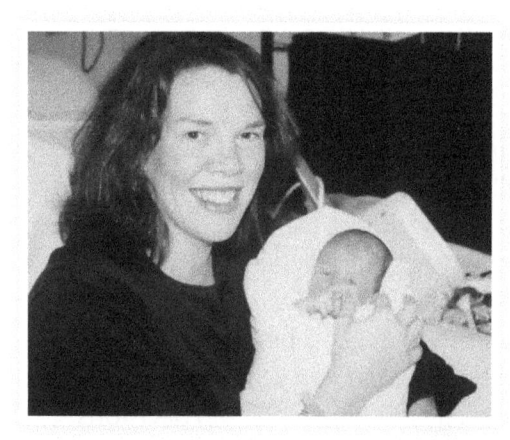

Paula's wish to be a Mom came true

At 3:05 a.m., Anna Paul was born, named after both our parents. Paula asked me to cut Anna's umbilical cord, and from that time on she affectionately called me "Grandma" when Anna was in my presence. Anna was born just eight months after Emily, which meant Lana and Paula were on maternity leave together. To see them bond even more deeply as mothers inspired an incredible sense of maternal pride all my own. We were three sisters raising five children. Our love for each other's kids was interchangeable and unbreakable. When we were all together, you never knew whose kids belonged to whom. Just like it had been on Coady Street.

At Thanksgiving that year, I felt overwhelmingly grateful. I was so full of love and gratitude that I took a page from Grammie's book and I wrote everyone a letter—a kind of love letter. I told each wonderful person in my life (including the dogs!) how much I appreciated them. In the letters to my sisters, I told them how lucky I felt for the sisterly closeness we'd maintained, the partners we'd found, the beautiful children we had, and the careers we'd nurtured. I assured Lana and Paula that we were living a good life, just as Mom and Dad would have wanted for us. I wrote that despite our incredible losses some things had turned out alright. If Mom and Dad had still been with us, all our lives would have been split between two places. They would have whisked the kids off to Cape Breton all summer long and spent a lot of their time commuting to Halifax for hockey games, school concerts, and in-service days. Instead, we had each other within a fifteen-minute triangle. I wrote that while we would always want to tell Mom and Dad about the time one of us got a promotion at work, or when one of our kids made a varsity basketball team, we still had each other and our growing family to celebrate each day with. For all that I felt very fortunate.

Cousins at Kenny Family Cottage PEI

Writing about such gratitude almost felt as if I was writing farewell letters to the pain I'd carried since losing my parents. As I rolled up the pieces of paper and set them as placeholders on our overflowing Thanksgiving table, I finally released the core-deep breath that I had been holding since Mom and Dad died.

Chapter 5

Christmas Love and Joy

"Christmas is a day of meaning and traditions, a special day spent in the warm circle of family and friends." —Margaret Thatcher

December 24th, 2005

The immense feeling of love, gratitude, and peace from Thanksgiving carried us straight through to Christmas. Since our parents had passed away we spent Christmas together. Our family celebration began on Christmas Eve and lasted until Boxing Day. Alain and I hosted until Lana and Paul bought their home; then we would rotate between the two. This sometimes provided comic relief when I attempted to transport a massive, often pre-cooked, turkey to Lana's house. Christmas 2005 was being hosted by Lana and Paul and I was so excited, as it would be the kind of Christmas chaos that creates lifelong memories, considering Emily was nineteen months old and Anna would be eleven months. They were at the perfect age of wonderment and awe. Tim and Connor were still "believers"--and if they weren't, they were too afraid to let the thrill of surprise go.

I felt like my "cup runneth over" and I, along with my sisters, was so looking forward to spending this magical, concentrated time together. Just a few days before Christmas I was looking after Emily, and I knew Paula was feeling a little stressed as they were in the process of buying a new home. I called her to see if she and Anna wanted to join Emily and I in a little retail therapy. I offered to pick them both up and when I arrived, Paula was writing in her journal and looking very pensive. Paula journaled faithfully and kept them all in a trunk I had given her years before, and yet after that day, I never saw any of them again.

Stockings made by Mrs. Ethel Boutilier

When Paula saw us, she snapped the book shut, smiled, and said she was ready to go. We went shopping and then to Montana's for lunch. It was just the kind of little happy outing that got us in the Christmas spirit–especially as we watched Emily and Anna devour the mini-ice creams they serve. Chocolate and vanilla dripped everywhere! I could just tell that Paula was completely in love with her baby girl and spending time together with the two babies was good medicine for us all.

Knowing I wanted to spend as much time as possible watching and playing with the children that year, I decided to cook the turkey prior to going to Lana's. Which is why on the afternoon of the 24th, I was running around our house, ensuring I had all the spices and fixings I would need to finish off the turkey, and that the boys had essentials like toothbrushes and underwear. Alain was loading our presents into the car and left a bottle of wine, a gift from someone at work, under the tree. We planned to save it for when we returned from Lana's on Boxing Day.

As I was finally closing the door to our home, the smell of turkey lingered in the air, with the promise of turkey sandwiches on fresh homemade bread to come. Once we were all in the car, I let out a sigh of utter contentment. I was simultaneously looking forward to having all eleven of us together and to when the rush and pressure of the formal holiday was over and Alain and I could share a quiet moment by ourselves. It was the mixed bag of emotions that only Christmas can stir up.

As it was Anna's first Christmas, Paula and Jason had lingered at home to do a video call with Jason's family, who were in Ontario. It was nice that technology made it possible for them to watch Anna open the gifts they had sent. Knowing they would be spending Christmas with our families, Jason had taken Anna to Ontario a few weeks before. Of course, as it goes, with your first child you take 100 pictures a day, not as many with the second, and hardly any of the third. What I appreciated about Paula's endless photos were the really funny captions she would add. They were meant to show Anna's blossoming personality when really, they were insights into Paula's love for her daughter and her light-hearted sense of humour.

In our family we actually eat Christmas dinner on Christmas Eve. That way I didn't have to spend all of Christmas day in the kitchen, like my mom did. Instead, after opening presents we enjoy a big brunch, and then relax, play with the kids, have some festive cheer. The menu for Christmas dinner was pretty typical of East Coast Canada. Obviously there was turkey, gravy, homemade dressing, and cranberries. For sides we could fill up on potatoes, corn, turnip, and carrots; we made sure we had a variety of vegetables for Jason. We always had the crackers you pull open with those most flimsy paper crowns and jokes inside. The crowns were worn throughout the meal and we took turns reading the jokes out loud.

Since I did the turkey, Lana and Paula were in charge of dessert. This year, Lana made sugar cookies and shortbread which just melted in your mouth. If anyone had room for more dessert, they could indulge in the requisite fruit cake, or nibble on the assortment of cookies and squares we likely all had brought home from our individual work parties. Throughout the meal and Christmas in general, Lana and I kept trying to heap more food and dessert on Paula. For someone who was in her thirties and had given birth less than a year before, she looked too thin in our overprotective eyes. Paula was slight to begin with, but it seemed she had lost a substantial amount of weight and it was concerning.

As expected, getting the kids to bed that night took some effort. The excitement of seeing the stockings Mrs. Ethel Boutilier had made, hung in anticipation of being filled by Santa, was even too much for Paul. Without a doubt, Paul was the Christmas energizer bunny—a kid at heart, he never lost his sense of Christmas magic. Paul was the official eater of the "cookies and milk for Santa." Not only did he munch away on the treats, he would leave the kids the most brilliant notes. Once the kids were nestled and snug in their beds, the moms began to fill the socks, while the dads pulled out all the toys that required "some assembly" and began the inevitable—and unenviable—hunt for batteries.

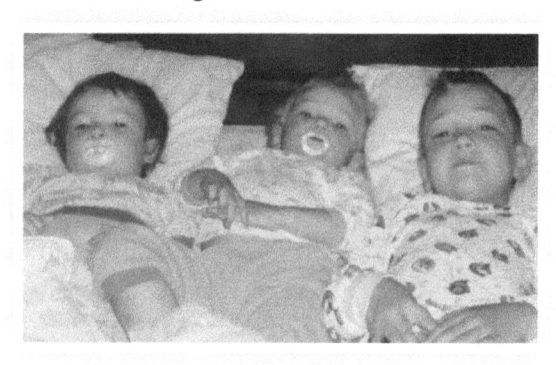

Anna, Emily and Dylan

We all went to bed that night with full bellies, eager to make more happy memories in the morning.

Christmas Morning

There is one silly, simple Gallant tradition that I hope my sons, nieces, and nephew carry on in their own homes on Christmas morning: permission to eat unlimited Quality Street chocolates before breakfast. I don't know where or why this tradition started, but I remember my mom and dad cracking open a can of these seasonal, scrumptious mixed chocolates before the first piece of tape was ripped off a gift. I distinctly remember the unique smell of the big can, a combination of chocolate and ink or dye from the wrapping. Of course, the cans were about the size of a wash basin back then, so it seemed like an endless tub of pure indulgence. Mom would hold the "chocolate cheat sheet" and remind us of our favourites as this was an annual, Christmastime-only treat. Lana, Paula, and I each had our favourites, and would be in such a rush to sort through what felt like a colourful treasure trove that we'd move or slap each other's hands playfully away to find the specific ones we wanted. Then we would dramatically slow down to untwist the first layer of shiny plastic, then carefully peel away the protective tinfoil layer without tearing it. I remember one chocolate also had a white outer paper wrapping, similar to those used on cigars. If you were careful, you could slide it off and use it as a paper ring for a little while. The sugary rush that followed only fuelled the anticipation of gift opening. All these memories came rushing back when Alain cracked open the tin this year. Except now, we had to share our brightly wrapped treats with our husbands and children, and I held the "chocolate cheat sheet."

Another tradition, which I am sure my sons, nieces, and nephew won't carry on is the requirement that children wait on the stairs until all the adults have consumed at least a couple mouthfuls of coffee or tea before they descend into the chaos around the tree. Paul, the only adult in

Cousins waiting for Christmas morning to start!

the house with the energy to match the kids, single-handedly amped up the anticipation and excitement at Christmastime. Usually, Paul was the first up, and he woke the whole house by blaring Christmas music and grinding beans for coffee that he would sweeten with a little Bailey's Irish Cream. At thirteen and eleven, this was all the incentive my boys needed to go from excited to euphoric. Paul would shake, rattle, and sniff each present before passing it over to be opened, or before opening his own, simply to tease the children and stretch out the enchantment of opening the gifts. Starting with the youngest, we would pass out a gift to one person at a time, and everyone else watched while that gift was opened. With eleven of us, it took several delightful hours to open our gifts.

By the time the gifts were open and wrapping paper picked up and sorted into recyclable and non-recyclable piles, it was time to start the prep for our big Christmas breakfast. Lana, Paula, and I headed to the kitchen while Alain and Paul kept the kids occupied with their new toys. Jason was going to run back home before breakfast to feed Coady and let her out. They had left Coady home this year as she was getting a little older, and a little crankier, and with the girls running around the commotion might have been too much. This gave us sisters a little gossip time while we sipped our tea and coffee in the kitchen.

Paula confided that she was not happy with Jason about his recent trip to Ontario with Anna. It seemed Jason had resumed living a fairly carefree life while he was there. Every time Paula called, he was out, with Anna being watched by his parents. She said his parents always made excuses for him. None of our husbands are perfect, so Lana and I just thought this was good, healthy venting. Looking back now, it's as if Paula was beginning to see a different person than the one she thought she knew and loved. Paula also mentioned she had met a friend from NSCAD for lunch a few days before, and when her friend got in her car, she asked if Paula had taken up smoking. This was a running conversation among the three of us, as Lana and I both thought Paula's car always smelled like someone had been smoking in it. Her friend was the first outside the family to confirm it. Despite Jason's vehement protest that he didn't smoke, we all thought he snuck the occasional cigarette—which was fine—we just didn't understand why he lied about it. Lana was convinced Jason had, in fact, smoked inside her downstairs bathroom. When Lana confronted Jason and told him there was no smoking allowed in the house, he denied it again and this time blamed the smell on his hair gel. This felt very demeaning to Lana and Paula, which triggered the "mama bear" in me, and may explain why I burned my finger making the stacks and stacks of pancakes that would be part of brunch.

Christmas brunch was nearly ready, but Jason still hadn't returned. While we waited we got the kids washed and dressed. The girls were close enough and young enough in age that we could dress them alike and it was still cute. So, like any good auntie, I bought them matching outfits for Christmas. Emily with her curly blond hair and Anna with her brown hair looked like a matching pair of dolls. It seemed whatever Emily unwrapped, Anna wanted, and whatever Anna opened, Emily wanted. It was nearly a perfect Christmas morning, except at one point when we had to break up a wrestling match between the girls over a toy—but not before we snapped a picture. For a moment, all we could see was a ball of black velvet and white frilly tights.

Anna and Emily's Christmas Wrestling Match!

Jason had been gone so long that Paula was visibly upset and quite embarrassed, especially as Jason wasn't answering his phone. When he finally returned, we could feel the tension between them. His excuse for making us all wait—including the kids and dear Aunt Marge (mom's first cousin, who was up from Cape Breton visiting another relative)—was that he'd fallen asleep. Regardless, breakfast brunch was enjoyed, then we gathered around to hang out in Lana's exquisitely decorated living room. Lana and Paul always had a very beautiful home, and their stairwell was the perfect backdrop for photos of the kids dressed in their Christmas best. We still make them pose for pictures today.

As I sat back and watched my beautiful family, I reflected on how in a way, Paula was similar to Paul, both equally engaged with the kids. Paula's natural instinct with children, especially with Tim and Connor, allowed her to slip into their world and share their joy, interests, and passions while bringing them all her love and learning. This was what made her an exceptional teacher and this morning was no different. Alain and I bought Connor a guitar as his big gift that year, while Lana had our childhood piano from Cape Breton, where Paula could bang out a few tunes. While she played the piano, Paula patiently coached Connor on the guitar. At one point Lana joined in by singing and I couldn't help but wonder at how Christmas past blended with Christmas present. In my mind's eye I was transported back in time to when Lana and Paula were little girls kneeling in front of the tree and giving Mom and Dad a private Christmas concert. After seeing Lana and Paula sing and Connor play his guitar, Christmas carols have never sounded the same.

December 26th

The next morning, we all got up and had breakfast and helped Lana and Paul return their home to some normalcy before we packed up and headed back to our respective homes to reset. Paula and Jason were eager to get home to Coady and to finish up some minor pre-sale renovation projects as they had made a conditional offer on a new home in Timberlea. Paula was anxious to sell her house and was keen to do some touch-up painting and cleaning before a showing later that week. On the 27th, Alain's sister, Auntie Di, had planned to take our boys to see *King Kong*, freeing Alain and I to plan our own date to go see the new movie about Johnny Cash. We packed all the gifts and some leftovers into the car, then hugged and kissed each other goodbye. It had been no small feat to fit eleven people under one roof at one of the most stressful times of the year. Of course, there had been some Griswold moments over the past 48 hours, but what

Paula and Anna Christmas 2005

resounded with me most was the love and the respect we all had for each other. It really was the most wonderful Christmas.

I was so happy that as cousins, Emily and Anna were developing complementary personalities, and I just knew they were bound to be best friends. What I didn't know was that they would eventually become sisters, when our idyllic Christmas ended in a horrific nightmare.

Chapter 6

Love and Death

December 27th

The next day, Auntie Di and her daughter Darcie—who was visiting from England—took our boys to see *King Kong*, a nearly three-hour movie! This gave Alain and me the opportunity to go see *Walk the Line*, the biopic of Johnny Cash. Despite the teasing from my sisters when I told them on Boxing Day that I wanted to see it, I really enjoyed the film—and enjoyed having some rare alone time with my husband. When we all left to go to the movies, it was one of those cold, clear, sunny winter days where the temperature hung around zero degrees Celsius. By the time we came out of the movie theatre, around 3 p.m., the wind chill brought it down to minus 10, with a damp, dark feeling that you often get during winter on the East Coast. It was the kind of day that made you want to hunker down with some snacks at home and watch some good TV.

I hadn't spoken to Paula since we all left Lana's the day before, and she was on my mind a lot that day. As we were driving out of the city on the 103 highway, I said to Alain, "We should drop in to Paula's and see what progress she's made on her projects." At this point in our lives, Alain and I had completely renovated our home, which had once been an old fishing shack, so we had some idea of what they might be experiencing. Since Jason often asked Alain for home maintenance tips, I knew he wouldn't mind, and Paula was used to her family dropping in unannounced. I thought they would appreciate us stopping by, even if it was just to make them both a cup of tea or play with Anna for a bit.

Just as Alain started down the exit ramp, that hunker-down-at-home-with-the-kids feeling took over and I changed my mind as I didn't really want my boys to come home to an empty house over Christmas. Instead of going to Paula's we stopped at New Release Video and picked out two movies to watch with the boys. The thought of hanging out at home another day in our comfy clothes, surrounded by our own Christmas decorations and tree, felt too tempting to pass up. Alain crossed the road and drove back up the on-ramp to the highway that would take us home.

The boys came home around 4 p.m. Soon after, Alain drove Tim to hockey practice and a Christmas party at St. Margaret's Bay Arena, then came home. This gave us time to watch a movie with Connor before Alain headed back to the rink to pick Tim up for 9:30 p.m. They were back by ten and we decided to indulge ourselves and watch another movie, *Bewitched*.

We had to paused the movie to get more snacks and to refill our drinks. Alain was in the kitchen and asked if anybody wanted a ham sandwich on homemade bread. I replied, "No, but I'll have a bite of yours." Which meant my sweet, intuitive husband of fifteen years made a sandwich and *a half* for "himself." On his way back to the family room, the phone rang. I looked at the clock and wondered who was calling at 10:20 at night. Naturally, I listened to the half of the conversation that I could hear.

Alain was saying, "No. No, we haven't. Well, just a second, I'll let you talk to Lynn."

Alain brought me the phone and said, "It's Jason," in a tone that caused an increase in my heart rate and a burst of cortisol that all parents feel when there's a possible threat to their kids.

Jason said, "I probably already know the answer to this question. Did you see Paula today?"

More cortisol pumped out, with a slightly faster heart rate. "No. What do you mean, did I see Paula?"

"She went out around two this afternoon and she hasn't come home."

I jumped up to my feet and started firing questions at Jason: "What do you mean she hasn't come home? Did you have a fight? Did something trigger her? This is not like Paula. Where's Anna?"

"No, no," he replied, talking over me. "She had to go to get diapers for Anna. And she didn't come home."

I said, "That doesn't make any sense."

And then he said, "Lana is here."

I stopped pacing. Something was definitely wrong. "Lana is *there*?" My free hand flew up to that worry spot where my throat joins my chest.

He said, "Yeah, I called Lana."

Everything went into slow motion as I processed.

I knew Lana and Paul had been at Paul's parents' house for supper, as his brother and family had flown in for Christmas. Apparently, Jason had left a very casual message on Lana's answering machine while they were gone. When they got home, Lana noticed the light flashing on the phone, asked Paul to get Dylan and Emily ready for bed, and she'd be up in a minute. Lana wasn't surprised to hear Jason's voice, especially as the message sounded so casual, until the actual meaning of the words sunk in.

"Hi, just wondering if you saw Paula today. She went shopping and isn't back yet."

The hairs on the back of Lana's neck had stood up as alarm bells started to ring. Lana called up to Paul and said she had to run over to Paula's, which in itself wasn't unusual, as we were always running things back and forth, sharing pots, pans, and other household items. *Mi casa es su casa* and all that.

Lana drove over there on her own. By this time of night, the sky had cleared and was a dark blue colour that made the stars look all the more bright. The trepidation of not knowing what she was walking into made Lana hyper-focused on the drive. She desperately tried to hold her biggest fear at bay—that something terrible happened to Paula. Since Paula would never, ever leave Anna, she wondered where Anna was and why Jason hadn't mentioned their daughter.

When Lana arrived at Paula's house, she tried to appear calm and somewhat casual—like one would approach a mad dog, or a wild animal you found in your shed. Which was why, knowing I would barge in like a sergeant major after a failed mission, she opted not to call me straight away. Lana opted to investigate first, to assess, and to use her own finely tuned spider senses before bringing me in as the blunt force. Thankfully, Lana was smart enough to make note of things that only sisters would see. When she first walked in, Lana could smell paint. Yep, that made sense. She could also smell paint cleaner or turpentine—again, made sense, if they spilled some paint or had to strip a baseboard or something first. Lana could also smell cigarette smoke—but having confronted Jason just days before for smoking in her own house, she kept this observation to herself.

Alarm Bell One went off in Lana's head knowing Jason had smoked inside.

Lana, in her brilliant wisdom, took a look at Paula's kitchen calendar—just in case we all forgot something Paula had planned. Thankfully, the kitchen calendar was used as a day planner and it was also where Paula attached sticky notes to remind herself of grocery items or other things she had to buy or pick up. There, on the calendar, was a sticky note that said *Batteries*—not diapers, as Jason had said.

Alarm Bell Two.

Knowing there was a possibility that Paula had simply grabbed the wrong sticky on her way out, Lana checked the closet where she kept the baby supplies. There was an abundance of diapers.

Alarm Bell Three.

By this point, Lana was desperate to bust into Anna's room to check and make sure her sweet little niece was okay. But she knew she had to keep calm, just like Jason was. Lana is whip smart, so she suggested that Jason log into their bank account online to see where Paula had been shopping that afternoon, figuring that would give them some way to track her movements—and would give Lana an insight into what Paula may have been planning or was up to. There were no banking transactions—Paula hadn't bought diapers.

Alarm Bell Four.

Lana was nearly bubbling with impatience to go check on Anna. She suggested Jason go out and drive around the neighbourhood to see if he could spot Paula's car. Maybe it broke down or she was at a neighbour's house. The nanosecond after Jason pulled out of the driveway, Lana went to check on Anna. To her utter, visceral relief, Anna was sound asleep in her crib.

My first alarm bell had gone off knowing Jason had called Lana first. Ever since he joined our family, Jason called Alain and me first, a hundred per cent of the time, for everything. On the day he should have called us first, he called us last. At the time, I figured it was because he knew I would call every police force in Canada, from the RCMP to Border Services, to the Via Rail Train Police. Hell, the US National Guard would have been on my list. My baby sister was missing; no stone would be left unturned.

Adrenaline joined cortisol and I was in full fight-or-flight mode.

I told Jason to hang on a minute and said to Alain, "You need to go to Paula's. Lana is there. You need to get Lana. You need to start looking for Paula."

I asked Jason if he had called the police and he said he called at 6 p.m. and 7 p.m., and they told him to call back after the malls closed, as they thought Paula might have just been shopping. He said he had called back since then too. I kept asking him to tell me where my sister had to go that day, what clothes she had on, and anything else he could tell me. He spoke in a very low, muffled tone and I had to get him to speak up several times. I knew in my heart that something was wrong, this was totally out of character for Paula. I kept asking why she took the car as she usually drove their SUV, as it had more safety features for Anna's sake. I kept thinking that maybe she had been in a car accident, maybe she hit black ice and her car went off the road. No matter what her physical condition, even if she was a paraplegic, she just had to be alive. No matter her condition, I—*we*—would take care of her. I wouldn't let myself even consider that she wasn't alive in a ditch somewhere. I could not imagine her not being alive.

Of course, I was trying to rationalize why Paula was not home where she belonged. But my gut knew something terrible was wrong. I told Jason I was coming too, and would call Alain's sister to come stay with the boys. If Paula had indeed gone to buy diapers at Costco or Walmart, I couldn't imagine anyone being able to harm her in the Bayer's Lake shopping area. I had been there that afternoon, and the place was packed with people. If someone had ever tried to grab her, Paula would have fought for her life and probably hurt them in the process. She was small but certainly very mighty and would have done anything to see her daughter again.

I called Auntie Di, who lived just a few minutes from our home, and told her I needed her. I didn't need to give her a reason. My two sons were in a state of shock at this point because I was completely beside myself. I got dressed and called my dear friend Andre MacLean, commonly thought of as our fourth sister. I told her Jason had called and said Paula was missing. I told her I was waiting for Auntie Di to stay with the boys. She told me she would meet me at Paula's. I didn't argue, I was not in good shape at this point, and I just needed to find Paula. I was still thinking "car accident" and wanted as many people as I could get to help me look for her.

Alain's sister and her daughter Darcie arrived within five minutes. Darcie said she would drive me. We left immediately. On the way, I called Alain on his cell to see if he had found her. He was out driving the #3 and the 103 highways, around Paula's community, checking the roads and ditches.

At the same time, Paul was making arrangements for his brother, with whom he just had dinner, to come stay with Emily and Dylan so he could join the search.

When we arrived at Paula's house, Darcie said she would go look for Paula. She said she was going to go back to exit 4. If Paula had gone to Costco, she may have taken a detour to stop by her new home. Paula had so many plans and dreams for it that maybe she'd lost track of time. She had talked about wanting to get some flooring samples, so anything was possible. Darcie left with my cell.

The first thing I noticed when I walked into Paula's house was the intense smell of paint. To this day, I remember commenting on how potent it was, and worrying about how unhealthy it could be for Anna to breathe in. I pushed that thought away as I had to concentrate on finding Paula.

Andre arrived within minutes of me getting there. Lana and Jason were in the living room. I looked around and saw one of Paula's half-full glasses of water that she left everywhere—it was like her trademark. I noticed that the living room window trim had been taped off and Lana confirmed they had been painting it. I talked to Alain on his cell and he had not yet seen any trace of Paula. I told him to come back, so someone could go with him. Lana offered to go help him look.

I asked Jason to give me the name and number of the RCMP officer he had been talking to. It was RCMP Constable Mansley. I phoned her and said I was Paula's sister, and in my (in)famous straightforward way, I asked: "What are you doing to find my sister?"

There was a sigh, and I was told that Paula had likely just got caught up while shopping and that she could have gone out for drinks with her girlfriends.

"No, you can stop there," I said. "If I need to form a human chain from Timberlea to Bayer's Lake to find my sister, I will. I can rally hundreds. I'm not going to be passive about this. This is totally uncharacteristic of her. Something is wrong."

She and I talked for some time, and I told her I had cars out looking for Paula. She promised to call me soon, and indicated she was heading over to check behind the stores in Bayer's Lake, including the dumpsters. When a police officer says they're going to check the dumpsters for a family member, all blinders fall off. The seriousness of the situation takes your breath away. Lana and Alain came back to Paula's at one point to check in, and with no updates, they went out again.

I thought waiting for news was what Hell must feel like.

When I hung up from speaking with Constable Mansley, I went and got a steno pad and pen out of Paula's sideboard. I needed to write things down so I could get things straight in my head. Jason was in the living room, hunched over his knees, his head hanging down. I walked into the living room like an end-of-career, crown prosecutor would walk into a holding cell, ready to kick ass and get answers.

I said in a voice that a mother would use with a hung-over teenager, "Lift your head and look at me. I have questions to ask you." At that moment, with those words, that pen and that steno pad, I started taking notes and haven't really stopped.

Jason and I went through the whole day.

- ✓ Paula woke up—like normal
- ✓ Took care of Anna—like normal
- ✓ Paula went out for paint in the morning—like normal
- ✓ Stopped at Lana's for a tea—like normal
- ✓ Painted the trim and other stuff—like normal

- According to Jason, Paula realized she needed diapers—somewhat normal
- ✓ She left to get them—like normal
- Jason took Anna for a drive while Paula was out—somewhat normal
- ✓ Jason gave Anna supper, washed and put her to bed—normal
- Paula not checking in, not coming home—not normal AT ALL

As Jason recounted the details of the day, I paced. I noticed that Paula's watch and wedding ring were still on the sideboard near the entrance. Paula and I both suffered from eczema, so she didn't wear a ring other than on special occasions, but she never left home without her watch. Her ring yes, her watch no—that was not normal. I made a note of that too.

Now that I understood how the day went, I wanted to know what happened in the last couple of hours before Paula went missing, and what had Jason done about it, and how had Anna been?

"So who did you call to ask if they'd seen Paula?"

I immediately thought it was a weird list, but who was I to judge at a time like this? The names Jason listed were all people who were out of town, so that gave me a glimmer of hope: Maybe Paula ran into someone and Jason just hadn't called them. Then I started to call people. By this time, it felt like the middle of the night. I was nearing an adrenaline crash and was wobbly and scared. Things Jason was saying didn't make any common sense, but I thought it was just confusion on both our parts. I wasn't supposed to be able to make sense of how my adult sister could be missing. It was senseless. I was desperate to gain some sort of insight so that I could go get Paula and bring her home and my own spider senses and reasoning skills were in overdrive.

I needed Paula alive in order to breathe.

Jason appeared almost catatonic at this point. Andre was sitting across from Jason in the living room, her eyes as big as saucers as I relentlessly blasted questions at Jason and took notes to cross reference later. As she watched this inquisition, she noticed he had marks on his hands that looked like scratches. Knowing they were doing renos, she thought the marks could have been caused by anything, so Andre kept that observation to herself for the time being. I was questioning Jason about Paula's last words to him, trying to find a nugget that we could run with. There had to be a thread for us to follow, if only I could find it. At this point I remember asking him if he called Paula's teacher friend who lived one street over.

It was then that Andre said, "Has anyone checked the school?"

Jason answered my question immediately: "Jennifer's her name."

I asked for Jennifer's phone number and asked him if Paula was working on anything for Anna's birthday. He looked at me with a very blank stare and said, "I don't know."

At that moment I decided to call Jennifer. It was around 11:30 p.m., and I knew in my heart that we would find Paula if I called—I just knew there was a lead there. When Jennifer picked up I said to her, "I know Jason called you earlier and asked if you had seen Paula. Well, she still hasn't come home and I just have a question for you. Was she working on any big art projects, by any chance? Was she doing anything at the school for Anna's birthday?"

"Yes," she said. "Paula was doing a painting for Anna."

An explosion of light clicked on in my mind.

Paula *was* working on an art project for Anna's first birthday. It was a painting of her beautiful little girl on a swing and it was a big piece of canvas, so she left it at the school.

I remember looking at Jason and asking, "Would Paula have gone to the school?" Not waiting for him to answer, my mind raced ahead with possibilities and solutions, trying to process this new information.

Maybe Paula had gone to the school to work on the painting.

Maybe she got locked in.

Maybe she fell and hit her head.

The way Jason looked at me was like a light went on inside his head, too.

My breath was coming in short bursts. I found it! This was the thread I was looking for. I knew if I followed it, I would find Paula.

With sweaty palms and a heart rate matching a marathoner during the last mile, I called Alain and Lana and said, "You need to go to the school." They were in Lakeside, not near the school, so I told him I would go. Alain got a little mad and told me to stay put, to stay safe and to stay with Anna. As we were arguing, Paul walked in the door. Andre put her coat back on and said they were going to the school, leaving Jason and me alone at the house. I called Constable Mansley and told her she needed to go to the school, too.

It was only a few minutes later when Andre called me from her cell and told me Paula's car was at the school. I called Alain and yelled at him to get there as soon as he safely could. Jason heard this, and ran out the back door, in sock feet. I called Constable Mansley back and told her Paula's car had been found at the school. She may have muttered a curse and told me she was on the way and asked me to call the principal and get the custodian's name, address, and phone number to open the school. She also told me to tell everybody to stay away from the vehicle. Just minutes after Alain, Lana, Paul, and Andre arrived, fire, police, and ambulance crews pulled up to the Beechville-Lakeside-Timberlea (BLT) Elementary School in the middle of the night, in the middle of Christmas vacation, to check to see if one of the school's most beloved teachers was ok.

As desperate as I was to run to the school, to check under every desk, look over every inch of that building, I stayed at Paula's. My instinct and desire to stay with Anna was overpowering. I knew she needed every ounce of my love, loyalty, and protection. I wasn't leaving that precious little girl.

It is my understanding that they had to wait until a specific RCMP team was on site to open the car and trunk. While they were getting everything arranged, Jason was apparently running from window to window looking in the school to see if he could spot Paula.

He went nowhere near the car.

Before the car was opened, one of the RCMP officers leaned over to Lana, Alain, Paul, and Andre and said, "That's a well-rehearsed actor right there."

The officer who actually opened the trunk had gone to school with Paul. For that moment, this personal connection offered a small comfort by creating a belief that the next steps would be done with compassion and circumspect. They opened the trunk and discovered Paula's body. She was in a fetal position, covered with a blanket, her shoes laid out at her feet. The officer asked someone to identify the body. Without hesitation, Alain stepped forward to complete this unimaginable, horrific task. Jason had collapsed and was curled up in a ball on the sidewalk.

When I saw Alain's truck pull up to the front of Paula's home, and I saw he was alone, I knew. My heart knew before he even told me. I walked out into the middle of that cold, crystal-clear night and met him on her front lawn. What he should have told me was that a piece of my soul was ripped from my life's essence. He should have told me that my life was now an unimaginable night-terror that would replay itself every day for the rest of my days. What he should have said was my life, as I knew it, was over.

Instead, my loving husband had to tell me that they found my beloved, bright light of a baby sister dead in the trunk of her own car. I will never forget the sensation of falling while standing stock still.

Of being instantaneously, simultaneously hot and cold.

Of feeling like every cell of my body was being set on fire.

Of blackness crowding my periphery, until all I could see was my husband's face.

Of feeling like my core had been hollowed out with a dull, hot blade.

Of feeling the nothingness that is loss.

Of screaming until I had no voice.

Of knowing my heart stopped beating that night.

The police told Lana, Paul, Andre, and Jason to come back to Paula's house, where someone would come by later. We waited, not knowing what to do or when to do it, staring at Christmas decorations Paula had so intently and lovingly hung, whose joyous purpose now seemed to mock us with the memory of what should have been.

I remember we sat in the near dark, too shocked to think about trivial things like light switches. We were all frozen in our own state of trauma. I don't know who, but eventually somebody turned on a light and had the wherewithal to put on a pot of coffee. I don't think anyone drank it; I think it must have burned. Since that night, when that pot of coffee had the audacity to sit there percolating as if it were a lazy, hazy Sunday morning—its proud aroma blending with the lingering scent of fresh paint and paint thinner, creating a false sense of normalcy—I have never had a cup of coffee again. Because for me, it tastes like murder.

At some point, Jason lay down and put his head on my lap and slept. He actually slept.

I was told that adrenaline overload can do that to you. Then I got furious that he could find enough peace to sleep. Nobody talked since we were barely able to breathe so Lana, Alain, Andre, Paul and I simply stared at each other. Yet, Jason slept like a babe in arms. I woke him up and asked how he could sleep and he said, "I don't feel good," and asked us to call an ambulance. The paramedics came and checked him out and told him he was fine considering everything he had been through. When the paramedics left they suggested that Jason get some sleep. So he stayed upstairs in the bedroom he shared with Paula. All night long, I kept calling Constable Mansley, sometimes asking, sometimes demanding, sometimes begging and pleading for information about what would happen next. I needed her to understand that our life had become a still photo of suspended pain.

My next memory is that it was brighter outside. Day was breaking. It might have been five or six a.m. when the police finally returned and took Jason to the station for questioning.

That was the beginning of our living nightmare.

Chapter 7

Love Will Find a Way

"People who consider themselves victims of their circumstances will always remain victims unless they develop a greater vision for their lives." —Stedman Graham

On the morning of December 28th, despite the crushing weight of loss that paralyzed us, the sun rose. We were all still sitting in Paula's house unable to process the night before. Trying to comprehend what we just lived through seemed impossible. My brain simply couldn't compute that my baby sister was dead. In your worst nightmare you could never imagine the depth of pain we felt. The self-protective part of your brain wants you to believe it is just a nightmare. Yet, every other minute I felt the pain of truth. I felt like my heart stopped beating and that my whole body was being consumed by concrete, trying to figure out how this horror came into our life. With every breath I had an endless circle of questions.

Who's going to come and make sense of this?
Who's going to tell my boys?
Who's going to hold me?
What happens next?
Who did this?
What happened?
Who will tell our family, our Coady Street family, our friends, Paula's friends?
What about Paula's students, her colleagues, her community?

Every cell screamed in agony: Why, why, why?

The feeling of helplessness was amplified with each passing second. I didn't know how to fix this. I needed somebody to fix this. Surely murder was the worst thing that could happen to a human being. There must be a team of people who were going to come in and take care of everything, and us.

As the morning unfolded, Lana, Alain, and I went to the police station to give our statements. On the drive down, I remember saying to Lana privately: "Jason couldn't have done it. Paula loved him too much."

"We need to keep an open mind," Lana offered as a comfort.

"But Lana, Paula loved him with her whole heart and soul. He couldn't have done it."

All Lana said was, "Nothing makes sense right now, Lynn."

I wanted so desperately to believe Jason could never do this. Jason was the man who took my kids to play golf, to play football on the beach. He loved it when Tim and Connor had sleepovers at Aunt Paula's. Jason was never confrontational; he was always smiling and keen to help.

Walking into the Halifax police station, wearing the same clothes I had thrown on when we paused the movie, was like an out-of-body experience. I'd never even had a parking ticket let alone had to give an official police statement. I don't remember the wall colour, but I remember it smelled like dread. The station could have had rainbows painted on the wall and a cotton candy machine, but the unmistakable sense of oppression and ego was like a haze we had to walk through. They put us in separate rooms. They came in and told us not to talk to one another. Not to share our thoughts or our observations. This felt counterintuitive. This was when I needed to talk to my husband, to my sister, to my boys. It scared me to be cut off from my intimate and familial support network. There was a risk I would self-combust without sharing my thoughts, without comforting my sister. They instilled the threat of a court case as the reason we had to keep our thoughts a secret. It felt like a ridiculous ask to keep quiet and not to share our hearts and minds with each other. But the risk seemed too great to disobey. So we suffered in silence.

They asked about Paula's state of mind. Could it have been suicide; did she have enemies; was she having an affair? During it all, I just wanted to scream, "No!" None of their questions made sense. All the officers working on Paula's behalf were strangers. If they knew her, they would know these questions weren't relevant to my sister. She loved Jason with her whole being. They may have had questions, but I had more. Yet, we were sent home. Without answers. Without direction. Without a plan. We were sombre and numb.

I went straight to Paula's after leaving the station. I craved Anna. I needed to see her alive-ness. I needed to feel the heat of her little hands. I also figured someone would be showing up soon to tell us what the next steps were. This was not Halifax's first murder, surely, an entire team of professionals would show up and give us some answers. *Please God,* I prayed, *have a team show up that is going to have all the resources and support that my whole family needs.*

Nobody helped us to prepare. No one told us what to expect. The first thing we encountered when we returned from the station was the media, waiting for us outside Paula's home. It was like a tsunami of curiosity when the news broke and people began to find out. At the time, BLT was the largest elementary school in Nova Scotia and Paula had left a profound mark with all of the ways she contributed to that school and that community. It was like a roar went through the community when news of her murder broke.

My thoughts quickly turned to Grammie, our extended family, and our Coady Street family. I wondered if they would be awake, because I had to phone them ASAP. I had to let them know before they saw the news. To this day, my hands still shake and I get a visceral reaction when I think about the phone calls I made that morning. I started every phone call the same.

"Hi, it's Lynn. Sorry to call so early. Are you alone? Is somebody there with you?"

I know we told Tim and Connor at some point. At their age, their lives were full of joy and innocence. They were carefree boys who loved skateboarding and going fishing. After learning their aunt was murdered, they became numb. They became afraid of the dark. Every night we read the book called *The Next Place* that the IWK Children's hospital provided. I started sitting with Connor until he fell asleep; I often slept there as well, as neither of us could sleep through the night.

I didn't want to go to sleep that first night or any night thereafter for a really long time. I wasn't afraid of the dark like my boys were. I just knew that when I went to sleep, dawn would eventually break through, and I would lose the welcomed detachment that even a broken night's rest offered. And when I woke, I would remember that my little sister had been stolen from us all over again. My aliveness, my circadian rhythm, became a cycle of madness. Saying it was unfair or inexplicable didn't seem adequate. I watched the world continue to move and knew people went on with their lives. I was desperate to join them, but I was a prisoner in a place where extreme grief was the torture of choice. I thought, *This must be what purgatory feels like*—waiting for somebody to tell us either it was a dream, or to help us live in this new reality. My mind and body seemed to have no choice but to go into shock. I remember asking my doctor if she had ever seen someone living without a beating heart. Because that's how I felt. When I used to put a hand over my heart, it felt like I was unable to feel my heartbeat; I figured it was because it was shattered.

I don't remember the rest of December 28th or the individual days during those first couple of weeks. I only remember moments. It just felt like a day from Hell that would never end. We were told by a retired RCMP friend to take notes on things like who came to visit, who brought over necessities, any details that we might need down the road.

Over the next few days people came to Paula's house to bring food, to offer their love and support, to help make and take calls, to clean up, to do anything that was asked. Most of my tribe took over Paula's downstairs rec room while other visitors were in the living room or kitchen, or with my boys. It was like they were gathering around us, forming a circle of love and insulation. As if they could bring enough of their love and untainted energy to buoy us. At one point, it was like I stepped outside of myself and could see love swirling around Paula's house. I tried to tap into it to fill up my bucket and find a bit of reprieve from sadness. At the same moment, Jason caught my eye, and I felt bad. I looked at him, and it was like he was just hovering around, afraid to land. Or maybe he was more like a caged animal, prowling from room to room keeping an eye on everyone but not really seeing anyone. His physical discomfort was obvious. We all thought it was a bizarre way to show grief. Since we each had our own coping strategies, maybe he thought our way was strange too.

I do remember that sometime that first week, I went to Paula's school on my own. I was so lonely, so full of loss and pain, I just needed to sit where she was last and see if I could feel her presence. I thought about her students and the school. I must have been sitting in that parking lot a while as Andre had come to find me. Two RCMP officers eventually pulled up as they were preparing to provide support for the teachers. At first, I was angry and confused. While I knew Paula's peers and friends would need help, it felt as though no one was supporting us.

I leaned into the car window and asked: "When will my sister's body be ready so we can plan her funeral?"

I will never forget the tone, the lack of empathy, or the words spoken by that officer.

"If you want to hamper this investigation, then we can release the body today. But right now, her larynx is sitting in the lab being analyzed. Maybe you just need to pull back, as her larynx is integral to the case."

What was I meant to do with a comment like that? How was that helpful? How was that kind? Repulsed, I went home to be among people who cared.

Then, on January 1st, 2005 as people were making plans for the start of a new year, we held Paula's wake. The funeral home was filled with Paula's art and the sweet smell of fresh flowers. It was a peaceful setting that should never have been.

Lana and I stood there beside Paula for the duration of her wake. We never moved. In my opinion, I needed more time with her. I wasn't ready to say goodbye forever. I already knew what that felt like. I didn't want to do it again with someone who should have still been alive save for an act of inexplicable violence. I remembered when our parents died, we needed more time; our family and friends needed time to say goodbye, and I think we needed more time to mourn. Which is why I wish I had not listened to Jason when he said he couldn't bear the thought of a long funeral service, and he only wanted one viewing. Jason was her husband and I wanted to respect that position in Paula's life. I could only hope the time we had would be enough for everyone to say our final goodbyes.

Throughout my dad's service, my mom had stayed near the coffin, wanting to remain close to his body as long as she could. Likewise, Lana and I stood guard over Paula, physically propped up by Connor. Alain, Paul, and Tim were ushers and organizers. Jason stayed in the very back corner of the funeral home, the farthest he could physically be from Paula, his head buried in his mother's arm. He never greeted anybody. He never came to the casket to say goodbye. The outpouring of love for Paula nearly burst that funeral home at the seams, so many people attended. I was told there was a lineup for miles of people wanting to offer their sympathies and words of encouragement. Considering the state was Jason in, I doubt any of that love reached him. I felt sorry for him. We all tried our best to support him despite our own loss.

When Dad died, so many people touched my heart deeply. I knew they had come to support us because of the love and respect they had for my dad. During that time I wanted to hold on to their love, to keep their words of comfort with me forever. So I began sewing an imaginary quilt, not a real one, because I have no clue what to do with a needle and thread. With each person who came to pay their respects to Dad, I imagined taking a beautiful, unique piece of fabric and sewing it together to create a blanket of love. Naturally, my quilt grew with the death of my mom as I received more love, and more words of peace and comfort. I imagined that one day this quilt would offer me peace when my own death came.

While the quilt was imaginary, the love was real, and I wrapped it around my heart and "felt" the care of the many people who had come into my life. At Paula's funeral I remember standing by her coffin and worrying she would be alone and cold. In my mind, I gently took my quilt and visualized tucking it around her, and with that, wrapping her in all my love and the love of the many people who loved our parents. My quilt had served the greatest purpose it ever could: to keep my sister wrapped in love. For just a moment, that thought made me feel a little bit better.

On January 2nd, 2006, we held Paula's funeral service. Sacred Heart Church was standing room only. I was told people were outside for the service as well. Father Jim Richards, the parish priest, was visibly shaken during the Mass. He had married Paula and Jason only a few years before, had baptized Anna less than a year ago, and had been a great source of support and hope to us in the days following Paula's murder. Susie Quackenbush, a dear friend and colleague of Paula's, filled the church with her beautiful, angelic, and mesmerizing voice. Heather Syms, our 1 Coady Street "sister," and Richelle Gallant-Williams, Paula's friend and colleague, did the readings. Our fourth "sister," Andre MacLean, wrote and read the eulogy:

We are here this morning to celebrate Paula's life and how she touched each and every one of us in so many different ways.

Paula was like a shining light amongst us. I would compare her to a diamond which consists of many facets that catch the light and transmit brilliance. I would like to talk about some of the elements in Paula's life that contributed to the many facets of who she was.

We all know one of the most fascinating qualities about Paula was the diversity she brought into her life in both the things she did and the people she associated with.

She always displayed a wisdom and maturity beyond her years and even though she was still very young, life's lessons had taught her not to sweat the small stuff, and to take time to appreciate and enjoy what was most important.

When you look at the many facets of Paula, and the influences in her life that led her to be the beautiful, caring, individual she was, you must first go back to Coady Street.

For those of you that don't know, this is a tiny street in Glace Bay where Paula grew up. Those close to Paula know about all the neighbours and the tight bond those families shared—and the significant influence they continued to have in Paula's life even after the passing of both her parents. They took the Gallant girls under their wings, and with Paula being the youngest, they especially held her close. That caring, love and compassion was a great example to Paula . . . it helped mold her and she lived by those principles as well.

Another facet to Paula was her education and pursuit of her dream to teach young children. This was a passion; it was not simply contained to within traditional school hours. Paula always spoke so glowingly about the students to her friends and family. She recognized the special qualities that each and every student had, and always brought creativity into the classroom so learning was fun.

That drive for creativity highlighted another facet of Paula with her pursuit of her art. On today's program, you see displayed a depiction of a recent creation called "Four Elements." When Paula presented this at the Nova Scotia College of Art and Design, she drew a correlation between the four elements and her life.

I would like to move on to what I consider the most important facets to Paula, and that consisted of her love for friends and family.

Paula had a multitude of friends from different walks of life: the teaching community, the art community, school and university friends. She had the Boutilier's Point "Poolside" crew, and then there was what I will call the group of twelve who gathered every October for a weekend getaway.

It was in these types of gatherings, either by the poolside, or on weekend jaunts, parties, wedding and baby showers, that you truly appreciated Paula's zest for life and her great sense of humour.

Everyone gravitated toward her because she truly was the life of the party. We all know she loved the limelight. Paula was never too shy to get up and dance in the middle of the dance floor as we all saw at her wedding, or to dress up in a Halloween costume like she did when we went away this past October, singing for all she was worth with Nancy—and I even hear she has been known to dress up as Superman! You could always count on Paula to be the entertainment. Her friends loved and appreciated this.

But the single most important and significant facet to Paula was her love of family. Her relatives and grandmothers in both Cape Breton and PEI meant so much to her . . .

And then her sisters . . . Lynn and Lana. The times were few that they were not together. The love between Lynn, Lana and Paula is one of the most powerful forces I have ever personally witnessed.

Alain . . . you became the father that she lost. You looked over her and protected her until she was old enough to forge her own way . . . and still continued to do so.

Paul . . . you became a brother to her, and it goes without saying your great sense of humour and dry wit was a great match for her.

Timothy, Connor, Dylan and Emily—niece and nephews that she became more like a second mother versus an aunt to. She loved you all so dearly.

And then there is Jason. When Jason came into Paula's life, we saw the light and sparkle in her eyes. She loved you so much. You brought her so much joy and happiness . . . and you brought her Anna. We have all watched Paula this past year, beam with pride and adoration at the family you became.

We must all take our next steps, and I would ask that we all reflect on the imprint Paula has left on each and every one of us.

After the service we filled the church hall and were soothed by the sounds of harpists Ardyth Robinson and Jennifer Wyatt. This too was arranged by Paula's friends. There was an endless stream of people, all offering their words of comfort and support. Although there was plenty of food, it seemed no one could swallow it down. I remember thinking about how it was the start of a brand-new year, and we were at my sister's funeral. It seemed this nightmare would reach into the next year.

When Paula was buried, we chose not to place a headstone right away as we couldn't decide what to have written on it. To be honest, the thought of seeing her name etched in stone wasn't something we had the strength to do. There was something too real, too cold, too permanent about a headstone. To temporarily mark her grave, a neighbour of the Kenny family made a beautiful wooden cross that we placed at the gravesite.

Anna was born on January 6th, 2005, the day of Epiphany. Our mom honoured the Epiphany tradition by keeping our Christmas tree up until January 6th, as this was "Old Christmas." I remember Father Jim, the parish priest, saying Anna was special as she was born on Epiphany. This also meant Anna's first birthday was just ten days after her mother was murdered. This was incomprehensible to me; I couldn't get these two milestones to reconcile in my mind.

My grief dove deeper, and I didn't realize I had another layer of mourning until Anna's first birthday when I wept for a future that would never be. I sobbed in the shower for all those future moments that my sister would not be here for, like seeing her daughter in a birthday dress. Now I would only be able to imagine the fabulous themed parties Paula would have dreamt up. I found depths of despair that I couldn't even fathom before. Which was maybe why we were not invited to Anna's first birthday party. Jason held a party for his adult friends; there was beer and pizza, and I am sure some gifts. But it wasn't a little girl's first party; it wasn't what Paula would have done and that bothered me a lot. There were no pictures of Anna with cake all over her face. There were no pictures of Anna's older cousins helping her blow out a sparkly number one candle. It didn't feel like she was celebrated at all.

I mourned that Paula would not be here to give her all-encompassing love to Anna. I vowed to channel Paula, and to shower Anna with as much love and care as I had for Tim and Connor. Lana felt the exact same; she and Paul promised to love Anna like their own. As her godparents, Alain and I committed to always being there for that baby girl. Paula always said if anything were to happen to her, she would want Lana and Paul to raise Anna, with Alain and me playing the role of grandparents. So that's what we did . . . I just couldn't help but wonder if Paula's decision was foreshadowing in some way.

In the days immediately following Paula's murder, our doctors tried to help in any way possible. Calls were made to various psychologists in the city to find one who was an expert in counselling victims of murder. The IWK Children's hospital provided books for the children and talked about their group counselling programs. Paula's neighbours, school community, and our dear family and friends took care of so much. Without their love and support we could not have functioned. Complete strangers–wingless angels who came to us through Paula's death—did whatever they could for us, the teachers, the children, and Paula's students.

In the weeks following Paula's funeral, there were many people and organizations who tried to offer services and information. We met and talked to some wonderful resources while we filled out an endless number of forms for assistance, for mental health support, for Paula's funeral, for tax information, etc. With so many forms and applications, someone needed to pay attention to all details that were needed. Thankfully, the left-analytical side of my brain could function independently of the emotionally swamped right side, as I even had to fill out forms for Jason because he couldn't cope with the questions and answer boxes.

While most of this time was a blur, I do remember this: I used to get phone calls on an almost-weekly basis from various victim support agencies via the RCMP or Halifax Regional Police. Volunteers started their call with, "We are here for you. How can we help?"

At first, I would say, "I don't know," in part to be polite, and in part because I doubted they could actually help. The last time I got such a call was from a lady named Marie. She probably retired after that phone call because, unfortunately, when she asked, "How can I help?" my capacity to be polite was at an all-time low, and I answered with brutal honesty.

"Can you come over to hold my sons at night while they sob until their noses run and ears ache?"

"Can you get my groceries, as I am too embarrassed to walk into a store with my puffy eyes and blotchy face?"

"Can you make some hot meals for my sons and Paula's infant daughter, as I can hardly remember to bathe, let alone cook?"

"Can you come wash some clothes, as I can't face the mundane when my world has imploded like this?"

"Are you going to call my son's teachers, so they're prepared for spontaneous breakdowns when school reopens?"

"Are you going to explain death to my son's friends and let them know their playmate is forever changed?"

Very, very quietly she said, "I can't do any of that for you. I'm sorry."

I was so enraged at the system that made a complete stranger call us, unsolicited, then read through a script from a binder, written by someone who didn't know what the hell had just happened to me.

I said, "Then please don't bother us again because I need somebody to help put our life back together."

A cruel chaos existed in our little world. Not the kind that previously filled our daily lives. It was a solemn, subdued, eerie chaos that felt insidious. The phone rang constantly and we just hoped it was someone on the other end with a relevant offer of help or insight into the next steps. We sat a lot, not knowing what to do or when to do it. So we waited. Those first couple of weeks all I remember is waiting for the doorbell to announce somebody had finally come with a plan. We needed someone in a superhero cape to say, "Okay, this is what we're going to do. Here's a roadmap for how to live while a murderer is being sought."

Sobs filled the silence with an unpredictable regularity, each of us taking turns breaking down. I prayed that darkness would not fall. I didn't want my friends to ever leave my kitchen because then I would be left alone to feel.

About two weeks after Paula's murder, I got a brochure in the mail: Help for Homicide Survivors, from Victim Services. I am sure the intention was good, but not only did it come too late, the generic messaging was not helpful. Where were the people who were going to help us, to specifically guide us through being a victim of murder, to lay out the roadmap on how to live until Paula's murderer was caught? When I asked for the kind of help that outlined the next steps, I was told it was hard to come by, or that it would be offered later, and I had to understand that it was Christmas and people were on vacation. To add further insult to injury, this particular pamphlet and other "experts" kept referring to what happened as a "homicide." When someone is murdered, we need to call it murder—it's graphic, it's brutal, it's crass. Sugar-coating murder with a "nicer" word is simply demeaning.

On January 24th, 2006, I received a letter from Victim Services with an opening that read: *It has come to our attention that you are a witness in the case involving the accused—unknown.* It outlined how to prepare a testimony, and what typically happens in court. If I was interested, I should call the noted number. I also got a letter about a Criminal Injuries Counselling Program with lengthy application forms to complete. I was still in a fog of grief, still unable to breathe deeply or truly comprehend what had happened in our life. While I checked the mail, I didn't necessarily know what to do with the mail. It just felt overwhelming. All I wanted to do was scream out loud over and over and over, not try to understand legalese, or complete official forms. I needed all my energy to care for others and to concentrate on the investigation that was ongoing. Wasn't it?

Over and over and over again, I was told "they" were working on solving Paula's murder. At one point, I questioned the same RCMP staff sergeant-in-charge that I met at the school on that cold day in December, asking why they didn't have a search warrant for Paula's house. He said without evidence or cause, Jason had to invite the police in to look around. Paula's house was the last known place she was seen alive; wasn't that sufficient "cause" to get a search warrant? I found out weeks later that Lana and two other people who were at Paula's house on December 28th saw one of the little silver hoop earrings that Paula wore 99% of the time lying on the floor between the rec room and the storage room in the basement. Apparently, the head of major crime at the time dismissed this observation and said they "couldn't count that as evidence, because women leave their earrings everywhere." This was insulting and chauvinistic. Paula's earring in that spot on the floor was a key piece of evidence that could have, at least, given them justification for a warrant. Perhaps with a warrant, they would have discovered other pieces of evidence in the house sooner, instead of Lana and me finding it years later.

In the beginning, I "gently" questioned the police. I felt I needed to be nice—particularly to this one RCMP staff sergeant who was meant to be our ally, our person in a superhero cape. I had to regularly push down and reconcile the misogyny with my need for his service and skill. The clash of power imbalance between officers and us felt like physical punches to my soul. As I was told "You get more bees with honey," I repeatedly committed to trying that tactic with the policing resources involved.

One of the most treasured blessings I had in this nightmare was taking Anna to church, when Jason allowed me to. As her godmother, this gave me precious alone time with Anna. It was a time of peace, of music, prayer, and sometimes there was light. I would pick Anna up, spoil her a bit by giving her a snack or two, and just bask in her presence in a place that offered love and care for the spirit.

On one particular Sunday, after a sleepover at my place, I was bringing Anna home when I noticed what looked like a dirty dish rag on the steps. I immediately thought Paula would be devastated, especially since two teachers also happened to be there at the same time to drop off vegetarian food for Jason. Which was ironic to me, as he stopped being a vegan the day Paula died. When the door opened, it was evident that Jason had a party the night before. The smell of cigarette smoke, stale booze, and empty wine bottles and discarded pizza boxes littered my sister's beautiful home. The house was a pigsty. I walked in and Jason was standing, leaning against the kitchen cupboards with his arms folded like he was waiting for me to react. The teachers must have sensed my anger and left quickly, saying they were there for anything anyone needed. I remember all the self-control it took to not react. Only my love for my sister and niece kept me from chastising Jason, as I would have with any other younger family member—including Paula, if the situation had warranted it. Instead, I just stood there trying to compose myself, desperate to make sure I didn't strain my relationship with Jason as he was Anna's gatekeeper. I needed Jason, because our family needed Anna in our lives.

I hugged and kissed Anna goodbye and told her I would see her next week. I picked up the dirty dishcloth and went to the laundry room, attempting to make some sense of the unkept state of Paula's home—which still felt like an extension of my own. I was staring into space contemplating this when a feeling of coldness swept through the room. A sense of darkness came over me. I was standing with my back to the doorway when all of a sudden, the hairs on the back of my neck and arms stood up. It felt like the air had been sucked out of the room and I couldn't breathe. My core body temperature spiked, while shivers ran down my spine. I turned slowly and found Jason standing behind me. A wave of fear washed over me that I have never known before or since. Sparks of knowing went off behind my eyes as my mind registered what my gut had been saying all along. I looked into Jason's eyes, which appeared black, and I knew I had met the devil.

I mumbled something about how I would see Anna next Sunday and left. I went home, and without speaking, curled into a ball in my bed. I was sick mentally and physically. I wanted to crawl out of my own skin. The level of grief, self-loathing, anger, and betrayal lasted days.

When I could think straight, I called Lana.
"I know Jason did it."
All Lana said was "You have to tell the police."
I explained that I didn't know what to tell the police. He was married to Paula. He was our brother-in-law, uncle to our kids, and a welcomed member of a tight-knit family. I was embarrassed that I hadn't known a murderer walked among us. I couldn't comprehend his duplicity, arrogance, and my own ignorance. I didn't know how

I'd missed the signs. Shouldn't the magnitude of love Paula had for Jason have insulated her from something like this?

It took me a week to process the revelation. The following Sunday I called Lana again. I was rather snippy with her, because I was scared and angry that the truth had surfaced within me. I said, "Arrange a meeting with our policing contacts, but it needs to be secret." It felt like Jason was now watching my every move. I reminded myself this was a murder investigation and I couldn't talk about my suspicions to anyone. I wouldn't do anything to jeopardize a court case. Talking was too big of a risk, so I kept my fear and intuition to myself. I remember the day I met with the detectives, and it felt like I was betraying Paula by talking about her husband this way–ven though I knew deep inside the horrible, dark truth about the man we loved and had embraced whole-heartedly into our family. The following is an excerpt from the formal statement I submitted to the investigation team in early February 2006.

> As I sit and reflect on Jason's personality and his involvement in our life, some key themes keep emerging in my thoughts . . . he is sneaky, he is a liar, he has no depth, he is conniving, and Jason is evasive . . .
>
> What I have to come to terms with is the fact that he has always been these things but what he was able to so successfully do the last five years in our life was project himself as a very quiet, agreeable, unassuming individual. A man who had a great childhood, who loved him family dearly, had moved to Nova Scotia because he loved it here . . . and had fallen in love with the woman of his dreams . . .
>
> And now I know he is not the man I believed he was . . . and I wish I could say this just based on the fact that he stole from me, or based on the fact that he smoked marijuana, or based on the fact that I caught him in small lies . . . but no, this reality really

came to light in the hours and days following the murder of my sister . . . the lies got bigger, the evasiveness intensified. I was made to feel like a stranger in my sister's home. His behaviour did not support the level of grief one displays when they lose someone they love so dearly. He could care less about the care of his daughter. His life seems to be better than normal . . . he does not have to go to work, Mom and Dad are picking up his dirty socks, no one making him accountable for managing money, he's hanging out with friends watching football and playing cards, back to smoking cigarettes . . . . . . even eating fish and beef gravy . . . big change for a man who needed to use different utensils to flip his burger on the BBQ. Every minute of every day the lies just keep getting bigger and bigger . . . and now we feel as if we have spent five years of our life with a stranger.

On February 8th, 2006, forty-one days after Paula was murdered, Jason was taken in for questioning. It so happened that I had Anna that day and I went to Lana's so our two families could be together during his questioning. Andre and two of Paula's other friends were there and the police called throughout the evening to keep us up to date.

"They interrogated him for twenty-three and a half hours, trying to get him to confess. But they couldn't break him. The words from the RCMP staff sergeant were haunting me: *"We'll only ever solve this if he tells the truth . . ."*

Jason's lawyer at the time was an ex-police officer who had left the force to get a law degree. I was told local police hated the guy because not only did he leave the force, he became a defence attorney. Which is the exact opposite of everything the boys in blue stood for and had sworn to defend. Jason's lawyer, therefore, knew all the interrogation tactics and tricks used to get criminals to confess. Apparently, one of the tactics defence attorneys use is to give their business card to the accused with the words "*Do not talk for 24 hours*" written on the back. Jason didn't talk and within twenty-four hours, life was good for him again. When he was released the next morning, he headed to church to see Father Jim. I remember speaking with Father Jim later and asking him what Jason said. "Did he confess? Did he show any remorse?" Of course, Father Jim didn't tell me anything. He simply told me, "When there are no words, there are no truths." A family friend had this quote cross-stitched for our families and it remains on my wall to this day.

This arrest changed everything, and everyone. Over time Jason changed and stopped letting us see our sweet Anna. As it turned out, I was changing too, slowly, over time.

Chapter 8

A Survivor Made by Love

> "In the final analysis, the question of why bad things happen to good people transmutes itself into some very different questions, no longer asking why something happened, but asking how we will respond, what we intend to do now that it happened."
> —Harold S. Kushner

    Paula's murder was a defining moment for so many people, the effects of which will never be truly captured. With a broken heart, a tired mind, and a soul in despair, I realized my search for a hero was in vain and that I needed to become the "fixer" we had been waiting for. At some point, you can choose to stay on the path of being a victim, accept the status quo, and move on as best as you can. Or you can stand up for the rights of victims and be the voice that impacts change. I chose to stand up and survive.

    I was drowning in all the love I had for Paula that had nowhere to go. My sense of loyalty and injustice for her wouldn't let me rest until change was made. I decided to use my love for Paula for good. I turned that love into advocacy and awareness about the impact violent crime has on victims, especially those who lost someone they love to murder. I expanded my love to include those who had experienced domestic violence and didn't have a voice. It was my hope that our experience could provide support to other victims on their journey, through a system that sometimes caused more harm than healing. I saw firsthand that the system needed to stop being a maze and instead help victims navigate their trauma with empathy, dignity, and, most importantly, respect.

When I found my strength and decided to funnel the love for my sister into advocacy and awareness, three goals came to mind:

1. Influence effective change within government for victims and the services they have a right to expect.
2. Keep Paula's story alive until justice was served, and we were reunited with Anna.
3. Advocate for Paula, and all women and girls who are impacted by men's violence.

> *I am only one,*
> *But still I am one.*
> *I cannot do everything,*
> *But still I can do something;*
> *And because I cannot do everything*
> *I will not refuse to do the something*
> *that I can do.*
>
> —Edward Everett Hale

In tackling the first goal, I first needed to look at the plethora of cold, impersonal "business" that had to be completed as a victim, as if having a family member murdered was an everyday occurrence. I had a long list of things that, from a victim's perspective, I felt were broken or needed to change, so I figured I would start there.

Trying to drive change within various levels of government is not an easy task. My efforts to share our experience with decision makers took months, which became years. I went to hundreds of public forums hosted by ministers, mayors, and other politicians and policing agencies just trying to be heard. I very quickly realized that as a murder victim/survivor I represented a minority. Everyone can relate to eroding health care, classroom sizes, seniors' needs, and crime in general. Very few people can relate to murder. Who knew how uncomfortable telling people your sister was murdered would be for the listener? Attempts to silence my voice were made and many, many people just wished I would go away. When I walked into a room, I could see people move away from the black cloud of murder that seemed to follow me everywhere.

So I threw myself into changing how the "business" end of murder is handled. I argued, over and over and over, that someone in a bureaucratic office can't determine what level of support a victim of murder will need six days, six weeks, or six months down the road. I lobbied for support to be extended for up to one year after a conviction, not the murder. Because when that conviction takes place, there is a hailstorm of emotional instability.

This is an excerpt from a letter I wrote to the Department of Justice in 2008, about our experience, which highlights some of the issues we encountered:

> If ordinary people don't demonstrate moral courage on the job as well as at home, if they don't have the will to do the right thing even when it costs more than they want to pay, the bad guys will always win.
>
> —Michael Josephson

In the first couple of weeks following Paula's murder, when we were functioning at a minimum, we did receive support for acute/urgent things from resources and volunteers... but that quickly faded and the phone calls stopped. We were left to move forward without a roadmap. Try and just imagine what that would feel like. Your sister is murdered. You have no experience with a life event as horrific as this. There are very few professional resources in Halifax with the skills and experience to assist victims of murder, and the one department you think will be there provides very limited services with conditions attached. This is a tragedy in itself and it needs to be changed now.

On January 24th, less than one month after the murder, we received correspondence from the Department of Justice Policing and Victim Services stating the following: "It has come to our attention that you are a witness in the case involving the accused, unknown. We provide services to victims and witnesses of crime as the case proceeds through the Criminal Justice System." We also received correspondence encouraging us to apply for counselling support and to request information and assistance regarding Victim Impact Statements, which we robotically did based on this expert advice being extended to us.

At this time, we were also told repeatedly by the investigative team working on Paula's case that it could take years to solve based on the complexity of murder investigations and that we had to prepare ourselves for the long haul. We were confused, conflicted by the different messages we were getting, and had no one to guide us.

When we received the applications for support, we applied as recommended. My sister Lana and I are the only two surviving members of our family. Paula was our younger sister. At the time of Paula's murder, my children were 11 and 13 years of age. Lana's children were 1 and 5 years of age. My husband Alain was like a father to Paula, and Lana's husband Paul was like a brother. Each of us applied for support.

In late February and April, each of us received individual letters from the Department of Justice with their decisions pertaining to our request for support:

- Lana, my husband, Alain, and I were each awarded $2,000.00 for counselling (with conditions which should never be imposed in this type of circumstance).
- Lana's husband was denied. He was with Lana and my husband that evening when her body was discovered. He watched his childhood friend, who is now an RCMP officer, open the trunk and say, "I think it is Paula." Yet, he was denied any counselling. How can this be justified? How did he not suffer what we did? Is it just because he's the brother-in-law? It's an insult for someone to evaluate their relationship and his loss.
- Our children were denied—they were not "affected" by this tragedy according to the department! Who could make that type of decision? Were they here holding my boys late at night as they cried themselves to sleep? There has not been a week that has passed in the last twenty-five months that they have not had a bad dream, cried out in their sleep, been afraid to go on a class trip, been inattentive in school because they think of Paula and the fact that someone murdered her; they have questions—so many which there are no answers for—and were and still are at a very vulnerable age. No, they were not "affected" by this at all. How dare you take this request lightly and tell us to appeal if we are not satisfied.

We simply did not have the energy to appeal at that time. We did not have the mental or physical capacity to disengage from the resources our family doctors recommended in the first few days following Paula's murder. Try and imagine two months after the murder, starting to tell the story all over again. Just when you are trying to heal the wound, the Department of Justice wants you to start again . . . this is a sad testament to the fact that you know absolutely nothing about the type or level of service a family needs in these circumstances. You are in a position to make it right but have chosen to do nothing to improve this at all.

We have tried to meet with former Minister of Justice Murray Scott to present our situation but this did not happen. We have written to our MLA, Judy Streatch. We have publicly asked for someone in government to address this issue at various forums including the Minister's Meeting on Safe Streets and Communities, as well as the Mayor's Roundtable on Violence. We requested a meeting with the new Minister of Justice, Cecil Clarke, but have had no response.

The funds we were granted expired and we did not use any of the funding as we have been told to prepare for the long term . . . we could use this support when someone is convicted and we have to sit through trials . . . but with a two-year time frame, a cap, and a limit, we have had to resort to our own resources at a huge expense.

All of our efforts have fallen on deaf ears. There is not one support group in the province for Victims of Murder. Try and walk in our shoes for a day . . . I am sure you would make the required changes necessary.

The Department of Justice also sends out a really long list of "approved" counsellors, but it's up to you to sift through and decide, in your extreme grief, which one would be best suited. I met with three. None of them had any experience dealing with victims of murder. One actually had the gall to say to me, "It would be great for you and me to work together because then you can teach me a victim's perspective, which would make me a better counsellor." As if that was my job or responsibility! I came for mental health support, not to educate someone else. Lana had the same experience. It was a complete farce and a waste of money, especially their approval process.

It was this moment that I began the transformation from victim to survivor. The depth of love I had for Paula, for Anna, for Tim and Connor and all the children of women murdered by intimate partners inspired me to become what some call a "wounded healer." My grief fuelled a drive to make things better, to create a roadmap for others. At some point it was less about our family and more about the next family that was going to walk a similar path, because there would be another one.

My asks to the Department of Justice included:

- A dedicated Victim Support Resource be assigned to each family, trained specifically in supporting victims of murder. This professional would possess the skills and expertise to understand the complexities of the process and guide victims through the system with care and competence.
- The Criminal Injuries Counselling Program:
    o Extend support until one year past the date of conviction.
    o Extend benefits facilitated by the Victim Services Officer in partnership with the family and any professional resources required, on a case-by-case basis.
    o Eliminate the program cap for counselling.
    o Alternate therapies (massage) be included in the program and receive the same funding as "traditional counselling."
    o Funds to support victims of murder be increased.
- Resources such as training, handbooks, seminars, and support groups be established and made readily available for victims of murder.

To the very best of my ability, I turned all my love for Paula into partnering, educating up, and networking and was able to achieve the following outcomes:

- ✓ "Alternate therapies" were included as acceptable counselling therapies.
- ✓ The maximum counselling award was increased from $2,000 to $4,000, and available funding for "alternative therapies" is now made at the discretion of the CIC Director.
- ✓ The program cap was increased to $85.00 per session. At the time of writing (2024) this cap is still $85.00 per session. How many counselors do you know who would work for this amount?
- ✓ Support is offered up to one year beyond the date of completion of the court process.

While these are wins, there is still work to do, especially around the $85.00 cap on a counselling session and alternative therapies, as well as their thirty-plus pages of approved counsellors mailed to victims.

In early February 2006, I also questioned why Nova Scotia didn't have a reward program to solve crime. I was told you cannot catch bad guys with money! I couldn't argue, as I had no experience, but knew that other places had adopted a similar idea and common sense told me a little motivation couldn't hurt. A good family friend worked with us to create a $50,000 reward poster that we planned to distribute in Paula's neighbourhood on February 25th. I didn't have $50,000, but to me that was a non-issue. If someone stepped forward and the monster who murdered my sister was convicted, I knew we could come up with the money someway, somehow. The lack of money was not going to be a deterrent when solving my sister's murder was on the line. There was nothing I wouldn't do, or pay, for justice.

The reward poster was ready for print, but the police told us we couldn't distribute it. I said, "Unless you give me a good reason not to, or you distribute it, our family and friends will." The then police took on the task of canvassing Paula's community and distributing the poster, but not before they removed the 50k reward from it. I was savage.

On May 12th, 2006, the late Honourable Bill Estabrooks, NDP MLA for Paula's area, stood in the legislature and acknowledged Paula's murder and the impact on the BLT community. Here is an excerpt:

> " . . . we have been enduring as a community, in Beechville-Lakeside-Timberlea, the terrible tragedy of the loss of a popular school teacher, a wonderful young mother, and of course, a person who is sadly missed each and every day . . . Paula was a special woman, she taught in a school where I often visited and I had the opportunity to be in her classroom on numerous occasions . . ."

This sincere gesture by Honourable Estabrooks motivated me, and others, to persevere. I thanked my dad for my tenacity as I wrote to Premier MacDonald, every minister involved in justice, along with the Minister for the Status of Women and every policing official who claimed to have authority and accountability. The Conservatives were in power at this time.

Finally, our voices were heard. In August of 2006, the Minister of Justice, Murray Scott, announced that a new reward program for unsolved crime was being created. The program officially launched on November 28th, 2006. The Department of Justice offered a cash reward of up to $50,000 for information leading to the arrest and conviction of individuals responsible for crimes against for the following five people:

- Paula Anne Gallant (homicide)
- Jonathan Reader (homicide)
- Tyrone Layton Oliver (homicide)
- Jason Allan MacCullough (homicide)
- Kimberly Ann McAndrew (missing persons)

Did that make me happy? On one hand, yes. I was relieved that Nova Scotia now had a rewards program, and that our voices were heard. On the other hand it was upsetting that the program only applied to specific individuals. To me, and to others I am sure, it felt like Paula's case was being viewed as more important than someone not listed in the program. This unfairness was not acceptable, and made me feel anger on behalf of the families whose loved ones were not included. I turned that anger into energy and I wrote more letters, gave more presentations.

I realized very quickly that I was being politically appeased. I then rallied the political opposition with the help of an amazing woman I had met at a Mayor's Roundtable on Violence, Bronwyn Burke, a beautiful soul who worked for the Honourable Geoff Regan, MP—a Liberal. Ms. Burke said, "I'd like to see if we can help." So, we met with Geoff and he listened. Then he, too, started writing letters.

I'll tell you one lesson I learned quickly: it only takes a few letters from the opposition to shame the government in power into taking action. Bronwyn, with the support of the Honourable Geoff Regan, orchestrated a strategy that opened doors for me. The aforementioned MLA, Bill Estabrooks, Liberal MLA Diana Whalen, and Liberal MLA Michel Samson were soon on board and became strong advocates for change. With their help, I was finally granted a fifteen-minute meeting with the Deputy Minister of Justice, Ms. Marion Tyson, and the DOJ Director, John Joyce Robinson.

On July 16th, 2008, I provided them with insights into our experiences as victims, the challenges and needed improvements within Victim Services and the Criminal Injuries Counselling Program, as well as the Rewards Program that had been launched in 2006. As part of my presentation I wondered out loud if the Ten Commandments' "Thou shalt not murder" would be the worst offense you could ever do to another human being. Clearly, at the time within the Nova Scotian Department of Justice (DOJ), murder was not the worst thing you could do, or there would have been more resources. Granted, the DOJ had developed programs and services, which likely started out with good intention. However, individuals offering the program and the program material simply didn't fit the experience of a victim. It felt like they hadn't consulted with victims when they designed the program or rolled out resources, causing a huge gap between what they offered and what was really needed.

In this meeting I detailed how *I* had to lobby for the launch of the rewards program. I explained that I threatened to launch one in Paula's name before I was taken seriously and any action was initiated. I told them that while I was happy the program had launched, I was extremely disappointed with its exclusivity–available only to select individuals—and the inadequate $50,000 reward. We had been told by the police that if a program like this would work (many still didn't think it would bring any value) that it would need to be a substantial reward amount to have any impact. I insisted that the amount should be no less than half a million dollars. Of course, I was then told they didn't have the budget. I countered by pointing out that the police themselves weren't confident that a reward would lead to any arrests, so it was unlikely they were actually going to spend the money. Then they said that no other province offered such a high amount. My reply was simple: "Perfect! Be the first. Set the standard and challenge every other province to treat victims with the dignity they deserve. We're talking about murder here."

I further advocated that the Rewards Program should apply to every unsolved case in the province, rather than "selecting" certain cases, with criteria only they knew about. From a victim's perspective, the current program made it seem as if Paula's case was more important that someone not named. This was wrong on so many levels. I equated their program to getting a deer licence: If your number gets drawn, you get named in the program and if not, too bad, apparently your murder is not worth solving. I shouldn't have had to explain to public servants how their program diminished the lives of those not listed. I was disheartened that I had to explain that every unsolved case, every victim, every loved one left behind deserves equal attention and respect.

I went in knowing I had 15 minutes, but the meeting ended two and a half hours later.

For some, two months seems like a long time. Yet, it is quite fast for the government to make a change like they did on September 4th, 2008, when Minister Cecil Clarke held a press conference that announced the Reward for Major Unsolved Crime would increase to $150,000. In my heart, I knew we were instrumental in making this change happen, even though we were not even invited to the press conference to share the news. By this time, I had allies in the media who told me about it, so Lana and I went. This particular minister had never come to an awareness event, never accepted a meeting request, and to be honest I am not sure he gave a care about Paula and the changes our love for her demanded . . . until there was something in it for him and his political party.

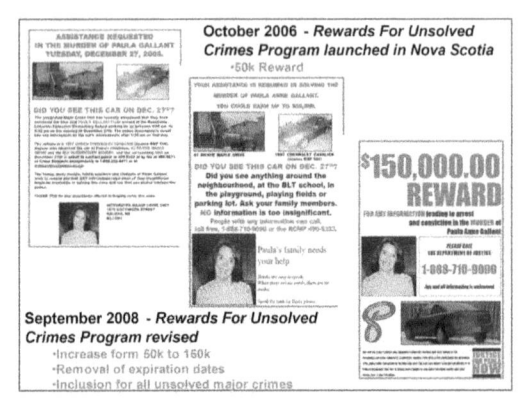

Paula's reward poster

With that press conference, I felt that my first goal—to influence effective change within the government and the services they provide for victims—had been accomplished. Then without a pause, overlapping time frames, I was on to Goal #2—Keep Paula's story alive until justice was served, and we were reunited with Anna.

I had been told many times that "these types of cases" often went unsolved, making it critical to ensure the policing agencies involved kept Paula's case a priority. I hated when people said "these types of cases." It made me want to grind my teeth and scream. What are "these types of cases"? It was like people still weren't considering domestic violence or intimate partner violence a crime. As if, if you were murdered by your husband, you had an asterisk on your case file.

Murder is murder, no matter who the victim is or if they knew the perpetrator!

I believed that all murders, including Paula's, should be taken seriously. I knew squeaky wheels get greased, which meant I had to keep talking, so the police would know I wasn't going to be silent and Paula's file would not collect dust. I also needed to remind the person who committed this heinous crime that he had messed with the wrong family. His actions may have silenced Paula's voice, but our collective voices would speak loud and clear for her, until justice was served.

In terms of keeping her story alive in the public, our family had to build relationships with personnel from the media. Thankfully, a family friend organized some very unofficial media training for us that offered practical insights into creating "key messages" and the dos and don'ts during interviews. Paula soon became a household name and the media advocated for her and our fight for justice. They kept her story in the news and treated our family with respect and compassion. We quickly learned who had integrity and wanted to report the relevant facts and stories and would help achieve our end goal of justice. Our family had encounters with many reporters throughout the five years we lobbied for the truth. With the exception of one or two overzealous reporters looking to get that one scoop that would elevate their career, we met incredible men and women committed to truth and justice. Our family will be forever grateful for their contributions.

Just as quickly, I realized that the policing agencies involved in Paula's investigation were disjointed. I was confused as to who owned the case; her murder happened in RCMP jurisdiction so I assumed it would be led by the RCMP, but Halifax Regional Police (HRP) were also often involved. What I hadn't realized was that in

2005, the Halifax Regional Municipality introduced their Integrated Policing Model with Halifax Regional Police (HRP) and the RCMP. The need for such a model came from the Perivale and Taylor report entitled *Partners in Policing*. The city mayor at the time said: "There is no other jurisdiction in Canada that has this policing model. We believe that the delivery of policing services between HRP and the RCMP can be seamless. The end result for our taxpayers will be elimination of any duplication in services and improved service in many communities."

In a profession that relies on egos, testosterone, endless paperwork, and highly detailed processes between "alpha" organizations that had a long and colourful history of competition, this was indeed a very, very big vision. Unfortunately, in our experience we did not witness seamless, improved service. What we saw was that the proposed and enacted changes created a power imbalance within each organization and among individual officers as they tried to (re)claim their turf. To support this integration there had been politically appointed reassignments of staff within the Major Crime Unit. I couldn't help observing that there was a dose of nepotism in the reassignments, resulting in a great deal of inexperienced leadership.

While our city now had this overarching integrated model, I witnessed on the ground power struggles between individuals in the HRP and the RCMP. I asked repeatedly, who was the *one person in charge of our case*, and never got a straight answer. I asked for an organizational chart, but none was provided.

What I didn't understand immediately was that Paula's murder was considered a high-profile case, and so both policing agencies wanted control. I watched grown, professionally trained men (as there wasn't a female officer in sight) fight over a murder and jockey for the lead position like gladiators. I was fascinated and frustrated at the same time. I knew my experience as a victim was not unusual, as I received too many pat answers for us to be the exception. Knowing there were people out there who were either in the middle of the storm, or about to enter it, I knew they too would need *one person in charge* to find a path through all the paperwork and egos. Yet none could be found.

I distinctly remember when I realized there was no *single* person in charge. It dawned on me that I was going to have to tackle this divide and be the bridge and the liaison between these two organizations. It was up to me, again. I was going to have to be the one person in charge of my sister's murder. The fact that I had no policing skills, no money, no experience, no resources, and only my love for Paula and family to fuel me should have raised concern. Instead, I was relentless and never backed down.

In the first two and a half years following Paula's murder we had to remain vocal, diligent, and focused on ensuring her case remained active and a top priority. I remember saying over and over, "I'm sorry my sister was murdered on December 27th as I know it's the holiday and this is a big inconvenience but I need_____." This feeling of being a bother, or an inherent inconvenience, remained through much of the investigation during this time. I constantly felt like we were disrupting the lives of people whose job it was to help us. The things I witnessed, the comments made to me, and the lack of leadership experience did not give me confidence that Paula's murder would be solved. Coupled with some key factors and specific events, my belief in the investigation process eroded–until I was left with no choice but to be *the one person in charge*.

Aside from the mistakes made at the start in Paula's investigation, I often felt like I was being patted on the head, appeased like a schoolgirl, often being told, "Don't worry, the big guns have this." After repeatedly asking for and being denied a meeting with those officers in charge, I finally said, "If I need to bring ten thousand people here to stand in front of this police station until you start taking our family and this case seriously, I will. Have you ever heard of a phone tree? I have one on speed dial. Do you really want to mess with the moms of children that Paula taught?"

As it turned out, one of the officers in that particular chain of command was wise enough not to mess with moms and I got my meeting. It should never have come down to a threat like that to get a meeting in a murder investigation.

As there were gaps in leadership, breakdowns in communication and processes, I had to question everything and make notes of every conversation. No one liked the record of events that I was diligently crafting, but my life as I knew it depended on it. In fact, many other lives would be impacted by the outcomes of this investigation. I wasn't there to make friends, I was there to get justice for Paula and to change how others would be treated in the future. I never apologized and promised to continue to advocate for Paula until I took my last breath, if that was what it would take. Our family had to fight for her; her voice had been silenced. We heard repeatedly that money was an issue, staffing was an issue, leadership was an issue, the integrated model was an issue, egos were an issue. It felt like they lost sight of the actual issue: a murderer was on the loose.

Interestingly, in April 2023 an independent Policing Model Transformation study conducted by the Price Waterhouse Cooper consulting firm highlighted that:

- The current policing model in Halifax Regional Municipality is disconnected and essentially has a truly dual policing model.
- HRP and RCMP do not operate in an integrated policing model today.
- The RCMP and HRP have totally distinct and independent operating models that are independent of each other with little to no coordination or integration.
- They have different approaches to people, processes, services, and enablers.
- Leadership is disconnected and does not provide a consistent operational strategy.
- The integration between the two organizations was never strong but has deteriorated in recent years.
- There is little to no coordination of resources and limited interoperability.

If these points sound familiar, it is because what Price Waterhouse Cooper noted in 2023 was the same list I made in 2006, and lived through seventeen years earlier. Just imagine how many victims fell into the gaps created by Halifax's (un)integrated model of policing during that time.

I apologize if it sounds like there were not any great individual policing resources—there were. We met several officers in both the HRP and RCMP who cared deeply, had genuine empathy, were highly skilled in their jobs, and were as committed to solving Paula's case as we were. You know who you are and what you mean to our family to this day. Thank you for all you did for us and for Paula. We will be forever grateful.

Naïveté can be a blessing and a curse. I was not aware of how prevalent men's violence was against women and girls until Paula's murder. I believed murder only happened to bad people, done by bad people. I believed after Paula was murdered that the wheels of justice would quickly prevail, and that the "system" would work to support us through the unimaginable nightmare. As you have read, that was not the case, but what I have learned is that through relationships and community, love will prevail.

I also naïvely believed that the federal justice system would work not only with offenders but also with victims, as stated in the Canadian Victims Bill of Rights. When you read the Act, you feel as if your rights as a human will be honoured. *"Whereas victims of crime and their families deserve to be treated with courtesy, compassion and respect, including respect for their dignity."*

After first reading the Victims Bill of Rights document, I was inspired; I was hopeful. At the time of writing this, I have been a registered federal victim for thirteen years and can say with confidence that this is yet another area of justice that needs *one person in charge*. On numerous occasions, my own family has seen how the federal system is so broken that the needs and the privacy of offenders take precedent over the victims.

We have been on repeat for years, asking both the Parole Board of Canada and Correctional Services Canada for their staff to do better. We have experienced issues and challenges that should never have happened to victims. This year alone, nearly twenty years after Paula's murder, I had to file two formal complaints with the federal ombudsman highlighting staff mistakes and oversights that re-traumatized me and my family. If I wrote two complaint letters in one year because mistakes were made, how many other mistakes have actually been made? How many other victims have also written to complain? How many others have been negatively impacted by ignored phone calls, missing information, or forgotten steps in a process meant to keep victims feeling safe? Is anyone counting or monitoring this?

In our experience, the system apologizes, but doesn't change.

Chapter 9

Love Leads to Advocacy

"The only things that stand between a person and what they want in life are the will to try it, and the faith to believe it's possible." —Rich Devos

I finally had to stop waiting.

I stopped waiting for somebody to treat me like a victim of murder and help me navigate this foreign, misogynistic, egocentric world of policing and justice. I prayed for a hero, and none came. I realized that no one was going to save me or Lana or even Anna. I looked to the heavens and thanked my dad for being a feminist and giving me the ability to walk into a room full of men and see only humans. I thanked my mom for the independence to be me, and I asked them both to help me take charge once again. I realized I was a survivor now and not a victim.

So, all of the things that happened to me, fuelled me. They didn't make me weaker. They didn't make me curl up into a ball and be a victim. They strengthened me, so others could join me and together we could raise the voices of all those who have experienced domestic violence. While I continued to seek justice for Paula, to one day get a conviction, I knew I had to do more.

Which brings me to my third goal: advocate for Paula, and all women and girls who are impacted by men's violence. This naturally happened in conjunction with advocating for system level change, but it was a different kind of work; it was very personal. Each presentation and event allowed me to bring Paula into the room, and give a little piece of her joy to those who attended a gathering. Which meant Paula's spirit was multiplying and the love and passion we had for her fuelled some and comforted others. It made the time I spent away from my own boys and family a little less painful.

There were dozens, if not hundreds, of events and presentations that achieved this goal of advocacy for justice and to create awareness about the prevalence of men's violence against women and girls in our society. The media coverage for every event was amazing, and we had the privilege of working with some exceptional people, including Jackie Foster, formerly of CTV News, and Sgt. Joe Taplin, Media Relations for the RCMP, who both provided us with guidance, respect, and compassion. We were also joined by politicians and key policing members who attended as allies for justice. Paula's spirit was kept alive by all who loved her and by those who came to know her through the collective work of so many. Below, I highlight some of the main ones that gave us the opportunity to partner with her school and community.

December 5th, 2006 – Paula's 37th Birthday

Paula's community, including the BLT school community, supported every initiative we held to raise awareness in her school. I was overwhelmed with the love they extended to us because of their love and respect for Paula. It came as no surprise that her school community wanted to do something to memorialize her. They engaged our family, and it didn't take long for us to agree on the perfect way to honour her. Paula was curious and passionate about all things artful, so to carry on her love of art and love for her students, we chose to transform the old industrial arts room where she used to teach art and run an after-school arts program.

The condition of the room and the lack of supplies never deterred Paula from her goals. She had told one of her professors at the Nova Scotia College of Art and Design that she one day hoped to transform this room into a beautiful space. Paula saw beauty and good in every aspect of her life and this room was another example of the potential she saw . . . the diamond in the rough! People were very touched and energized by this renovation project and gave generously of their time and financial support. An auction was held to fund the project and almost 400 businesses donated auction items and cash donations needed for this transformation. This room gave Paula's students and teachers a space for hope, healing, and peace. In 2007, in our hometown of Glace Bay, money was raised to help support the ongoing art supplies for Paula's Place.

Paula's Art Room Transformation Both Before and After Pictures

PAULA'S PLACE

This Art Room is dedicated to the memory
of teacher Paula Gallant.

Her passion for teaching, especially of the Arts, kindled
learning in her students and inspired colleagues.

"When love and skill work together, expect a masterpiece."
2006

Through a very generous donation from an anonymous sponsor, local artist Ineke Graham was commissioned to do a portrait for Paula's Place. Two of Paula's former students unveiled the magnificent painting at her birthday celebration at the opening of Paula's Place. Hundreds of people came to the BLT Elementary School to visit this space, listen to the children sing, hear speeches, and share stories of a woman they loved dearly. That space will forever be known as Paula's Place, and that night I looked around and thought, *Love did this.*

Mother and daughter
by Ineke Graham

Artist's Note: "It is my hope that this painting of Paula and her baby will play a tiny role in keeping the memory of Paula alive, always . . ."

October 10th, 2007 —Paula Street

My sister Lana and her family were approached by a member of their community asking if they were comfortable renaming the street that they live on after Paula. HRM needed to approve the name change and so a petition was created to get community input, and it was approved.

Paula Drive

December 5th, 2007 – Paula's 38th Birthday

It is important to our family that Paula be remembered for who she was and all the things that made her Paula. She was and is so much more than the "murdered school teacher." The idea of setting up a website, as well as using the letter "P" from Paula's actual signature, as part of the awareness campaign was discussed. Once again, family and friends rallied to make this vision a reality.

Paula's P by Lynn MacEachern   Paula's Magnetic P by Lynn MacEachern

Our long-time family friend, Lynn MacEachern, designed the *P* logo from Paula's signature. Her love, support, creativity, and passion for justice are evident in all she has done for Paula. Paula's signature *P*, which in life seemed insignificant, in death represents a great deal. The purple hue which washes over her *P* is representative of and stands as a voice for violence against women. Woven into the ribbon of the *P* are the words: *Paula, Peace, Perseverance,* and *Prosecution,* which are the four themes of Paula's story, and words Lana and I came to live by. With help and generosity, the purple *P*s went all over the world. You can still see them on vehicles in our city.

Paula's unique signature *P* also inspired the layout and theme for the website. Four key themes were highlighted: *Come Meet Paula, Perseverance, Prosecution,* and *Peace*. It was a beautiful labour of love brought to life by many hands. Paul, Lana's husband, patiently and meticulously designed the site—his very first–and took the lead putting it all together. What a masterpiece it turned out to be! As a brother-in-law, Paul fiercely loved Paula, and his pride in this project was evident to anyone who visited it. Paul's feelings and sense of loss were palpable in every detail. There were hundreds of views from its inception until it was shut down after Paul died unexpectedly in April 2020. I have managed to capture some of the highlights from this site, which you will see in Chapter 13.

A postcard was also developed to support the key messages of the awareness campaign which were to:

- Remind the public of the wonder and beauty of Paula's life and spirit as an inspirational friend, daughter, sister, teacher, and mother.
- Remind the public that her murder was unsolved, and the public's help is needed to achieve a conviction and to encourage anyone who has ANY information or observations to get the information to police either directly or indirectly.
- Encourage the public to think and talk about violence against women, and remember how Paula's life ended on December 27th, 2005.

We held simultaneous awareness launches at BLT, hosted by Lana, and at the Savoy Theatre in Glace Bay, which I hosted. The attendance was overwhelming, and our guest speakers spoke from their hearts. Music, birthday cake, and the sharing of Paula stories could be heard throughout the events. There was a renewed sense of hope with this launch.

October 2008

I was asked by the Nova Scotia Department of Justice to consider writing a submission for the 2009 National Victims of Crime Resource Guide. It would assist the many agencies, support groups, service organizations, and most importantly, other victims of violent crime, by providing a connection to the emotional and personal experience of a victim's insight. In April 2009, _How One Victim of Murder Chose to be a Survivor_ was published as part of the National Victims of Crime Awareness Week.

December 5th, 2008 – Paula's 39th Birthday

On Friday December 5th, 2008 at the BLT Elementary School, our family extended thanks to the entire community of Beechville-Lakeside-Timberlea, who opened their hearts and provided unconditional support to Paula's family and friends after her tragic murder. Those in attendance placed purple ribbons over their hearts in support of the National Day of Remembrance and Action of Violence Against Women.

At the event, Lana talked about Paula and her involvement and connection to that community. Many kilometres of stories and laughter were shared between Paula and her friends on the BLT trail, and both her daughter Anna and her dog Coady were known to enjoy a walk with their mom on many occasions. Paula was an avid outdoor enthusiast and encouraged her students to live an active and healthy lifestyle. In planning this event, we talked about the importance of the community support we had received, and the fact that Paula would want us to give thanks to her community for all they had done and continue to do for so many on this journey. We knew Paula would be pleased if we found a project that would benefit the majority—including the young, the old, and, of course, the dogs!

That fall, Lana and I met with the BLT Rails to Trails Board and presented a donation from the Family and Friends of Paula Gallant in Paula's memory. The Board advised us the donation would be used to purchase a history panel that would be erected on the trail near Paula's school. A plaque would be placed on the panel in memory of Paula.

Once again the Honourable Bill Estabrooks was a proactive voice for Paula, and during this event, he presented Lana and me with the 250th Democracy Award for our efforts in seeking justice for Paula and for our work with Victim Services in creating awareness about men's violence against women and girls.

Children's Book by Louise Christie

Another long-time family friend, Louise Christie, then presented the book she wrote in loving memory of Paula and dedicated it to Anna. Louise invited children in the audience to join her at the podium as she introduced *Miss Gallant's Favourite Season,* and shared the wonderful artistry of Joan Power, an artist from our hometown, Glace Bay, Nova Scotia.

The night concluded with a birthday cake to celebrate Paula's life and a "A Walk to Remember" on the BLT Rails to Trails for a ribbon-cutting ceremony marking the area for the dedication.

And with each step taken, it felt like Paula walked beside us.

December 6th, 2008 – National Day of Remembrance and Action on Violence against Women.

Louise Christie and I attended the 20th anniversary of the Montreal Massacre and the National Day of Remembrance and Action on Violence against Women. We were thrilled to be asked to speak at the event and presented a cheque from the proceeds of *Miss Gallant's Favourite Season* to the Transition House of Nova Scotia Association (THANS). *Miss Gallant's Favourite Season* is another amazing tribute to Paula and has helped improve the well-being of abused survivors. It is times like this that I feel so privileged to have had such a wonderful sister in my life.

The executive director at THANS wrote a thank-you letter to our family: *What an amazing and wonderful gift. It feels very honoured to think that I belong to an organization that is thought of so highly by a family who has suffered so much injustice and pain.* I was always proud of Paula, but I am proud in a different way now as I see goodness the legacy her tragedy has had in our society.

This is the kind of goodness that Paula would expect us to work toward. Our loved ones leave behind spaces in the world that can never be filled. They also leave behind love and light in each of us that can spark joy and hope in our hearts, and give strength to our souls and others. There was much good done, so many gaps filled, and programs changed all because of Paula, because of the love we shared as sisters, because of the love she had for her fellow teachers and her students and their families.

By August 2009, I was exhausted to my core and my soul was tired from grief and wrath. I had emptied my bucket and my voice was tired of screaming at deaf ears. I was pretty sure I had done all I could do. We had auctions, vigils, walks, the art room, and countless presentations. I couldn't think of a new way to advocate. Until one call filled up my bucket just enough to keep going.

By some luck of the draw or fate, we were assigned the best media relations resource the RCMP had, Sgt. Joe Taplin. Joe was a household name in Nova Scotia at the time, and a bright light of optimism and hope. His policing experience combined with his compassion and commitment to justice provided the media guidance we needed. In the fall of 2009, Joe met with Lana and me, and asked what we were planning to honour Paula's memory at her school on what would have been her 40th birthday–December 5th, 2009. I admitted to him that I was done, that there was nothing left in me to call, plan, or give. I admitted that I had employed every strategy I could think of. Joe looked at me and Lana with understanding, but said in his deep-timbered voice, "We need you to do it one more time."

I looked at Lana and I thought about my family: my boys, who, for the last four years, had lived with a grieving, distracted mother, and of Alain, who was ever my rock, and accepted without complaint how I channelled my love for Paula into advocacy and system change. I balanced that guilt with the fact that Joe had never asked anything of us and gave all the support and trust he could, whenever we asked. So, I said, "Okay, we'll figure something out."

December 5th, 2009—Paula's 40th Birthday

A Parade of Hope and Peace took place in Paula's community on her 40th birthday. Forty wreaths, adorned with purple ribbons, Paula's *P*s, and dedication notes were hung through her community. I left a special note for Anna on the wreath I hung at the end of the street that led to Paula's house, letting her know we wouldn't stop until justice was realized! Anyone who knows me knows who my message was really directed to. After the walk, we went to the BLT Elementary School gym for remembrance, song, cider, and some homemade Cape Breton sweets!

Wreath for Paula's 40th Birthday

Once again, all who loved Paula walked shoulder to shoulder to be a voice, her voice and the voice of all women and girls impacted by men's violence. Policing officials and politicians spoke about their commitment to justice and once again, thanked Paula's community for their support.

Jason never came to a single event and for a long time he didn't do any media interviews. Then on August 18th, 2009, he did an interview with Dan Arsenault with the *Chronicle Herald*. During the interview Jason described Paula as his "best friend." He said, and I quote, "She was my life and was taken away from me. I'd never do anything to hurt her."

Chapter 10

Love Gets a Conviction

"When I despair, I remember that all through history the way of truth and love have always won. There have been tyrants and murderers, and for a time, they can seem invincible, but in the end, they always fall. Think of it--always."
—Mahatma Gandhi

After two and a half years advocating for Paula and others like her, I finally felt like the policing agencies (HRP and RCMP) realized I was never going to stop fighting for justice and the system level changes that needed to happen for whoever came after. I was on a mission, and I wouldn't—in reality, I *couldn't*—stop. Every cell, every fibre of my being, knew there were answers out there. Somewhere in my notebooks and binders, somewhere in my emails, I knew in my heart and mind there was a path to justice. I just hadn't found it . . . yet.

I remember this deeply personal moment, when someone who was in a position of power, who was "in charge" and as a result held influence over me and actions that needed to be taken, told me to my face that I was "hard to deal with." In the years before Paula's murder, I likely would have taken that to heart and internalized it a bit. As a successful, professional business woman, I would have reflected on my interactions with that person and wondered how I could have done better. Instead, I stared right back at him, and said with an equal amount of conviction, "Good. Get the job done and I'll go away!"

As I already said, we did work with some great people in policing in those first couple of years. There were leads to follow and possibilities to discuss, but from my observations, it seemed those competent individuals kept hitting one roadblock after another, mostly from their superior officers, mired within this integrated policing model.

And finally, change came. We were first introduced to Frank Chambers as the newly appointed Detective Sergeant-In-Charge of the Halifax Regional Police and RCMP) Integrated Major Crime Section. Apparently, Detective Sergeant Chambers was previously in charge of Major Crimes, until the integrated model came into effect and political appointments changed everything. After meeting Detective Sergeant Chambers Lana asked me, "What do you think?"

I said, "He looked us in the eye when he shook our hand. That's got to be a good thing."

In fact, when Detective Sergeant Chambers looked me in the eye, he said something I will never forget for the rest of my life as it made my shoulders drop away from my ears a little bit, made my jaw muscles relax just enough that I could chew gum without getting a cramp.

"This is not your fight anymore, and you no longer have to be *the one person in charge*, Lynn. I will do my very best, with my team, to try and solve Paula's case. I promise you that one of two things will be the outcome—it will be me telling you we made an arrest, or the case cannot be solved."

With those few words, Detective Sergeant Chambers lifted the weight that had been crushing my heart and lungs. I am not sure if anyone noticed, but in that moment, tears of hope formed in the backs of my eyes and stung my nose a little. For two and a half years, that's all I had been waiting to hear. With that, I could finally take a breath deep enough to move my diaphragm. I think that's when my heart began to beat again. I felt a sliver of optimism as a single ray of sun broke through the dark cloud of murder that had been hanging over my family and friends.

Through my finely crafted wall of perceived invulnerability, my response was simply:

"I didn't want to be in charge. But for two and a half years I searched and desperately tried to find that one person who was going to fight for my sister like I would. And no one stepped forward."

With Detective Sergeant Chambers, I felt unexpected sincerity. I felt like I had encountered genuine professional commitment to justice. After all this time fighting, lobbying, advocating for change and justice, I certainly wasn't going to be naïve and completely hand over the reins. He knew it, and I knew it. But my level of weariness, laced with anger, made me feel desperate to trust him. My gut said I could, so I did. I decided I was going to give this man and his team a chance. I sat back just a little and waited and watched.

Frank Chambers had decades of policing experience, a profound corporate memory, and an impressive professional network along with the highly skilled resources needed to take over the case with confidence. By no means did Detective Sergeant Chambers say or do anything to appease me or my family. He did things the "right" way, on a timeline that only he knew about. I admit that was frustrating as there were plenty of times we were unaware of what was happening. Nor did he say things he thought I wanted to hear—there was no patriarchal patronizing. This was refreshing and replenished a little faith in the system. In fact, Detective Sergeant Chambers never sugar-coated anything. He and his team just did their job; they sought justice for Paula. That was what we wanted all along.

Despite being in the dark about what was taking place in the investigation, I couldn't help but feel Paula was finally getting the focus she deserved. Detective Sergeant Chambers and his team instilled such confidence in our interactions simply by being honest and forthcoming with regular communication. With Detective Sergeant Chambers and his team now leading the policing elements of Paula's case, I had some bandwidth back. I turned my energy, focus, and commitment to justice into more advocating for others and making noise for everyone who could not speak for themselves. Together, Detective Sergeant Chambers and I worked in parallel–he on the policing, and me on the advocating and awareness raising.

August 17th, 2010—1,691 Days Since the Murder

The morning of August 10th, 2010 started out at 17 degrees Celsius, and the sun was going to break through the fog and haze at some point and sunrise would be around 6 a.m.—at least that is what the weatherman predicted. On this particular morning I expected to miss the sunrise, as Alain and I were asleep in our bed, until our landline rang around 6 a.m. Alain picked it up. Half asleep, he acknowledged the person on the phone. Then he passed it to me, and all he said was, "It's Frank."

Like many people who get phone calls at odd hours, my first thought was, *Oh crap, who died?* In the mere seconds it took me to take the phone from Alain, I mentally ran through the remaining members of the Gallant family who could have died. My beloved Grammie had already died, so who was left? Thoroughly expecting to hear Uncle Frank's voice, I took a deep breath to help prepare me for another phone call that was likely going to deliver more bad news.

"Hello?" I asked, trying to sound more awake and ready to face whatever the caller had to say head-on.

The man on the other line said, "Lynn, its Frank."

My still-sleepy brain paused. The man didn't say Uncle Frank, or Uncle Francis, as we called him. *Hmm.* I tried to register the voice.

The man said, "I need to speak with everyone. Should I come to your place or Lana's?"

Suddenly, with those words, in that tone, the voice registered.

I asked, "Is he dead?"

He said, "Lynn, which house should I come to?"

"Come to mine."

In fact, the sun rose at 6:11 a.m. on August 10th, 2010, and I was up to see it after all as I was phoning Lana.

"I'm sorry but you need to get your babies up and bring them here. Frank is on his way." I couldn't help but add, "He better have his gun holstered and double locked if he's coming with bad news. I don't know what I'll do if he's coming to tell me he's closing the case. "

Lana assured me, "He's not coming at six-thirty in the morning to tell us he is closing the case."

Alain and I figured it was best to wake up our boys and prepare them, instead of them waking up on their own and seeing the police here. I especially remember waking Connor and saying to him that Frank was coming to talk to us. He asked if we knew what it was about. I admitted that I didn't know. Connor speculated that Frank wouldn't come this early if it wasn't good news. It sounded logical, but I could not let my guard down.

When Lana and Paul arrived with their precious, bewildered children, we made it a special treat for Dylan and Emily by letting them curl up in our bed and watch TV. Tim and Connor were now eighteen and sixteen years old, respectively, so they stayed downstairs with us. They were old enough to hear the truth. They were only thirteen and eleven when Paula was murdered, and we tried to shield them as much as possible from the full gory truth of what happened to their aunt. It was what my heart told me to do at the time. In hindsight, I know they deserved the truth then too. But as their mother, I was and still am driven to protect my kids and I did what I thought was best at the time.

Detective Sergeant Chambers, known to all of us now as Frank, arrived. He started making small talk, checking in with the boys, asking about school and sports while frequently looking at his watch. I couldn't tell if he had some other place to be or if we were boring him. Frank then suggested we have a cup of coffee and so I made some for the others. There was still no way I was drinking that stuff—it brought up many psychosomatic responses. A pot of tea was made for Lana and me.

Even though Frank looked at his watch again, it somehow felt like time had stopped.

Finally, slapping my hands on my knees, I said, "Frank, get on with it!" somewhat more forcefully than I intended.

He said, "Let's go sit in the living room." We all knew it was another delay technique but went along with it, simply because it looked like Frank had something important to say, and I knew my heart needed to hear it. In the living room as we all stared at him, he checked his watch again, then his phone. I was about to lose any shred of patience and sanity I had left. Again, Frank looked at his phone as if willing it to ring, and then it did.

He got up and took the call outside. By this time of the morning, the air was close and the humidity was rising, in parallel to our stress levels.

He came in and looked at his watch for what felt like the thousandth time. Just as I was about to self-combust he said, "We've just arrested Jason and charged him with first-degree murder in Paula's death."

For the second time in my life, my whole world paused as it felt like the universe stopped on its axis. There was a fraction of disbelief before a flood of welcomed relief: The day of reckoning had arrived.

They arrested Jason on the Bedford Highway at a roadside safety inspection checkpoint. Someone wise, and someone with a great deal of awareness and empathy, made the decision not to arrest Jason at home because they knew Anna would be there. Who knew how someone who murdered his adoring wife with his own hands would react if cornered in his own home? Though it was never confirmed, I know it was Frank who made the decision. I know he would never do anything to put Paula's little girl at risk.

While the rest of us adults sat still, trying to recalibrate with the impact of what Frank said, Connor was the first to speak: "So, first degree murder is twenty-five years."

Frank nodded. "Yeah, it is."

Connor was clearly processing this information faster than us adults. "And the five years it took to get him, that'll be added on to a sentence?"

"Sorry, Connor, no, it doesn't work that way," Frank explained.

"What about the money you spent to catch him? How much did you spend to catch him?"

"I'd have to guess over a million dollars," said Frank.

"Will he have to pay that back to society? He should be made to pay that back," Connor insisted, completely transparent with his unabashed sense of right and wrong, and definitions of fairness and of justice far beyond his age.

March 2nd, 2011—1,891 Days Since the Murder

After a five-year police investigation, the following statement of facts was agreed upon and submitted to the courts, along with the victim statements. Please use caution when reading the statement of facts; it contains the graphic details of how Paula was murdered by her husband and it could be (re)traumatizing.

THE STATEMENT OF FACTS

R.v. Jason Wayne MacRAE

The accused, Jason Wayne MacRae, (DOB: May 12, 1973) and the victim, Paula Ann Gallant (DOB: December 5, 1969) were married July 5, 2003. The couple had one child, Anna Paul MacRae, born January 6, 2005. They resided together at 41 Silver Maple Drive, Timberlea. Jason MacRae worked in the call centre at Nova Scotia Power and Paula Gallant was a grade 3 teacher at Beechville lakeside Timberlea School. At the time of Paula Gallant's murder, the couple were preparing to purchase a new home on which they had an accepted offer.

On December 27, 2005, at 8:12 p.m., Jason MacRae contacted the Halifax Regional Police to seek advice, reporting that his wife had failed to return home from shopping. About 45 minutes earlier, MacRae had contacted his wife's sister, Lana Kenny, to inquire of his wife's whereabouts, telling her she had been gone since about 2:00 pm. Ms. Kenny had spoken with Paula at about 1:30 p.m., and Paula had said she was not going out. This was the last known conversation with Paula Gallant. Ms. Kenny went to her sister's home, and together with Jason MacRae, began phoning Paula's friends, and checking her bank and credit cards on-line for indication of use. Jason MacRae left his home and allegedly drove to the Costco store where he reported Paula had gone to purchase diapers, to see if her car could be located. Family members and friends began a search for her.

Having turned up nothing, MacRae called 911 at 10:14 p.m. and reported his wife as a missing person, prompting an RCMP response. Four of the friends and family members searching for Paula, brothers-in-law, Paul Kenny and Alain Blackburn, sister Lana Kenny and friend, Andrea Maclean, went to the school where Paula taught, walking distance from the MacRae-Gallant residence. There, at 12:30 a.m. on December 28, 2005, they located her locked vehicle. Calls were relayed back to the residence, and to the RCMP, and Jason MacRae attended the school while Paula's sister, Lynn Blackburn, remained with Anna. With his brother-in-law, Paul, Jason MacRae banged on the doors of the school, seemingly to try and determine if Paula was inside. Once the police arrived, and a second set of car keys were obtained from the residence, the vehicle was opened. The body of Paula Gallant was found laying in the fetal position in the trunk under a grey blanket. She was dressed in jeans and a black nylon jacket with her shoes positioned near her head. Her purse and car keys were inside the passenger compartment of the vehicle. She was not dressed in appropriate clothing for the weather, as she had been when she was observed out earlier in the day.

An autopsy was performed on the body of Paula Gallant. The cause of death was determined to be asphyxiation and the method of death, strangulation. Significant findings included marks on her neck, petechial hemorrhaging in both her eyes and a contusion on the back of her head. There were no signs of defensive wounds. There was biological material found on the crotch of her jeans. She was wearing only one earring. The degree of brain swelling observed was consistent with an interval of at least several minutes between a lack of oxygen supply and death.

Jason MacRae was formally interviewed by police on December 28, 2005, January 10, 2006, January 11, 2006, January 30, 2006, and on February 8, 2006, when he was arrested. In each interview, MacRae claimed that he had no knowledge of his wife's murder, and maintained that she had left their home at about 2:00 p.m. on the date in question to go shopping, never to return.

Throughout the extensive investigation, Jason MacRae remained the primary suspect in the murder of his wife, though there were no indications of previous domestic violence, or serious marital discord, and friends and family members described a loving marriage. Investigation did determine that an on-line gambling debt of $700.00 that MacRae had hid from his wife, and blamed his brother for, was a source of friction between the couple. Police were easily able to re-construct the last days of Paula Gallant's life, which were not marked by anything out of the ordinary. She and Jason MacRae spent Christmas Eve, Christmas Day and part of Boxing Day, together with their daughter Anna, at the home of her sister and brother-in-law, Lana and Paul Kenny, and their children, along with sister and brother-in-law, Lynn and Alain Blackburn, and their children. The holidays were relaxing and joyful, by all accounts, marking Anna's first Christmas. Paula Gallant and Jason MacRae returned to their home with Anna on December 26th, and were intimate. On December 27th, Paula Gallant visited her sister Lana in the morning, dropped by a hardware store, and began to do some painting in preparation for listing their home for sale. She thawed chili from the freezer for supper that evening.

In the years following his wife's murder, Jason MacRae continued to reside in the home he once shared with his wife, along with his daughter Anna, and his mother. The mortgage on the home was paid out by insurance. He collects monthly C.P.P. and N.S.T.U. survivor benefits on behalf of himself and Anna, and received a one-time C.P.P. death benefit ($2,500.) MacRae submitted a claim on his wife's life insurance policy of $100,000. but was denied by the insurer. He did not pay the bill for her funeral expenses ($5,500.), nor put a headstone on her grave. The unsolved homicide generated intense media interest over the ensuing years. Against the advice of legal counsel, MacRae gave an interview to the Chronicle Herald newspaper in December, 2007, in which he described himself as "heartbroken", and "trying to get through day by day" without the woman he described as "my best friend" and "my life". On the same date, he issued the following public statement:

> *We live in a very close-knit community, everyone says "Hi" to everyone in the street, and there are always people on the streets in our neighbourhood, everyday.*
>
> *I can't understand how something like this tragedy could have happened in the middle of the day, and no one see anything. If someone knows something and is afraid to come forward, it is not too late. Any information, even the smallest detail, may lead to a break in this case.*

> *My little girl is growing up without her mother because we have a killer walking amongst us. I do not want this to happen to someone else.*
>
> *If anyone knows anything about this case, please contact the police or Crime Stoppers.*

MacRae contacted the C.B.C. national news program, The Fifth Estate, saying, in an interview, "maybe something done nationally might create more awareness and actually bring something to light" (to catch her killer).

In October 2009, a covert under-cover RCMP operation was undertaken. Through the means of a ruse, MacRae was introduced to an undercover officer who, over time, befriended him and purported to offer him work for a crime syndicate. An undercover operation began, utilizing a number of scenarios to gain the trust of MacRae. In April 2010, MacRae voluntarily quit his job at Nova Scotia Power to work full-time for the alleged crime syndicate.

On August 6, 2010, MacRae met with an undercover operator he was led to believe had learned that the police had something on MacRae, had connections and could possibly make his "problem" go away. The undercover operator maintained that he was the head of the crime syndicate and that MacRae would have to tell him everything about what happened to his wife, in order for him to understand MacRae's situation and what the operator would have to do to assist MacRae. Pursuant to a Judicial Authorization under ss. 184.2 and 487.01 of the Criminal Code, this interview was both audio and video recorded, unbeknownst to MacRae. Jason MacRae disclosed the following details to the undercover operator with respect to the events of December 27, 2005:

- He killed Paula Gallant on December 27, 2005, between 2:00 and 2:30 p.m. at 41 Silver Maple Drive, Timberlea, Nova Scotia.
  He describes the layout of the house and the basement area.

- He and Paula were arguing about a debt on his Visa and that he lied to Paula about it. This argument took place in the basement of 41 Silver Maple Drive.
- He said Paula was on the computer, sitting on a chair, back to him when he went upstairs and returned with a piece of 2 x 4 wood and struck Paula on the back of her head while she was seated. He described how he hit the wall with the wood while he was swinging it towards Paula.
- He states Paula did not go down after being struck but turned and stood up and faced him and screamed.
- He states he then grabbed her from the front around the neck and pushed her back into the laundry room area.
- He states he strangled her for a couple minutes with both hands. He states Paula may have peed herself as her pants were wet.
- He states he knew she was dead because he put saran wrap around Paula's face and head to see if she was breathing and left it there for about 20 minutes.
- He states he covered Paula with a sheet and left her in the laundry room.
- He states he went upstairs and fed his daughter, Anna, while Paula was in the basement.
- He states after finishing feeding his daughter he goes outside to see if anyone is around.
- He returns to the basement, pulls the sheet off Paula and sits her up and puts a black pullover windbreaker jacket on her and puts loafer type shoes on her.
- He states he wraps Paula in the beige sheet and slides her out a window adjacent to the driveway.
- He states he puts Paula in the trunk of her car, a Chevy Cavalier.
- He state he covers her with a grey blanket that is taken from an emergency kit in the trunk of the car.
- He states one of her shoes fell off and picks it up and puts it in the car next to Paula.

He states he left his daughter in her highchair and drove the car over to BL T school and parked it there. He backed the vehicle into its parking spot.
- He describes leaving the keys in the console between the driver and passenger seats.
- He then runs home. Near his home he stops near the mailbox.
- He states he takes his daughter and goes for a drive around 4:00 p.m.
- He states he went to the area of Halifax Shopping Centre and got rid of the 2 x 4 and the saran wrap by throwing them in a dumpster.
- He states he went to the Credit Union and deposited $100.00 dollars into an account he had.
- He states he went to a Needs Store on the way home and bought batteries.
- He states he had a small nick on his hand after getting back home.
- He states the next day, he found Paula's earring in the laundry room. He took it upstairs, and disposed of it in a garbage can at a Tim Horton's three days later. (This earring had also been observed by others, at the same time.)
- He states at the funeral he checks Paula's nails and observes they had been clipped.

Following this discussion, the undercover operator persuades MacRae to provide a re-enactment of the crime, in the house, in order to assist in understanding how the crime boss can best help MacRae to elude justice. On August 9, 2010, Jason MacRae disclosed the following details to the undercover operator about his crime; this interview also audio and video recorded.

- He went to the basement of his home and indicates that Paula was sitting at the computer.
- He states that they argued once he told her about his gambling debt and lying about it.

- He shows how he went up the stairs and grabbed a 2 x 4, came down the stairs, and with a right hand swing shows how he hit Paula in the back of the head.
- He shows the operator the damage to the wall indicating specifically which spot it was that he hit just prior to hitting Paula in the back of the head. The damage to the wall is about the same height as the operator's head as he sits at the computer desk.
- He also indicates that he patched the wall later the same day of the murder.
- He shows the patch work which is still visible.
- He shows the operator how he strangled Paula by demonstrating on one of the operators. He grabs the operator by the front of the neck and pretends to strangle him in the same manner he strangled Paula.
- He pushes the operator back into the laundry room floor and onto the floor.
- He states he squeezed as hard as he could. He states that while Paula was on the floor, she said, "what are you doing, stop."
- He states he pushed her into the left side of the laundry room away from the doorway with her head further from the laundry room door.
- He describes how Paula made gurgling noises after she was lying unconscious on the laundry room floor. He states he could hear his daughter waking from her nap on the baby monitor as he strangles Paula.
- He states she was making some gurgling noises after strangling her.
- He describes how he went upstairs and got the saran wrap and wrapped Paula's head with it 3 or 4 times to make sure she couldn't breathe.
- He states he covers her with a beige bed sheet.
- He states that after wrapping Paula's head in saran wrap, he goes upstairs and gets his daughter up and fed her lunch in her highchair.

- He then states after about 20 to 30 minutes he finishes feeding his daughter and leaves her in the highchair and then goes outside and checks for possible witnesses or neighbours.
- · He states he goes back inside and back downstairs to the basement, sits Paula up and puts a blue windbreaker on her and shoes on her and wraps her in the beige blanket and slides her out a window by the stairs.
- · He shows the operators the window and indicates it is driveway level and the cars trunk is right next to the window and the car was backed in the driveway.
- · He states as he moves Paula from the driveway to the car, a shoe falls off and he picks it up and puts the shoe in the trunk next to her.
- · He states he places Paula in the trunk of the car.
- · He demonstrates how he placed Paula in the trunk to the operator by moving the operator into the same position.
- · He places the operator on their left side in the fetal position facing away from him, indicating this is how he placed Paula in the car.
- · He states he covers Paula with a grey blanket from the emergency kit that was in the trunk of the car.
- · He details that the shoes fell off while putting Paula in the trunk.
- · He demonstrates how he placed both shoes next to Paula in the trunk.
- · He directs the operators over to BL T School, indicating and travelling the route he took on December 27, 2005, and indicates this was between 3 and 4:00p.m.
- · He shows how and where he parked the car. • He shows that he backed the vehicle into a parking spot.
- · He walks with an operator the route he took on foot back to 41 Silver Maple Drive, crossing the soccer field and using the path to Tiger Maple Drive and to his house at 41 Silver Maple Drive.

- · He describes that he ran from the corner of the school, across the soccer field, onto Tiger Maple Drive and then walks when he gets to Silver Maple Drive
- · He walked past his house to the mailbox on Silver Maple Drive at Red Maple Drive then returning to 41 Silver Maple Drive.
- · He describes that he stopped by the mailbox so that if anyone saw him outside he could state he was getting the mail.
- · He describes how he left the car keys in the console between the passenger and drivers seat.

During the re-enactment, MacRae was asked questions by the undercover operators about whether he had planned the murder. The following exchanges occurred:

p. 55 line 1334 - 1345

> Voice 3: Urn. Just curiosity, like 'cause, I, I, At what point, did, did you know you were gonna fuckin' whack her? (Short laugh)
>
> MacRae: Um. Honestly, I had thought about it before. I didn't think I would ever do it. Um, then, yeah. I pretty much knew I was gonna do it when I did it.
>
> Voice 3: But did you wake up that mornin' and say I'm gonna tell her and I'm gonna fuckin' whack her right after, or (Short laugh)
>
> MacRae: No
>
> Voice 3: It just happened like that?
>
> MacRae: Just ah. yeah. It just happened.
>
> Voice 3: But you thought about it before?
>
> Voice 4: Yeah

p. 56 line 1355 - 1375

MacRae: Um, so yeah, I had had thoughts about it but I didn't think I would ever do it, but

Voice 3: How long before that did you have last thoughts that you were gonna whack her?

MacRae: The last time I had thought about it?

Voice 3: Yeah

MacRae: Oh, it was _ _ , Um, yeah, a coupla days before that probably (Short laugh)

Voice 3: A couple days, did you

MacRae: _ _ _ _ _

Voice 3: But, you were thinkin' like. Doing it that way, or?

MacRae: Um. (Sighs) Yeah, if I, I'm tryin' to think. I thought of it. I actually thought to myself how, how could I do this if I actually did do it. And ah, yeah, that was pretty much my _ _

Voice 3: Like what, what, what was it like

MacRae: _ _ , Yeah, like I had thought about like, do I wake up in the mornin' one day and just grab her or, in bed. And then, I had some different ideas and then that day it just

Voice 3: So what. your ideas. Well, was it, was it like what you did, or hit her, or choke her, or shoot her

MacRae: To choke her, that was my idea, to choke her

p. 59/80 line 1432 -1453

> MacRae: Honestly, when I look at this (looking at picture of Paula Gallant and Jason MacRae) I usually, think like, fuck, one day we were happy
>
> Voice 3: Yeah (Clears throat)
>
> MacRae: Like, we were really happy one, at one time. _ _ . She's just, she was everything in the apartment
>
> Voice 3: Yeah
>
> MacRae: Nothin' could be out like, fuckin'. Forget to take somethin' downstairs as soon as I finished with it, she'd get on my case
>
> Voice 3: Oh Really?
>
> MacRae: Yeah
>
> Voice 1: She really needed to be perfect, kinda like you (*name of undercover operator omitted*) (Short laugh)
>
> Voice 3: Um, um. That, that. that, that ah, that. A lot of women are that way though anyway~, But did you ah, like when you were ah. thinkin' thinkin' about it. I mean did ya know that, this is not gonna last One day she's fuckin' dead, or?
>
> MacRae: Um, I had, honestly yeah. I think I did (Clears throat.
>
> Voice 3: You did what?
>
> MacRae: I pretty much decided that this is, was gonna have to be done
>
> Voice 3: Like. whack her, or divorce her, or

MacRae: Um, You know, I can't believe _ _

Voice 3: You were gonna whack her?

MacRae: Yeah

p. 60/61 line 1457 - 1480

Voice 3: like when did you think you were gonna do it for. If you knew you were gonna whack her?

MacRae: Um, I think, like I say, it was probably only a couple weeks, maybe a month, that I actually started havin' ideas of, of doin' it

Voice 3: Yeah. But you, you knew you that. That was gonna happen, you just didn't know when or

MacRae: Um. I had pretty much decided. Yeah, it was gonna happen but. I don't know if I actually knew that I would go through with it

Voice 3: Yeah

MacRae: I mean, it was one day, I was like, fuck yeah, I'm gonna fuckin' do this and then the next day, no I can't do that

Voice 3: But that _ , that, that mornin" like ah. Okay, she bitches at you for whatever. Money, money. When you got up that morning, did you know you were going to whack her, or?

MacRae: No (Clears throat) No, in fact, like. When we got up that mornin' she went out. She went to the hardware store to get some stuff and then she came back. And then like I say, she wasn't in the door five minutes and she was just bitching at me about something and like, I think something just went off and I said, okay, apparently today is the day.

>Voice 3: (Short laugh)
>
>Voice 1: (Short laugh)
>
>Voice 3: Did you like ah, did you say, okay today's the day and then you just happened to see the wood. Or you saw the wood and say okay, now this is it
>
>MacRae: I saw the wood and said, yeah, this is it

During his meeting with the alleged crime boss, MacRae described his wife's murder as a "big fight, it got out of control" telling the crime boss, "you realize I loved her, I really did" (transcript, August 6, 2010, p. 36, 37) He elaborated on the fight in the following exchanges:

p. 48 line 1160 - 1169

>Voice 1: Okay. And then you guys had this argument, and you choke her. You guys weren't getting along or what?
>
>MacRae: (Sighs) No, I mean, we were gettin' along fine, it was. It was little things. Um. Little petty things, um. Like we'd have little arguments, but nothing too major. Um. But then she had just found out that I had just lost a bit of money gambling
>
>Voice 1: Um hmm. So she probably wasn't too happy about that
>
>MacRae: _ _ _ no, she wasn't happy about that
>
>Voice 1: Is that what you guys argued about?
>
>MacRae: Basically, yeah

p. 64 line 1557 - 1572

>Voice 1: Um. I'm just tryin' to think here what else it could be. (Sighs) so you were sayin' this started over some gambling debt? MacRae: Yeah Voice 1: How'd she find out about that?
>
>MacRae: Um. I actually ended up telling her. I lied to her about it at first and told her that I lent my brother the money
>
>Voice 1: Oh. 'cause this was money out of your bank account?
>
>MacRae: Yeah. And then ah. Ah, she just kept asking me and
>
>Voice 1: I imagine when she found out she was probably pretty pissed, eh?
>
>MacRae: She was really pissed
>
>Voice: Yeah, women generally don't understand that stuff too well
>
>MacRae: No they don't
>
>Voice 1: So, was that when that happened, right then and _ _ ?
>
>MacRae: Ah, yeah _ _ _ _
>
>Voice 1: This argument about the money?
>
>MacRae: Just, pretty much, yeah

In his 2006 police interviews, MacRae denied any link between this gambling debt and his wife's murder _ He initially maintained the story that the debt was his brothers, but eventually admitted that he lied and that the debt was actually his, but maintained that Paula died never knowing the truth. He described that fact as "something (I) have to live with every day. I lied to Paula about something." He stated in 2006 that he knew he had to tell her, but did not want to bring it up over the holidays, so his plan was to tell her after New Year's. He said she would not have been too happy if she found out and would have been surprised, but they would have worked it out.

Jason MacRae was arrested on August 17, 2010, and interviewed under caution. In his cautioned interview, MacRae made no specific admissions, but did not deny involvement in his wife's murder.

A warrant to search 41 Silver Maple Drive was executed the same day. A portion of drywall was excised where MacRae had showed the undercover operators he had made repairs to the drywall, and the drywall displays damage, beneath the repair work.

My love for Paula allowed me and my family to become survivors. Finally, two and a half years into this transformation, Detective Sergeant Frank Chambers walked into our lives. After five years of waiting, of keeping up the pressure, we finally found a man who valued justice and fairness just as much as Connor did.

Though he never showed us, I know Frank has a superhero cape somewhere.

Chapter 11

With Love the Truth Speaks

"A difficult time can be more readily endured if we retain the conviction that our existence holds a purpose—a cause to pursue, a person to love, a goal to achieve." —John Maxwell

When I look back at the pictures from our last Christmas together as a family, I see the change now. Those Christmas memories have played like a movie in my head over and over and over for years. Sometimes in the middle of driving to complete a mundane errand, other times in the middle of the night while I try to sob quietly to not wake Alain. I have replayed the scenes of those three days together endlessly, searching for a clue that all was not well. Obviously my perspective has changed with what I know now, and I can see Paula looking at Jason with tension in her eyes. Looking at the pictures with the benefit of hindsight, I see Jason was always just a little separate from our group. There are pictures where he could have stood closer to our family, or where he was just simply looking away. Like he was already distancing himself from us. I still feel ashamed about how happy and content I felt at Thanksgiving that year, and the notes I wrote to everybody thanking each of them for being in my family. With the early and close-together deaths of our parents, I thought I had suffered the worst pain I could ever suffer. But there's no way I can ever find words to describe the pain I felt when Paula was murdered by Jason.

In preparation for the court case and conviction, the following victim impact statements were written and are reprinted here with permission.

Victim Impact Statement

March 2nd, 2011
Victim's Impact Statement
Submitted by: Lynn Gallant-Blackburn

In memory of my sister Paula Anna Gallant who was born December 5th, 1969, and was murdered December 27th, 2005, at the age of 36.

As I reflect on my life without Paula since December 27th, 2005, and the violent way she died I struggle to find the words that will ever truly capture the impact. Everything changed, and from that day on, it would never be the same. I also struggle to try and describe how this murder impacted "me." I have never just been "me" as I have only ever known "us," which not only included Paula but everyone I loved, including her husband. I cannot partition or compartmentalize the loss and make it just about "me" as I am part of everyone that loved and lost Paula.

I am challenged with trying to condense the rawness and depth of emotion I have witnessed, experienced and survived since Paula died. Her murder should never have happened. But it did. If this was an act of violence that occurred "in the heat of the moment," and if the person responsible was truly sorry and really loved my sister then he could have ended it on February 8th, 2006, when he was arrested. The journey could have lasted forty-three days instead of one thousand, eight hundred and ninety-one days.

Who or what we become relates back to the people who brought us into this world and the experiences we endured. In trying to help you gain an understanding of the impact, you will first have to understand our relationship as sisters and the bond that existed in our family and in our circle of friends.

Three sisters raised by wonderful parents, in a humble, very loving home on Coady Street in Cape Breton. We lived in a peaceful, safe, trusting environment where we treated each other with respect, empathy and dignity. Our father taught us to be independent, to stand up for our beliefs, to work hard in all we did, to strive for the impossible. Our mother taught us compassion, to take care of everyone we loved, to have hope and faith, to be honest and to cherish our blessings. Our Coady Street family, including 23 Hillside Drive, was comprised of seven homes with twenty-one children, which taught us that one of the most important blessings we would have in life was the relationships we build in our families and with those who come into our lives. Family was at the core of all we did and all we knew, and we were guided by a solid moral compass that had been instilled in us.

Three sisters who experienced monumental loss early in life with the tragic death of our parents: our mom was forty-six, our dad only forty-nine when they died from cerebral aneurysms. Orphaned young by these tragic and untimely deaths, we believed that we had reached the boundaries of pain and sorrow one's heart could bear. There could be no deeper or more crippling pain imaginable in our minds.

Three sisters, bonded from birth, whose relationship and love was strengthened when our parents died, leaned on each other as we persevered forward in our lives. This experience provided us with a courageous and tenacious spirit and a determination to survive. We worked hard to find happiness again knowing it would never be the same without our parents, but as long as we had each other we would live a life our parents had encouraged us to strive for. I took on the parental role for my two younger sisters, and their relationship as best friends was truly one of love and loyalty. We were entwined in each other's lives daily.

Just as my husband and I had assumed the role of surrogate "mom and dad," Lana and Paula took on the "big sister" role for my two sons, Timothy and Connor, when they were born. We operated like one large family making decisions, planning vacations, celebrating milestones and holidays . . . always together, as one. Those who understood our past knew why we were so close and those who didn't soon came to realize you never knew one Gallant sister without getting to know the other two . . . our hearts truly beat as one. From our dad's wedding ring, our mom had three rings designed as a triangle. When she gave the rings to us she said "the three of us were equal sides of one triangle; created though our parents love and bonded for eternity."

The years passed . . . and as three sisters, our love, strength and desire to live a fulfilling life was being realized. Never ones to wallow in self pity, the laughter and carefree spirit in our souls reignited over time.

In 2001, my baby sister Paula, who I loved, protected and cared for as my own child, fell in love with Jason MacRae, a man she adored.

In 2002, Jason MacRae asked my husband and me for Paula's hand in marriage. He promised to love her, take care of her and be a wonderful husband forever. He said he was the luckiest man alive to have her in his life.

In 2003 I walked my beautiful sister down the aisle and gave my love and blessings to the happy couple as I welcomed Jason MacRae and his family into our trusting and accepting circle.

In the guest book at the cottage where they celebrated their honeymoon, Paula wrote, "I am truly blessed to have married my best friend."

In 2004, three sisters and our families enjoyed life and the closeness we shared together.

I was so proud of my sisters and all they had overcome at such a young age. I was also happy they both adored their husbands who had embraced the dynamics of the "Gallant family" and our relationship as sisters.

In 2005, Paula experienced the joy and celebration of her daughter's birth.

On January 6th, I held my sister's hand and whispered encouraging words of support and comfort during the birth of her first baby. At 3:05 a.m., Anna Paula was born and named after our parents. Paula asked me to cut Anna's umbilical cord and from that time on she affectionately called me "Grandma" when Anna was in my presence.

As Paula describes in the journal she kept to one day give to Anna: "It was the most amazing night of my life and my heart grew a hundred times with the instant love I felt for you. Anna, the second you were born, my life changed for the better. You are named after the two most important people in my life. I am so sad you will never get to meet them. I hope the stories I can tell you will do them justice. Meeting your dad allowed me to trust again.

"Now, meeting you has shown me the bond between mother and child. No matter what the next one hundred years bring us, you can always count on me and Dad. I love you so much."

In 2005, Paula experienced the shock and horror of her own death by someone she loved and trusted.

On December 27th, just one week before her daughter Anna's first birthday, my 36-year-old sister, Paula Anne Gallant, was violently murdered. Her lifeless body was put in the trunk of her car which was then driven to the elementary school where she taught. She was left alone, in the cold darkness of her own car in her school parking lot, and the person responsible did not give a second thought about the impact this senseless and selfish act would have on all who loved Paula, including the more than eight hundred students and fifty staff who were such an important part of Paula's life.

And from that day on . . .

Life as we knew it was redefined in the most horrific and unimaginable manner possible. Someone living amongst us made a conscious choice to end Paula's life, to take away her right to be the mother of her 11-month-old baby girl, to end her career as a teacher and artist, to end her ability to fulfill her life as a woman, friend, sister, aunt . . . and so much more.

Making the choice to end Paula's life severed the most sacred bond that exists . . . the bond between baby and mother. No longer would Anna be comforted by the sound of her mother's voice, the gentle touch of her hand, her mother's scent, her heartbeat, her breath on her cheek. She would no longer hear her mommy's laughter or feel her embrace. Anna would never have the chance to inhale her mother's beautiful spirit or be blessed with Paula's physical presence guiding her through life. Paula would never have the chance to see Anna's first steps, hold her hand the first day of school, see her run on the beach or fly a kite. She would never be able to share stories of her life as a child, or pass on traditions, family recipes, religious values, anecdotes or tales of her grandparents, all of which was so important to Paula.

When Anna was only twenty-one weeks, Paula wrote in her journal, "I can't wait to get to know you and who you'll be when you grow up." Paula was denied what she always dreamed of . . . being a mother.

Anna was denied the right of having a mother and she was burdened with the truth she would one day have to face.

And to think that less than twenty-four hours before her murder, we had all hugged each other goodbye after spending Christmas together from the 24th to the 26th . . . all under one roof, three sisters and their families. As we raised our glasses during our Christmas meal to give thanks for all that we had, one could never have imagined that the acts of another human being two days later could bring such pain and devastation to this loving and happy family.

In the days immediately following Paula's death my main focus was to take care of my sister's husband, the man she loved and trusted and the man who I had also loved. He was an important member of my family and he had always looked to my husband and me for guidance and support. I coddled him like a child and provided unconditional love and compassion. He portrayed himself as a helpless, devastated, broken-hearted husband who looked to me and my family for everything, including taking care of Anna, making travel plans for his parents, planning his wife's funeral, picking out Paula's grave plot, arranging his grief counselling, working with his employer to understand his benefit entitlement, ensuring the bills were paid off, working through all the paperwork for the many benefits he would receive as a result of his wife's death . . . which he was very attentive and engaged to pursue . . . the list was endless. My husband and I covered all the expenses during this time on his behalf with his reassurance he would reimburse us.

This, of course, never happened even though he received several monetary gifts of support from family and friends along with other benefits including the CPP death benefit. My brother-in-law kept me very preoccupied and focused on his needs. I was operating on autopilot and truly unaware of the fact that I was caring for him at the expense of my well-being and that of my family; especially my sons Timothy, aged thirteen, and Connor, aged eleven.

I was patient in trying to understand why Paula's husband was not grieving the way my mom did when Dad died but I argued with myself that everyone grieves differently. I was patient with his vague responses, his apathy, and his inability to stand with me and Lana by our sister's casket at the funeral home. My two young sons bravely stood, devastated and broken-hearted, with me and Lana to thank all who had come to say goodbye while my brother-in-law was curled up in a ball in the corner at the back of the funeral room, shielding his face and shame from the hundreds who had come to pay their respects. I was patient, but challenged with the fact he did not willingly invite the police into his life, into Paula's home, or try and help find Paula's murderer. He never demanded answers from the police or asked for the public's support. He never truly fell apart like so many around me did. He never rallied anyone in his family or in his trusted circle to help the Gallant family in any way possible. But, because I loved him and he was part of my family and he was the father to a niece I adored and loved, he remained my top priority. Whatever he needed, my family and I provided, without question.

During this time I was also intent on getting answers to understand why this happened to Paula and how . . . as well as who was responsible. We needed something, anything, logical to help us understand the world we now found ourselves living in which was completely foreign to all we had ever experienced. I was like a tenacious bulldog demanding action and accountability. I was immersed in everything I could do to end this nightmare we were living. The day we buried Paula, I promised to become her voice, for her, for Anna, for the children and for every woman who had violently and senselessly lost her life to violence. I vowed that as long as I was able to breathe Paula's voice would never be silenced and that I would never stop seeking the truth until justice was realized. Paula's husband passively watched me endure this struggle to find answers. He observed the torment and guilt I felt in not being able to protect my baby sister. He saw the rawness of my pain and how I struggled with the unknown, especially with needing to know if Paula had suffered at the time of her death. He knew I was haunted with images of her final terror-filled moments. He saw my frustration and anger about the unfounded and appalling rumors our family had to deal with, the many calls I made to the police for updates and the efforts I was taking to try and shield my children from the horrors of the truth. He had all the answers and could have ended the suffering but instead moved on with his life, without any regard for anyone but himself.

As the days passed and I observed his easy transition to redefine his life without Paula, with no strong evidence of grief or with any ambition to aggressively and passionately work with the police to try and assist in solving her case, my autopilot switch flipped off and my patience was depleted. I began to distance myself from his needs, his control and manipulation. I became acutely aware of my pain and the suffering my family was experiencing. In the midst of their deepest despair and agony, I was providing support to my sister's husband. I realized he was completely insensitive to our loss, our feelings and our struggles.

Based on the tragic and untimely death of my parents I thought I had been exposed to the rawest level of pain and suffering I would ever endure, but what I felt after Paula's murder was far more severe and complex. I was consumed with shock, disbelief, numbness, confusion and fear. I kept hoping I was going to wake up from the horrific nightmare but then I would look into my children's eyes, see their fear, their struggle, and their inability to understand what was happening in their lives as it spun out of control . . . and I would feel a pain so deep, a pain so crippling that I could barely catch my breath. I prayed that darkness would not fall because then I would not have to wake up again to face the reality. My heart felt like it had shattered into a million pieces and I felt such extreme loss on so many levels . . . for Paula, for Anna, for my parents, for my sister Lana, for our children, for my aging grandmothers, for my family and friends, for Paula's friends and colleagues, for her students, for her community. I quickly came to realize the traumatic effect of Paula's murder was endless and had no boundaries.

Every morning, even before I was fully awake, Paula was my first thought. My heart felt as if it would beat out of my chest as I was consumed with an overwhelming sadness. I had to mentally replace the dark images of Paula's death from my thoughts with ones that reflected Paula in life. I needed to see Paula's smile versus the terror in her eyes. I needed to hear her laughter versus her screams. I needed to see her kissing Anna versus knowing that Anna would never feel the kiss of her mother on her face again. I would realize all over again that Paula was murdered . . . and the questions would begin.

Why was Paula murdered? Why was this the only option? How could this happen? When is it going to end? Only thirty-six years lived. Paula deserved so much more than that. Every day, as the reality became permanently etched in my heart and mind, the impact became more vivid. I lived in fear . . . afraid to get out of my car after dark, afraid to stay in my own home alone, afraid for the safety of my children, afraid of hearing the truth, afraid of the chaos that now seemed to exist, afraid I would never feel peace, afraid that I would never overcome the heartbreak. I lost my sister, my brother-in-law and our secure, peaceful, loving family structure. I knew it would never be the same and I would once again have to redefine "some level of normalcy" based on this life experience that was forced upon me and my family by the choice and actions of someone we trusted, loved and respected.

Every night when I closed my eyes, I would realize, yet again, that my sister was gone forever. I was tormented with my thoughts around who I believed had done this to her. I worked so hard to push those thoughts from my mind and hoped and prayed that I was wrong. I wanted to believe that my sister really did go shopping and this was a random act of violence. Her murder was unfathomable . . . How did this happen to three sisters from a small town in Cape Breton? I began to realize no one was immune to violence and it did not discriminate

— it could and did happen to good people and most often by someone they loved and trusted.

As parents, just try and imagine telling your young children that someone they loved, who was a big influence and mentor in their lives, had been murdered and placed in the trunk of their car. Just stop for a moment and think of having to do this. I did and it was the most painful thing I ever had to do as a parent. As I spoke the words, it felt like a jagged knife was piercing my soul over and over again.

Of course, because of how they were raised, with family being core, they worried so much about their uncle, Anna and Coady (Paula's dog), but were glad they had each other. My eleven-year-old son was so overwhelmed with worry that he opened a trust fund for Anna and made the first deposit of the only money he had. Between January and the last deposit in March of 2006, almost five thousand dollars was deposited by all those who were touched by this gesture of humanity.

My two young sons who loved Paula like a big sister no longer felt safe. Their hearts were broken and they felt a depth of pain no child should ever feel, especially when it has been brought on by someone they loved as a "big brother." My children were afraid to go into the city, into Paula's community, afraid to sleep in a tent outside in our backyard, afraid to stay alone, afraid of the isolation and afraid the pain in their chest would never subside. They lost their youth, their innocence, their ability to trust, and their carefree spirit. Instead of thinking about their next hockey game, enjoying their new Christmas presents, or spending time with friends over the holidays, they were faced with horrific news about their aunt's death. They attended a wake and a funeral during the holiday season, talked to psychologists, missed school and did not go on their school trips which would have taken them from the safety of their home. They were incubated in this world of pain and felt isolated and different than their peers. They experienced an endless wave of emotion and confusion, and sleep did not come easily. I had one who roamed the halls at night and one who cried himself to sleep . . . the darkness was not their friend. Sleep came easier when the sky was light. Their uncle didn't even flinch when my boys had to be swabbed for DNA. Evil and violence invaded their precious, naïve souls.

My heart still aches when I think of how much my children have endured, how much they have suffered, how much they have lost. They lost the mom and dad they had before Paula died. They lost their mom as I spent countless hours advocating for Paula and keeping her voice alive. They lost the ability to live the life they should have lived versus the one forced upon them. They were exposed to this torment for almost five years of their lives because there was no closure, and would have had to face it for life if it wasn't for the dedication and mastery of excellent policing.

What would it have been like for them to have Paula in their life through their junior high and high school years, to have her cheer them on in the stands while they played hockey, to watch Anna grow up with them, to maybe even celebrate the birth of another child Paula dreamed of having? What would it have been like for them to feel safe, to feel uninhibited and carefree, to be a kid and to celebrate Christmas the way they always had . . . three sisters with their family, feeling joy and peace? This altered the course of their path in life and they had no say in the matter— it was a journey imposed on them and they were children . . . children who loved Aunt Paula and would never experience the life they should have been entitled to.

It didn't matter which direction I turned— the impacts of Paula's death were everywhere. Even the strongest had to surrender to the powers of violence. My husband, the one who took care of everyone and was always the anchor for our family, was plagued with an intense emotional conflict trying to support Jason but also trying to understand Jason's behaviours, his responses, his attitude and his actions the night of December 27th, 2005, and then in the days that followed. I felt so helpless in trying to provide any solace or comfort to him. I wasn't capable nor did I have any answers that would make it better. Alain had a very special relationship with Paula and she was a big part of his life. Perhaps it was the wonderful sense of humour they had, their ability to make other people feel good, or the quick wit they dished out to one another!

Whatever the reasons, they respected and loved one another very much and this was an overwhelming loss for him to endure. Alain was the one person Paula's husband called on for everything. Everything, except the night he would have really needed him the most . . . December 27th, 2005, when his wife went missing. Alain gave his time unconditionally to him and took him under his wing. It was Alain, that cold, dark Tuesday night in December, who stepped forward when the RCMP needed someone to identify the body in the trunk of Paula's car. My husband, who promised my mom when she died that he would take care of her baby girl, was put in that position by Paula's husband, a man Alain loved and welcomed into our family. The acts of betrayal were countless, including the day Alain and I took Paula's husband to make funeral arrangements for his wife. He was very despondent and non-responsive throughout the arrangement planning. He had asked us to act on his behalf and when the contract required a signature, he asked Alain to sign because he was so upset and needed to go outside for some air. Paula's husband never paid for his wife's funeral and when they tried to take legal action we were told he simply replied, "I didn't sign anything so you cannot come after me." He knew Alain was liable because he signed the contract and would not have given it a second thought if we had been taken to court. He felt no obligation to pay for this expense or put a headstone on Paula's grave, although he received a death benefit to offset the cost. Besides witnessing the anguish my children and husband endured, I also saw my younger sister Lana's intense sorrow. Besides their special bond as sisters, Paula and Lana were best friends. They were exceptionally close and loved to be in each other's company. When Anna was born, Lana's daughter Emily was eight months old. In 2005, my two sisters and their children shared many adventures together as they were both on maternity leave. I am so grateful that they gave each other the gift of their time which I know Lana will cherish forever. They should have had the ability to experience so much more, as sisters and as mothers, but that was brutally ripped from their lives . . . and from the lives of their children. Lana's courage, strength and perseverance these past five years is a testament to her devotion to and love for her best friend and sister.

Paula's death also affected a school community, a community in which she lived, a community in which she had been born and raised, a city, a province. Strangers were drawn into our lives by her story and shared their empathy and support. People started to understand that this could have been their daughter, their sister, their aunt, or their friend, through Paula's story. Hundreds came to pay their respects, brought food and notes of comfort, gave generously of their time and support, and felt an overwhelming sense of helplessness in knowing what to do. There were so many people who needed support and so few who really knew how to help. We leaned on each other and drew strength and hope from one another and from God. It was hard to comprehend that the acts of another human being could cause so much destruction on so many levels. It was endless, like the waves that rush against the shore . . . pushing, pounding, eroding with a fierce and steady force.

Paula's community, her colleagues and parents at the school, focused on Miss Gallant's Grade 3 class, on the children she had taught and the children waiting to someday be in Miss Gallant's classroom. Innocent victims, who lost someone they respected, admired and loved and whose lives were forever changed not only by the untimely and horrific loss but also because someone made a conscious decision to violate their safe place, their school. Paula loved her school and her students and played a significant role in their lives every day. The children wrote her poems, stories and created art in her memory.

They worried about Anna, Coady (Miss Gallant's dog) and of course her husband who she always talked about in such a loving and positive way to her students. Their pain and sadness was so apparent and although they tried to be brave, many slept with their lights on at night, walked to school holding their mom or dad's hand, cried out in their sleep and were paralyzed with fear. They experienced an intense sadness that no child should ever have to endure that was thrust upon them by someone else's actions.

Two sisters now, not three . . . one physical side of our triangle severed and the two remaining sides forever altered. I now have to live every day without my sweet baby sister in my life. I will never hear her voice again, or hear her laughter or feel the love of her warm hugs or comfort of her presence. She was my friend, she was the baby, my princess I loved to spoil, a source of inspiration and a wonderful person to be around. She made me laugh, knew when I was sad and why, understood me better than I sometimes understood myself, and reminded me that life was a gift to be cherished each day. She embraced life and truly danced, even when everyone was watching. Her vibrancy was refreshing and her smile infectious. We shared so much over her thirty-six years and had so many more memories to create. I felt close to my parents when Paula was with me as she was blessed to have the qualities I admired most about my parents.

Gone forever, my sister who loved her husband unconditionally and who would have worked through any issues they had with understanding, patience and love . . .

August 17th, 2010, the man who walked free among us for four years, seven months, and 21 days was arrested and charged with first degree murder in the death of my sister. My brother-in-law, Jason MacRae, who we embraced into our family and trusted with our life, was my sister's beloved husband, father to our precious niece, uncle to our children and friend to so many. The same man, who on February 8th, 2006, was arrested and pleaded his innocence.

Paula's death had a profound impact on so many lives, many of whom are here with us today. They represent the interests of all those I have spoken about . . . our family, our children, her students, her colleagues, her friends, her community, our society. We will be forever grateful to the countless number of people who persevered shoulder to shoulder with us in our commitment to prosecution so that we would feel peace in our souls. We are all survivors, not victims. Through our love for Paula and each other, we have endured this tragedy with courage, empathy, respect, pride and an unprecedented strength, just as Paula would have wanted and expected.

Her name is Paula Anne Gallant, she is my sister, and she did not deserve to die by violence.

Victim Impact Statement

March 2nd, 2011
Victim's Impact Statement
Submitted by: Alain Blackburn (Paula's Brother-in-Law)

On December 27, 2005, my life as I knew was about to change in a way I could have never imagined. At around 10:00 p.m. we received a phone call from my sister-in-law Lana that Paula hadn't returned from shopping. The events that would take place in the next few hours were something that you only ever witness in movies or happen to someone else, not our family as we were so very close. After what seemed like hours of looking for any sign of Paula's car, we received a phone call that her car was in the school parking lot where she actually taught school. After searching the school area everywhere hoping Paula would be okay, my worst nightmare was about to unfold. I would never again be the person I thought could deal with whatever life threw at me, like the loss of my grandparents, father and sister, aunts, uncles and friends from normal causes. I was approached by the RCMP officer that there was a body in the trunk of her car and could I identify if it was Paula. The decision I made that night, which was the only decision possible based on who was in the school parking lot from our family—I never believed that this decision would haunt me the way it has. Unlike what you see in the movies or hear of happening to other people, this was real. After seeing Paula there as if she is sleeping in the trunk of her car, I hoped she would just wake up and everything would be normal.

Well, everything from that day forward is far from normal. The counselling to teach me how to go back to sleep after I wake once, twice, I'm not even sure anymore how many times— I see Paula's face in the trunk of her car each night. My trust for people has changed, and my way of thinking has changed. Our family structure had changed in that we seem so distant. I miss our two- or three-times-a-week visits that turned into only seeing each other on special occasions. The time it took for my wife and sister-in-law Lana to start to heal was tough on our families, but the work they did to keep Paula's case in the media and Paula in our hearts was remarkable, which is a proud feeling to have at such a sad time. We are a stronger family but at a huge expense. Then you look at my niece Anna, who has lost her mother, and Anna was also taken from us in a selfish act at the age of three by the person who murdered her mother. She was surprised to even know she had an Uncle Alain in August of 2011. Well, I wish I would have never had a brother-in-law Jason MacRae. There were about 33 million people in Canada in 2001 when I first met Jason MacRae . . . How did I get stuck with this selfish, cowardly monster? To think of my two youngest boys growing up with this horror in their heads sickens me because there were other options: seek help, divorce, leave, or even better take your own life not someone else's. I often wonder what life would be like with Paula around, the wonderful mother she would have been, the loving aunt she would have been, the great friend she would have been, the asset to society she would have been, the influence she would have had on so many school children, and don't forget the fun-loving sister-in-law who was more like a daughter to me, especially after her father and mother died at an early age. Instead we have a selfish, cowardly monster that our tax dollars will have to look after, feed, clothe and rehabilitate, so someday he can return to the world he took from Paula.

We teach our children to do the right things in life, be honest, respect others, obey the law because there are consequences for those who wish not to. I really hope that after this proceeding is finished they will think that the consequences for taking someone else's life are what they expected. I'm sure it won't be enough for anyone who loved Paula, so another chapter will begin for my wife and me as the rest of the world walks away. This task I wouldn't wish on anyone else, anyway. Life is tough enough as it is if you have one at all.

Victim Impact Statement

March 2nd, 2011
Victim's Impact Statement
Submitted by: Timothy Blackburn

My name is Timothy Blackburn. Paula was my aunt. She was like my big sister. I am 18 years old now. I was 13 years old when she was taken from my life. I will always remember Paula as my young aunt. She was fun to be around and she had a "belly laugh" when something really funny happened. I remember when I was little that she took me everywhere. Sometimes I can't remember all the things we used to do, so I look at pictures so I won't forget. When I was 13 years old, my life changed forever. When my mom and dad told me that Paula was gone, I was confused and I was so sad. Looking back, I know I was in shock. I remember thinking, how—out of all the people in the world —could this happen to us in Boutilier's Point? After it happened, I found it really hard to cope. My friends didn't mean to, but they treated me differently. Everyone in my family was so sad because Paula was gone. I didn't feel as safe as I used to. It is hard for me to explain how everything changed but it did. Paula was my godmother. She helped me with my schoolwork. She never missed a significant event in my life. I miss her laugh and I miss her smile. I wish she was still here. I loved Paula, and I always will, but what I have learned from going through this is how many other people loved her too. Paula made an impact on many lives and I know she would be proud of me over the last five years because I am still able to laugh and find good in people. Paula would have wanted that.

Victim Impact Statement

March 2nd, 2011
Victim's Impact Statement
Submitted by Lana Kenny
(sister of the late Paula Anne Gallant)

When I was first told on Jan 20, 2006 that I was allowed to make a victim impact statement, my first thought was how could I ever express the heartache and emotions I was feeling? The second thought was I get to face the person who murdered my sister, and then I thought, if they could committee murder, how could my words have any impact whatsoever on that person?

That evening, I immediately started writing my statement. These are my words from five years ago . . .

No words can, could, or will ever express how this horrific, heinous and senseless tragedy has affected my whole being and that of my entire family. I have so many feelings inside of me that I never thought I would ever feel again in my life. I have and continue to feel numb, lonely, sad, angry, scared, raw, exposed, helpless, insecure, and mostly, I have a heart that has been broken forever.

I never thought after losing Mom and Dad at such a young age that I could ever feel such raw and intense pain in my heart but this was a different kind of pain I was feeling, as this was based on a loss through someone else's choice, not God's.

As three sisters who've had to endure what not too many young people should have to or have gone through, we were as close as three siblings could be. We relied on each other through all that life dealt to us and were there to support each other throughout our lives. We shared our family holidays together, summer vacations, girls' weekends away, weekend family dinners, pool days and pretty much all facets of our lives, not just the significant dates.

We were one very close family unit.

On Dec 27, 2005, our family unit was torn apart. We only had each other left and now that special bond has been taken away and our integral part of that chain has been forever removed.

Not only have I lost my sister but my best friend. Paula and I shared a special bond that only she and I knew and understood. She was the most kind, loving, thoughtful, humorous, compassionate and loving human being ever to touch so many lives. She was my maid of honour at my wedding as I was at hers.

We bought our first house together at 41 Silver Maple Dr., lived together for many years, enjoyed many evenings and weekends at each other's homes, shared part of our maternity leave together with our children and had a connection that was indescribable.

The conversations Paula and I shared will always be a special part of our bond and will always be a part of me. Paula's biggest fear was loving someone and having them die on her, like Mom and Dad. Someone did die as a result of her love, but it was her.

She finally was able to open her heart and trust again and I'm sure never thought that the person she considered her best friend would murder her.

My children, Dylan and Emily, have also lost their beautiful aunt Paula. Paula's kindness and patience were certainly qualities that she instilled in the children. My son, especially, loved Paula's quick wit and humour. She was like a magnet and my kids were drawn to her energy and zest for life. They miss going to Aunt Paula's for a sleepover and her giving them special "treats," no reason, just because. The day my husband Paul and I had to tell our children that Aunt Paula was killed— not just died, but someone had killed her— was one of the hardest days of our lives. Dylan (five at the time) had so many memories of his time with Aunt Paula, and unfortunately, my sweet, precious Emily had fewer memories as she was only one-and-a-half years of age. Dylan immediately broke down and starting crying and we did our best with the resources available to comfort him and offer him protection. Poor little Emily just cried along with her brother even though she had no idea of what she had just been told, nor the magnitude of what was to come.

What child would, at one-and-a-half years of age, or any age?

My children have lost the innocence of their childhood with this horrible nightmare and they've had to grow up way too fast and know more information that any child should ever have to. No child should ever have to experience the death of someone so close to their family at the hands of another person. It's hard enough for children to grasp death, but murder is unthinkable.

To see my husband Paul torn up by this tragedy and wanting to take away any pain inflicted upon his family but there is nothing he can do but stick with me— his support means more than he will ever know . . .

To see my sister Lynn, who basically raised Paula and myself, and Alain, who was a father figure to Paula, go through the heartache of basically losing a child, tears you apart . . . you wish you could take away everyone's pain. My nephews, Tim and Connor, who have very vivid memories of Aunt Paula, to see their pain and anger destroys you and you want to be able to do something, anything, to erase the nightmare they are living with.

These are young boys who should be able to live life to the fullest, worry about sports, school and girls, and yet they are faced with the same question everyone asks: Why???

When I arrived at Paula's house on Dec 27, 2005, I instantly knew that something was wrong and she was not coming home . . . it's that intuition that we all have but I was forcing it away and trying not to have those thoughts . . .

From the night we found Paula stuffed into the trunk of her car like garbage, at the school where she taught Grade 3, I have been haunted by what my precious baby sister went through. Did she know she was going to die? If so, how did she feel knowing that she was going to die? Was she scared, crying, fighting, praying or begging for her life? These are the images I have in my mind when all is quiet and my mind races.

Those were the words written five years ago . . . Now, in February 2011, the emotions from Dec 27, 2005, are still as real as they were on that day. Even though I now know more about Paula's death than I did five years ago, it just raises more questions. In any normal grieving process, you mourn, you suffer your loss, you get by day to day, but then at some point, you're able to move on . . . Trust me, I know this only too well from the deaths of my parents. You never forget but you move forward with one foot in front of the other and make the most of your precious life on this earth.

Through the past five years, with the tremendous support of my husband Paul, Lynn, Alain, and our families, friends and co-workers and professionals, I was able to move forward with keeping Paula's memory alive. I am proud of all the memories our family has created in Paula's name. My children will always know who Paula is and was. I will continue to mourn my dear sweet Paula for the rest of my life as she was taken from me at the hands of another being. This, I will never understand. I will, as I have continued to do for the past five years, move forward in life, enjoy each precious moment I have with my children, husband, and my family and friends. Someone had a choice and the choice they made was to kill Paula. We all are faced with making choices every day of our lives . . .

I am forever grateful that I got to spend three wonderful days during Christmas 2005 with Paula. I will always treasure that last Christmas as a family—talking, laughing, singing in front of the Christmas tree and sharing childhood memories with our children.

I will hold close to my heart the memories I have of Paula when we were growing up as children on Coady Street, as young women who had two paths to choose after the death of our parents and we chose the correct ones, sharing in the joy of her Teacher's College Graduation, sharing our first apartment together, buying our first home together, buying our very first new car together, her engagement, her wedding day, the birth of her beautiful daughter Anna, and being a part of each other's lives and the special bond we shared as sisters. NO ONE can take away my memories I have of Paula.

When I had to tell my son most recently of the person responsible for the death of his aunt, he had one question for me, "Why would he do this to Aunt Paula? She loved everybody?" I asked him how he feels when he thinks of Aunt Paula and of course he broke down and cried and told me he feels very sad. I told him to try to remember all the good memories he has of Aunt Paula and he told me that he's starting to forget them . . . As a parent this tears your heart apart and there is absolutely nothing you can do to stop an innocent child from having these sorts of feelings, but at the same time you would do anything to protect their feelings. As adults we are expected to accept things and move forward— my children should not have to endure the pain they have felt and will continue to feel with the absence of Paula in their lives . . . That in itself is a crime.

This is what I have mourned:

- The sister who will never be in my life again.
- My children who have had to endure this horrific nightmare no child should ever have to experience.
- Paula not seeing my children grow up— seeing my sweet Dylan's personality and shyness, and Emily's spunk of life and humour.
- My children not having Paula in their lives.
- My husband for having to endure my grief for a lengthy period of time.
- My husband for his loss of his sister-in-law with whom he shared the same quick wit and humour.
- Anna not having a mother to love and nurture her. Paula missing her birthdays, her first steps, her first missing tooth, her first day of school, her prom, her graduation, her wedding, her first child . . .
- Our "girls" having the close bond that Paula and I shared, we talked about this often, how Emily and Anna would be at each other's house every other weekend. We wanted them to be as close as we were . . .
- Tim and Connor for the pain they have been through and will continue to go through as young boys and men.
- Paula's friends . . . for missing out on the wonderful friendships Paula treasured.
- Paula's colleagues for having to drive into that school parking lot where Paula was found.

- Paula's children that she taught or impacted, for the pain of loosing their Miss Gallant and her Happy Fridays with Double Bubble Gum.
- For all those who never had the privilege of meeting Paula and never will.

Although I've tried to capture as best I could my feelings, there are absolutely no words to ever describe the past five years and the pain I have endured as a result of this senseless tragedy.

I will leave you with words written by Paula on her honeymoon:

"July 8, 2003—What a honeymoon spot. We arrived yesterday to the most breathtaking day imaginable. It seemed to take forever for the sun to set. Lana, Paul, Lynn and Alain left some delicious treats for us which we promptly dived into. My husband is sleeping now and I'm listening to the cries of seagulls. I am truly blessed to have married my best friend! We plan to enjoy the beach and some great food while here. A welcome retreat after a fantastic, chaotic and memorable wedding. Thanks, Jim and Bert, for sharing your paradise with us! Paula and Jay, the newlyweds of three days."

Paula never would have imagined that her life would be over two-and-a-half years later . . . at the hands of the person she thought was her best friend.

Victim Impact Statement

March 2nd, 2011
Victim's Impact Statement
Submitted by: Paul Kenny

I had a wife who was able to laugh and relax and enjoy life . . . Jason took that away from me.

I'm fortunate that Lana was strong enough to overcome the pain that Jason caused her and our family and is once again a woman who knows the joys of life and the happiness that can be found through friends and family.

I had a son who was outgoing and ready to meet new people and face every challenge . . . Jason took that away from me as well, but through the strength and love of our family, Dylan has again become a confident, respectful young person who is willing to try new things and make new friends.

I have a daughter who will only know of Paula through our stories and memories. The experiences Paula could have shared with her as she grew up has been taken away by Jason.

I have a beautiful niece who will never feel her mother's touch, hear her voice or share in moments only a mother and daughter can share together . . . Again all taken away by Jason.

I was able to go to sleep without double-checking that the doors were locked and setting the alarm . . . Jason took that away.

I was able to close my eyes at night and not be woken by every creak in the house or car that seemed to drive slowly up our street . . . Jason took that away.

I used to trust and enjoy meeting new people . . . Jason took that away.

I could walk out my door and not worry whether my wife and kids were safe . . . Jason took that away.

I used to have a beautiful, funny, smart, caring wonderful person for a friend and sister in law . . . Jason took that away.

I was able to say that I hated no one . . . Jason took that away.

I used to have a simple life . . . Jason took that away.

As much as I feel Jason stole from me when he selfishly committed this heinous act, I know that as a family we have fought back though the support of both friends and family over the past years to achieve a "new normal" without Paula in our lives. Now that Jason will be gone, the fear of him causing further grief in our lives is gone.

Victim Impact Statement

March 2nd, 2011
Victim's Impact Statement
Submitted by: Elena DeCurtis

    My life changed forever on December 28, 2005, when I received a call telling me that Paula had been found dead in the trunk of her car. I can remember that moment very clearly as I immediately panicked, desperately hoping that I was in the middle of a nightmare and that it wasn't actually happening. In the days following, while dealing with my own shock and grief, I did what I could to support Paula's husband, both emotionally and financially. I did this because I considered him a very close friend and also believed that this is what Paula would have wanted me to do. After about six weeks, I began to come to the very reluctant realization that this support was clearly misplaced and I felt the intense horror and betrayal that I imagine Paula must have experienced on the day of her murder on December 27, 2005.
    This criminal act has taken away my best friend and confidant, my sense of personal safety, my basic trust in others, including those I love, and also completely shattered the trust I have in my confidence in being a good judge of character.
    After Paula's murder I began experiencing very vivid nightmares and often would wake myself up screaming. While they have lessened over the past couple of years, I do continue to have very intense nightmares, where I am dreaming that I am Paula and I am in the midst of being murdered by the man that I love and trust. This criminal act also left me with the inability to sleep in my home alone due to feelings of fear, and as a result, I needed to make plans to either stay with friends or would have to ask friends to stay with me when my roommate or husband was away. My level of independence was also negatively impacted in that I no longer felt safe going places alone, even during the day and also at times felt very uncomfortable in my own home. As an example, I

could not stand comfortably at the kitchen sink with my back to the rest of the room and started doing dishes standing on an angle so that I could keep an eye on what was behind me. I consistently had vivid images of someone coming up behind me and killing me. It's important to note that this level of fear and anxiety lessened since I moved away from Halifax in August 2009, and again this August, when Paula's husband was arrested. However the feelings of fear and anxiety did resurface again when I learned this past fall that a request for release on bail had been made.

This crime has also negatively affected my relationships with others. It has made me seriously doubt my sense of judgement of others and I no longer have basic trust that people are good, or that I will be able to recognize when someone is being completely deceitful. It has taken great effort and counselling to not let it negatively affect my relationship with my husband, which at the time of the crime was a fairly new relationship. I used to make new friends easily and prided myself on being very observant of interactions between people. Now I am hesitant to make new friends and no longer trust my ability to know whether someone is being truthful or dishonest, including at times being concerned about their potential to conceal a "dark side."

I have left explaining the loss of Paula to the end as it is very difficult to put into words and I continue to have a lot of anger and rage associated with the fact that her life was ended so prematurely and senselessly by the man that I truly believed she loved and trusted. The last time I spoke to Paula was the week before Christmas. I was travelling to Ottawa and she called me before I left to tell me the news that she and her husband had just purchased her dream home. I can clearly remember the happiness and excitement in her voice, as she gave me the details of how they had made the deal and we made plans for the housewarming party they were going to host as soon as they moved in. At the end of the conversation we confirmed our plans to celebrate New Year's Eve together at my house and she made me promise to call her as soon as I got home. I never would have imagined that, instead, I would have been attending her wake on that very same day. I have not been able to celebrate the New Year again since then.

Paula had such a vibrant energy about her, it was impossible not to get wrapped up in her excitement and enthusiasm for life. She had an amazing sense of humour and was always able to draw people to her. I know that I am only one of her very many friends who continue to feel the loss of Paula from their lives.

When I moved to Halifax for work in the fall of 2000, Paula was my first friend. I didn't know anyone in the city and she warmly welcomed me into her life and as part of her family. The first birthday I celebrated away from my family in Ottawa, Paula helped plan a surprise visit from my cousins and a couple of my other close friends that she hadn't met yet. My cousins are like sisters to me and it didn't take long for Paula to also call them her little sisters. She picked them up at the airport during an intense snow storm and delivered them safely to my front door just to make sure I had a fun birthday. We spent a lot of time together and we spoke a lot about relationships, hopes and dreams. I was so happy for her when she met her husband, and often spent a lot of time with the two of them, both in their home and elsewhere. We also had other close couple friends that we spent time with, and unfortunately this criminal act has also led to the loss of that entire circle of friends.

I am deeply saddened by the loss of Paula in my life. I have already missed and will continue to miss sharing the happy milestones in my life, including my wedding day. I miss being able to call her to tell her about the things that I know only she would find funny and the things that I know only she would understand.

I believe that one of the reasons that Paula and I connected quickly and in such an important way was due to the fact that we both had lost parents at a young age unexpectedly due to brain aneurysms. We often spoke about the impact that this experience had on other parts of our lives and that for that reason, we had a lot in common.

We had very similar strengths, values and fears. Before getting pregnant, Paula had talked to me about her concerns about having children and how her greatest fear was of her child ever having to experience a similar loss or be in the position of being left alone by her parents. I know that Paula eventually worked through that fear and I always credited her relationship and trust in her husband, Jason, for giving her the confidence to bring Anna into the world with hope and happiness. I remember her beaming with joy the day she told me that she was pregnant. She had put one of my throw pillows under her shirt and walked into my kitchen, giggling and asking what I thought. This memory of her is one of the many memories I have of her that is now filled with extreme mixed emotions. I was so happy to see her and remember her happiness so vividly and at the same time I am filled with incredible sadness and anger to know that this happiness and hope for the future was ripped away from her, and mostly, I am devastated that her worst fear for her daughter Anna has come true in such a tragic and profound way. My heart breaks for both Paula and Anna, in that she was taken from her just days before her first birthday. I simply cannot put into words the intense emotions I continue to experience, knowing how Paula felt about the life she wanted for her baby Anna, and now knowing that Anna will have to live with the impact of this crime for the rest of her life, without the love and protection Paula would have given her.

Finally, while as described, I continue to experience intense negative emotions due to the impact of this criminal act, a portion of this was based on the fact that the criminal investigation and criminal case was unresolved for so many years. I now hope that the conviction and sentencing will allow me, and all those Paula loved, to draw upon her strength and positive outlook on life, and to move together toward healing.

Victim Impact Statement

March 2nd, 2011
Victim's Impact Statement
Submitted by: Lynn MacEachern

I have buried my father and I have buried my brother. And although heart wrenching for me, both I could accept, as there was a valid reason for their passing. It has been five long years since Paula was murdered and to this day I still struggle with the fact that her death was unnecessary.

I knew Paula pretty much her entire life. I watched her grow from a busy young girl, to a gangly teenager with a smattering of freckles, legs as long as Coady Street and a smile almost as big as her heart, into a graceful young lady whose outward beauty was only surpassed by her beauty within. While she started out as our "go-to" babysitter, she quickly became a member of our family. She was like an older sister to my children. I had the pleasure of seeing her in both of her white gowns: her prom dress and her wedding dress. We shared so many happy times and we also shared sad moments. I hugged her as she suffered the pangs of young love and breakups. The most difficult, however, were the many occasions I comforted her as she cried over the loss of her father, who passed at 48 from a brain aneurysm. Who knew that three years later her mom would suffer the same fate? I have never forgotten the conversations we had when she would question me why it had to happen, and the look of devastation and hurt on her face when no sound reason could be found.

Paula was magnetic; people were naturally drawn to her happy and accommodating personality. She was emotionally charged, loyal, fiercely independent, capable, and stubborn. She was kind and gentle and she was fun. She was a breath of fresh air. Paula had the ability to transcend age barriers, for she was as comfortable spending time with a three-year-old as she was with a 93-year-old. She was somebody who made you feel glad that you knew her, that someone who brought out the best in you. If asked to pick a word to describe her, it would be "comfortable." Paula was comfortable. She was a "one size fits all" type of person.

Articulating the effect Paula's passing has had on me is difficult. It has caused so many changes in my life, for life as I knew it is now divided into memories of before and after. "Before" represents laughter, innocence and arrogance about tomorrow. "After" represents reflection, regret, guilt for being so busy with life that opportunities were missed, and memories — bittersweet. So many things taken for granted, so many things taken away, so many words left unsaid, so many lost chances.

Over the past five years I have endured countless sleepless nights because of nightmares, dreams, and ongoing scenarios about her murder— and I know all too intimately how I struggle on a daily basis to come to terms with it. I also struggle with the knowledge that the choice was made to end Paula's life.

Paula's death has caused me to give away pieces of who I am. It has taught me to question things that would never have been questioned in the past and it has brought out a cynical side that causes me to second-guess. It introduced a darkness and unrest that have kept me awake for nights on end. How do you make it okay to feel such resentment when it has not been in your nature in the past? It has necessitated many hours of support from family members, from close friends, as well as the support of my family doctor. It has taught me distrust and has created a sadness within that I pray time will soften. For the longest time it caused me to question newly formed relationships, as my daughter introduced her latest love interest and, in turn, it caused my daughter to question the potential lack of character of the young man in question. There was always the "what if?" in the back of our minds. Paula's death has triggered in me an end to innocence and trust.

In a box, I have some cards Paula had given me over the years, but one in particular draws me back, for she thanked me for "being a role model." When I first received it I thought, "What a nice thing to say," but in death it reads, "Why did you not pay closer attention? Perhaps Paula would still be here if . . .". So many guilty thoughts, so much regret, such sadness. This is a burden I will endure for the rest of my life. I realize how blessed I was to have enjoyed innocence for now it is gone, and I mourn that loss. Murder is something that happens in movies but not in my world— especially not to someone like Paula. I mourn the loss of normalcy— life is forever changed not only for me but for my family as well. I mourn the loss of Christmases past for Christmas changed for me on December 27, 2005. Now, I relive that horrific day each December 27th; I remember every scent, I remember how the day sounded, I remember the sun creating crystals on the snow— just like the window crystals Paula used to twirl for my children so they could "watch the shadows dance." I mourn the loss of a happy ending, for that was so very important to Paula— she was all about the happy ending. Her plan for life was to become a teacher, marry, have children, a nice home, and to live happily ever after.

I mourn the loss of a mother and child bond. Paula shared her dreams for Anna with me. I have such a hard time accepting and understanding what a huge and overwhelming burden this child has been left to bear. It seems like yesterday that Paula told me she was pregnant. She was so happy and asked that I not tell anybody for she had not yet told "another soul" and while I suspected she did share her news, I played along—it was always important to Paula that you felt special . . . and I did feel special. I was honoured by her friendship. I think of the relationship I have with my daughter who is now expecting her first child, and it takes me back to Paula's dreams for motherhood. While I am overjoyed for my daughter, I'm reminded of Paula when she was at this very stage and what should be one of the happiest times of my life is tainted by her memory and what could have been.

Family was so very important to Paula. Her parents taught by example and lived the importance of love, compassion, respect and strong sense of family; this is a trait Paula and her sisters exemplified and you need only have been in her company a very short time to quickly realize this. I mourn her absence from that family circle for I could always look forward to a funny comment from her about something that had happened within the family. I mourn the loss of laughter with my friend. I miss her witty commentary and quirky slant on life, for she had a way of finding the bright side of any situation. I mourn so many things, but mostly, I mourn the loss of my beautiful friend.

"Tell me about my mom." Five small words which in my world would seem relatively innocent; however, for Anna this is her reality. She has been denied so many mother-daughter moments. As a parent, my first instinct is to shelter and protect my children, to give them the tools to make proper and informed decisions themselves, and I struggle in knowing this was not the case for Anna on December 27th. While I continue to be amazed by the strength and resilience of Paula's family, I struggle daily with the fact that Anna will be faced with so many difficult questions for which there will be no easy answers and which will only become more difficult as she grows and matures. The information is well documented and there is a beautifully carved cross marking her mom's grave—all, forbearers of a very sad and unnecessary life story for such a beautiful and unsuspecting girl. I can't stop thinking that, on December 27th, 2005, Paula was handed a death sentence; Anna and her family, a life sentence; and we, her friends, a life forever altered. On December 27th, my heart was broken in a way that can never be mended. Thank God Paula will never know she was at the root of so much pain and grief for all those who loved her so very dearly.

Victim Impact Statement

March 2nd, 2011
Victim's Impact Statement
Submitted by: Mary Stone

I would like to thank the court for allowing me the opportunity to speak today. It is customary to think of surviving victims as being members of the deceased victim's family. Paula Anne Gallant had another huge family, a family of co-workers, students and the school community at large, all of whom were deeply affected by her brutal death.

Her murder has left a void in the hearts of those who worked with her as teachers and colleagues. Our staff was fortunate to have counselling at the school made available to us in the days and weeks following Paula's tragic death. Although this helped us to cope with the immediate shock, the long-term effects have stayed with us these last five years and probably will, no doubt, linger for years to come.

We lost a very professional teacher whose dedication and leadership in the area of curriculum had a direct impact on the education of students. We lost her commitment to the idea of constant collaboration and cooperation amongst teachers. These aspects of Paula's educational professionalism helped to create a better education, not just for the children under her care at the time, but for all students. As one who asked questions and dug deeply for the answers, Paula had great potential to effect change and progress in the area of curriculum and education as a whole. The loss of this has been felt by her colleagues and unknowingly by her students. It is with bittersweet memories that teachers continue to make use of her ideas, materials— sweet to think of her creative, positive nature, but then bitter and angry to realize that future collaboration with her is needlessly lost forever.

Everyday, staff members are faced with a constant reminder of her murder as it is necessary to park one's car in the same parking lot where her body was left in the trunk of her own car. It serves to bring those days and her absence to mind every single working day. That knowledge reveals a sadness that, to this day, is not far from the minds of her colleagues even though some of us have retired or left the school.

Working and/or living in the same neighbourhood where her home still stands is also a grim reminder that cannot be changed. Community members and teachers who pass Paula's home are constantly reminded of what took place there. During the last five years, they were often haunted by the lingering possibility that the murderer still lived there and was amongst them. Transferring to another school and/or neighbourhood was, for some, the only way to enable them to put some distance between themselves and Paula's death. The community involvement in the yearly remembrances of Paula's death stands as a reminder of the grief and sadness still experienced by so many.

In the summer after her death, the BLT community and school rallied together to create a beautiful, useful art space in the school in Paula's memory. But, as wonderful as it is, that too stands as a reminder of what we no longer have in the form of friendship and of a life cut terribly short, a reminder of an artistic and creative teacher who could have been guiding and teaching hundreds of students.

Victim Impact Statement

March 2nd, 2011
Victim's Impact Statement
Submitted by: Patricia McCormack

My first introduction to the Gallant family was in 1972. I attended a baby shower for one of our neighbours and Paula's mom, Dianne, was present. We struck up a conversation and learned that we had many things in common. The next day we met again while walking with our daughters, Paula and Susanne. I was invited for tea and biscuits and while the girls played we talked about our children and swapped recipe ideas. This was the beginning of a long and wonderful family friendship. The men discovered a shared interest in hunting and fishing and my three children and Dianne's three all enjoyed the out of doors and camping. We spent family vacations together in Newfoundland and PEI, as well as camping weekends locally. Paula spent many happy hours at our house playing Barbie dolls with Susanne. If I close my eyes I can see her running through the tall grass between her back door and ours with a little case in her arms full of dolls and dolls clothes, while Dianne watched at her back door to make sure Paula didn't trip or hurt herself on the way over. Paula and Susanne soon became best friends and loved to dance together, dress up in high heels, and sing and perform. They took dance classes together and figure skating lessons.

Our neighbourhood was made up of young families. The children all played together and celebrated important occasions together, such as birthdays. They were always eager to perform concerts to which the adults were invited for a small charge, of course. The children played many hours of school and chased each other through the sprinklers, all of these activities under the watchful eyes of the adults. We as neighbours and friends provided a happy, safe, and nurturing environment for our children.

In 1985, Paula and her sisters Lynn and Lana were faced with the tragedy of losing their beloved father to an aneurysm. This was devastating and overwhelming for them. With the support of their mother, relatives and friends the girls found the strength to go on.

When tragedy struck these girls the second time it was almost more than I and all those who love them could bear. How could and why would this happen again? A gentle lady who was one of my closest friends and their precious mother was taken from them. This time they had to rely on their friends, relatives and most importantly each other to survive this terrible loss. Armed with the inner strength that their parents instilled in them and their love and support for one another they managed to pick up the pieces and take the next step forward.

Over time the girls each met and married their soul mate and settled down and began raising their children. The strong bond that always existed between them was now even stronger with the loss of both parents. The girls spent evenings, weekends, holidays, and all important occasions together, along with the many friends that they cultivated along the way.

When Lynn called and relayed the horrific events of December 27, 2005, we were paralyzed. The myriad of emotions that were felt at that time and still remain are of such a proportion that sometimes one feels swamped by them.

One of the first emotions was a strong feeling of DISBELIEF. How could something this horrific happen to one of our own girls, a wonderful young mother with so much to offer and who was so very, very, loved and needed? Then the SADNESS set in and this was overwhelming. How would Lynn, Lana and their families, as well as grandparents, relatives, students, co-workers, and best friends ever deal with this huge loss? ANGER then became a constant companion. Why can't someone fix this? Why is it taking so long? There must be other ways to find answers. Why does it seem like the authorities don't care? What kind of people do we have amongst us who would behave in such a beastly way? An emotion that is ever present is one of HELPLESSNESS. What can we do for the two sisters and their families that we love? How can we help them through this? It never seems enough to just be there and be a good listener. I RESENT the fact that I will never be able to watch Paula and my daughter Susanne interact with their children in my presence, and perhaps I would give a little chuckle and look up and ask Dianne if this is the way we would have handled that challenge. I resent the fact that my daughter Susanne will never be able to spend time with one of her closest childhood friends. I also resent the fact that I have had reason to question my religious faith. How could the GOD that I believe in let this horrible act take place? Why didn't HE intervene? We, as dedicated and protective parents, made sure that our children were always in a safe and protected environment, but who is their protector when they grow up?

During this emotional roller coaster there were times when I hated to go to bed because I was afraid to have that dream again. That dream that always seemed so very real. There were so many days that went by that all I thought of was Paula and the circumstances in which she died, and then realizing that if you felt that way then it must be tenfold for her sisters and their families. These are the times that the profound feelings of sadness and desolation step in because you hurt so much for yourself and your own family but also for Lynn's and Lana's and wish there was some way to make it go away. I am in complete awe of the many things that Lynn and Lana, with the help of dedicated friends and family, have been able to accomplish in the last five years. I am so very proud of them and to be part of their extended family. I am also profoundly sad that they were ever given a reason to have to bare their souls to the public, put their lives on hold for five years and live the rest of their lives without their precious sister. Paula did not deserve to die so young and in such bizarre circumstances, and her murderer must be made accountable to the full extent of the law. It is my hope and that of my family that this senseless deed enacted on a wonderful and cherished sister, loving mother, much respected teacher, and best friend to many, will be treated with the utmost severity that it deserves.

Victim Impact Statement

March 2nd, 2011
Victim's Impact Statement
Submitted by: Richelle Gallant Williams

Paula and I were many things: team teachers, aspiring art students, and kindred spirits. We taught side by side, learned side by side, and met challenges side by side. We stood at the stove and cooked lunch together every day, taught with our connecting doors open, convinced students we were sisters, laughed until our bellies ached. We spent hours in art class together, with as many hours spent on the phone working through assignments and studying.

The loss associated with Paula's murder is far too great to be captured in words. The lives that were changed are innumerable. I can only try to communicate the impact it has had on my life.

Death is an inevitable part of life, but living, after murder, is difficult. For five years, I've lived with excessive guilt, guilt about even the smallest things. None of these things are truly my fault, but yet they continue to cloud my every thought.

December 27th is my birthday. It is also the day Paula was killed at the hands of another. It will forever be a day marked by both a birth and a death. The guilt that plagues me is infinite. Each December 27th marks another year of my life, but another year of her death. It will forever feel wrong to celebrate this day.

Graduating from NSCAD felt unfair. Beginning each new school year feels unfair. Having a loving husband who protects me feels unfair. Watching my children reach milestones feels unfair. I am unable to be grateful without feeling a semblance of guilt. I live under the guilt of wonder, wondering why she lost her life and I didn't.

After stumbling through the initial days of shock, my brain quick firing and not allowing me to rest on any single thought, I started to question everything I knew about my world. I questioned my most intimate relationship. I questioned the people I thought I knew. I questioned my sense of judgement. I questioned if I really ever knew anything.

For at least a month, my ears were ringing. I had a burning sensation in my chest and could not take a full breath. Months later, I would still wake twice a night completely drenched in sweat. My body was reacting to the shock in the only way it knew how.

My mind was in a state of fear. Suddenly anything in this world was possible. No one was safe. No one could be trusted. No one was in control of their own fate. I suddenly believed that if this could happen to Paula, it could happen to anyone, including me.

I was wrought with fear and anxiety. I stood with my back to the wall while cooking at the stove, terrified of someone coming up from behind. I kept all the curtains closed, chasing images from my mind of someone peering in. I checked the locks on my doors obsessively, never remembering if I had previously checked them or not.

I felt unable to complete simple everyday tasks. Every day I planned to go to the grocery store. It took me months to get there. I couldn't go to my outdoor compost bin. I insisted my husband sit and watch the garage door touch the ground before leaving the driveway, for fear of someone sneaking into my house when his head was turned. I developed a fear of parking garages. I had become plagued with irrational thoughts that were altering my life.

As Paula's car was found at her school, I desperately grasped a theory that somehow students were to blame. My brain was struggling to make sense of the impossible. At the time, I was working with many challenging students. I suddenly didn't want them to know me. I didn't want to have any association with anyone who could prove volatile or unpredictable. I was afraid of my students or who they may become.

I was unable to work for several months, resulting in loss of accumulated leave time and income. I was worried I would be unable to return to the school. By the grace of God, I received a transfer to a new school. With supports in place, I was able to return to work.

After Paula was killed, I was conflicted about returning to art college. She and I were students who held hands through every course and assignment. I knew she would want me to finish, so I tried. Dazed, I went to the first class of the photography course we had signed up for. Feeling an obligation to her, I sat through the first class, struggling to keep my emotions intact. Later as I raced to my car in the dark, I was overcome by that same sense of fear and panic. I quickly recognized I did not have the mental or emotional capacity to continue at that time. Through various treatments, I would return six months later.

As I stood in line to graduate, I was solemn. Both being Gallants, I knew she would have stood directly in front of me, ready to walk across the stage. I was not standing there for me, but for her. After receiving my diploma and returning to my seat, I was moved to hear the speaker make a public acknowledgement of Paula's role in the shaping and ongoing development of this newly developed credited program. She spoke of how Paula's input had been valued and led to changes within the program. These changes would benefit the teachers and artists to come. The art community had lost a true contributor who came with a unique perspective.

While my well-being was affected, so too were my relationships. I did not want to be social. I suddenly felt so vulnerable. I didn't know who I could trust. At times, I slept excessively to escape the overwhelming fear and grief. In a haze of depression, I felt unable to care for my children in the ways I wanted to. My children were just six and four years old at the time. My memories from that time are cloudy, as though I was absent. Only in the last few years have I felt fully present. I will forever resent the toll that this, heinous, senseless act took on my family.

The relationship between my husband and me has been challenged to its very core. Paula's murder shattered my whole belief system. Suddenly I found myself questioning the trust I had in my own husband. I was questioning whether I really knew him. It made me wonder if he actually loved me, what his motives were and what he could be capable of. This, paired with his feelings of helplessness and frustration, created a great deal of pain and anguish. With support, we did make it. However, the scars run deep. To this day, each anniversary, event, newspaper article or mention of Paula's murder rubs salt in a wound that is still raw.

In looking back at all that has been lost, the greatest losses have been time and innocence.

Time with Paula: laughing until we cried, pulling gags on the staff together, getting back at her for that April Fool's Day when she convinced me school was cancelled, eating at Swiss Chalet with our kids, fruitless efforts to make her a Dixie Chicks fan.

Time spent talking on the phone with her at the end of a rough day, the comfort in her wise words and company. The laugh I would have gotten telling her not to trip just as she stepped onto that graduation stage.

Time with my family: tucking them in at night, going to the park, tickling them until they squealed, snuggling on the couch, and reassuring them the way a mother can.

We'll never get Paula back, the time we've lost, or our sense of innocence. Our glass has been half emptied. For we now live with the beliefs that we can never truly know someone. Others can control our fate, and there are some parts of our lives that, no matter how hard we try or pray, cannot be undone.

On March 2nd, 2011, 1891 days following the murder of my sister Paula, the monster among us, Jason W. MacRae, was finally found guilty of murder and sentenced to life in prison with no eligibility of parole for 15 years. Here is what the Honourable Justice Kevin Coady had to say.

Judge's Statement

CANADA   CRH 336925
PROVINCE OF NOVA SCOTIA

IN THE SUPREME COURT OF NOVA SCOTIA
Between:
HER MAJESTY THE QUEEN

and

JASON MACRAE

ORAL DECISION

HEARD BEFORE:	The Honourable Justice Kevin Coady
PLACE HEARD:	The Law Courts
Halifax, Nova Scotia	
DATE:	March 2, 2011
COUNSEL:	
Denise Smith	Crown Attorneys
Christine Driscoll	
Michael Taylor	Defence Attorney

COADY, J. (Orally):

All right. Just for the record, I'll indicate that I've signed an order authorizing the taking of bodily substances for forensic DNA analysis pursuant to 487.05 of the *Criminal Code*. I've signed that and I'll just give that to the clerk.

As well, I have before me a copy of a section 109 and 114 of the *Criminal Code* firearms prohibition for life in relation to Mr. MacRae, and given his counsel's comments, I've signed that as well. So I'll just hand that to the clerk and the parties who require those can pick them up from the court afterwards. Okay.

First of all, I want to thank counsel. It's not an easy task to be involved in a case like this. I can just tell from watching you folks do your thing that it takes its toll, and I want to commend both the Crown and the defence for the excellent materials that I've been provided. It's made all the difference in the world. And furthermore, balanced materials, materials that saw both sides of the issues, and I want to thank you both, both Crown and the defence, for that.

They say in this job the most difficult aspect of the job is sentencing people, and I think that's correct. You've made it a lot easier, and I thank you.

Let me just say at the starting position that we are involved in an adversarial process. The Crown get up and make representations to me about what they feel their considered position is to be, and the defence makes theirs. In the final analysis, it is my job, and my only job here today, to apply the law, and the law didn't just start today, it started a long time ago and there's a whole body of law you've heard reference to here today that I must consider in coming to my conclusion.

Jason MacRae has entered a guilty plea to the second degree murder of his wife on December 27th, 2005. The facts have been agreed to and are before this court as an exhibit called an "Agreed Statement of Facts." For our purposes, I accept those facts as being proven the same way they'd be proven if there was a contested hearing.

I need not repeat those facts as they have been fully canvassed by the Crown during submissions and not challenged in any significant way by the defence. These facts speak volumes about the character of Mr. MacRae. They show Mr. MacRae as a person who is able to be triggered into violence by small domestic disagreements, and in this case with his relatively new wife, to the degree that he could kill his wife in a violent rage under the same roof where their young daughter slept. The fact that Mr. MacRae maintained his guise of innocence for almost five years tells this court that he does lack, at least to some degree, a conscience, or I should say a conscience as we've come to accept that term. The fact that he could be enticed into the police sting operation speaks volumes about his ego and his own sense of superiority.

This, first and foremost, as Ms. Smith and Ms. Driscoll have indicated, is a case of domestic abuse, and that is the cornerstone upon which they base their submissions. Mr. MacRae, let me say, carries full responsibility for the death of Ms. Gallant. Ms. Gallant did nothing to bring this violence upon herself. The events of December 27th, 2005, that led up to the crime represent the usual issues that most new couples discuss without threat, intimidation or violence. The facts of this case are all about Mr. MacRae and his inability to control his anger in the face of normal human dialogue. It is he who has failed.

I've also had the opportunity to read or hear 11 victim impact statements. The loss of Ms. Gallant under these circumstances to her family and friends is palpable. There is nothing happening here today that will bring her back or that will restore the life that each and every one of you who have given these statements will have into the future. It is my hope that the provision of the victim impact statements will assist each and every one of you in moving on after this day is over, although I am sure that Ms. Gallant's death will leave a huge void in your family and in your community.

Mr. MacRae has entered a guilty plea to second degree murder. The *Criminal Code* dictates the sentence in section 235, and I quote:

> "Everyone who commits first degree murder or second degree murder is guilty of an indictable offence and shall be sentenced to imprisonment for life."

Subsection (2):

> "For the purpose of Part XIII, the sentence of imprisonment for life prescribed by this section is a minimum punishment."

Given this direction, it is not my role to determine Mr. MacRae's sentence. That is predetermined, and Mr. MacRae knew that when he entered his plea this morning and acknowledged such. My only and my limited role is to set Mr. MacRae's parole ineligibility period at a place between 10 and 25 years.

Section 745(c) of the *Criminal Code* governs this issue. Section 745 says:

> "Subsection to section 745.1, the sentence to be pronounced against a person who is to be sentenced to imprisonment for life shall be:
>
> (c) in respect of a person who has been convicted of second degree murder, that the person be sentenced to imprisonment for life without eligibility for parole until the person has served at least 10 years of the sentence or such greater number of years, not being more than 25 years, as has been substituted therefore pursuant to section 745.4."

Let me make it very clear as a starting point, the sentence for murder is life, and that is the sentence that Mr. MacRae will receive for this crime today. My only discretion today is to decide how long it will be before Mr. MacRae is eligible to be considered for parole. Whatever my decision is, that does not mean that Mr. MacRae will be approved for parole at that time or will suddenly be released from prison. I am not making an order as to when Mr. MacRae is paroled. Rather, my order deals only with the issue of ineligibility for a period of time.

It is also important to acknowledge that, even if Mr. MacRae is approved for parole, he will still be serving his life sentence for the rest of his life. The only difference will be that he will be serving, if granted parole, that life sentence in the community under very strict supervision.

We are not a society that locks people in a cell for the remainder of their lives as retribution. We are a society that recognizes that people can learn from their mistakes and sins and become contributing members of our society. We are a society that recognizes rehabilitation as a goal of sentencing and we are a society that sees rehabilitation of an offender as the most effective way to protect society.

Not all offenders find rehabilitation while in jail for those long periods of time. Those persons who do not, stay in jail until the end of their sentences, but many offenders are rehabilitated. It is all up to the offender. Some reach for the light at the end of the tunnel and others do not, for a wide of reasons.

Section 745.4 of the *Criminal Code* provides as follows, and I quote:

> "Subject to 745.5, at the time of the sentencing under section 745 of an offender who is convicted of second degree murder, the judge who presided at the trial of the offender or, if that judge is unable to do so, any judge of the same court may, having regarding to the character of the offender, the nature of the offence and the circumstances surrounding its commission, and to the recommendation, if any, made by a jury . . ."
>
> Which does not apply here.
>
> " . . . may, by order, substitute for 10 years a number of years of imprisonment (being more than 10 but not more than 25) without eligibility for parole as the judge deems fit in the circumstances."

So clearly there are three factors that I must consider in determining Mr. MacRae's parole ineligibility period: (1) the character of Mr. MacRae himself; (2) the nature of the offence he committed on December 27th, 2005; and (3) the circumstances surrounding the commission of that offence.

Section 745.4 uses the language, "substitute for 10 years a number of years." That dictates that the starting point is 10 years of parole ineligibility.

The Supreme Court of Canada in a case called *Shropshire* discusses the appropriate standard to be applied when considering parole ineligibility periods. The court stated at paragraph 29, and I quote:

> "As a general rule, the period of parole ineligibility shall be for 10 years, but this can be ousted by a determination of the trial judge that, according to the criteria enumerated in section 745.4, the offender should wait a longer period before having suitability to be released into the general public assessed."

The Supreme Court of Canada also stated at paragraph 25:

> "The only difference in terms of punishment between first and second degree murder is the duration of parole ineligibility. This clearly indicates that parole ineligibility is a part of the punishment and, thereby, forms an important element of sentencing policy. As such, it must be concerned with deterrence, whether general or specific.
>
> In permitting a sliding scale of parole ineligibility, Parliament intended to recognize that, within the category of second degree murder, there will be a broad range of seriousness reflecting varying degrees of moral culpability. As a result, the period of parole ineligibility for second degree murder will run anywhere between

a minimum of 10 years and a maximum of 25, the latter being equal to that prescribed for first degree murder."

The *Criminal Code* also sets forth many objectives of sentencing that apply to all offences and also apply to parole ineligibility, and the case of *Shropshire* endorses this principle. Section 718 of the *Criminal Code* states:

> "The fundamental purpose of sentencing is to contribute, along with crime prevention initiatives, to respect for the law and the maintenance of a just, peaceful and safe society by imposing just sanctions that have one or more of the following objectives:
>
> (a) to denounce unlawful conduct;
> (b) to deter the offender or other persons from committing offences;
> (c) to separate offenders from society where necessary;
> (d) to assist in rehabilitating offenders;
> (e) to provide reparations for harm done to victims or to the community; and
> (f) to promote a sense of responsibility in offenders and acknowledgement of the harm done to victims and to the community generally."

There can be no question that Mr. MacRae's crime requires a generous application of the principles of denunciation and deterrence, specifically aimed at other members of our society who might be inclined to commit a similar crime. Rehabilitation is also an objective and applies.

Section 718.1 of the *Criminal Code* states, and I quote:

> "A sentence must be proportionate to the gravity of the offence and the degree of responsibility of the offender."

Section 718.2 lists a number of other sentencing principles, not all of which are applicable to Mr. MacRae. It requires me to weigh all aggravating and mitigating circumstances. It requires me to craft a sentence that is similar to similar offenders who commit similar crimes in similar circumstances. I have considered the relevant objectives in deciding Mr. MacRae's period of parole ineligibility.

Now, while I must consider 718, 718.1 and 718.2, the clearest directives for this case are found in section 745 of the *Criminal Code*. Often the codified objectives are subsumed in the objectives set forth in section 745 of the *Code*.

The Crown takes the position that the correct number is 20 years, whereas the defence calls for 12 years plus. The defence suggests the range is 12 to 17 years. The Crown relies on the words of Iacobucci J. in *Shropshire* respecting the Nova Scotia Court of Appeal decision in *Doyle* as articulated at the time by Chipman J.A. in, I believe it was, 1981, and I quote:

> "The *Code* does not fix the sentence for second murder as life imprisonment with no parole eligibility for 10 years. The discretion conferred on the sentencing judge by 742(b) and 744 is not whether to move from a prima facie period of 10 years but, rather, what is a fit sentence, applying the proper guidelines. Unusual circumstances are not a prerequisite for moving away from the 10 year minimum, although, as the cases illustrate, they certainly play a role in the proper exercise of the judicial discretion.
>
> It is not the law that unusual circumstances, brutality, torture or a bad record must be demonstrated before the judge may exercise his discretion to move above the 10 year minimum. Nor is there any burden on the Crown to demonstrate that the period should be more than the minimum."

In relation to the character of Mr. MacRae, in many cases this factor usually amounts to a mitigating factor. In the case of Mr. MacRae, that is not as much the case, though not aggravating. He is not an addict, as we often see. He had a solid employment history and I understand that he enjoys strong family support. As the Crown stated in their brief, he enjoyed a normal middle class life. But his true character came out when he killed his spouse and took steps to avoid detection. He obviously presented as a normal person, but the reality is that he is a very dangerous person under certain sets of circumstances. Mr. MacRae's potential for violence is real. He did not kill his spouse in a rage or after provocation. He just decided to do it, more or less to settle an argument.

Notwithstanding that fact, rehabilitation is an achievable goal. Mr. MacRae may take a long time to achieve rehabilitation but his character can make the necessary changes. He is not suffering any deficits, mental, intellectual or self-induced, and he has no history of violence other than this particular incident.

A man with Mr. MacRae's character would have to search hard for any excuse or explanation for what he did to his wife. On the other hand, those characteristics should assist Mr. MacRae in his long-term rehabilitation, should Mr. MacRae avail himself of those opportunities. If he does not, he'll probably spend the rest of his life in jail.

The nature of the offence: This was a particularly disturbing crime. It was a domestic crime. It was not provoked. There were no triggering events. It was committed on a domestic partner by a person in a position of trust. This was all about violence and settling things with violence.

The third factor is circumstances surrounding the commission of the offence. This crime did not stop with the death of Ms. Gallant. It continued with the hiding of the body and the guise of missing her and it continued with the coverup that went on for five years.

Now, in relation to aggravating factors, I'll list those: (1) as per section 718.2(a)(ii), this was a spousal homicide; (2) as per section 718.2(a)(iii), committed by a person in a position of trust; (3) the attack was the product of Mr. MacRae's thinking process and not the product of external factors; (4) Mr. MacRae's post-offence conduct; (5) there are elements of considering committing the offence as disclosed in the agreed statement of facts; (6) a young child was present at the scene; (7) Mr. MacRae's willingness to attach himself to a criminal organization in the wake of his wife's death. It would appear that in Mr. MacRae's case what everyone has seen over the years was not an accurate representation of his total character.

In terms of mitigating factors: (1) Mr. MacRae entered a guilty plea very early on in the process, that is the first step on the road to remorse and recovery; (2) he did not possess a criminal record at the time of the crime; (3) he has the support of his family; (4) he does not suffer from addictions or mental illnesses; (5) there is no evidence of prior spousal abuse; (6) he is still a young man who has shown for many years that he can live a pro-social lifestyle, and that speaks well for rehabilitation.

Now, sentencing requires a balanced approach. Justice Wood in a British Columbia decision called *R. v. Sweeney* (1992) 71 CCC (3d) 82 (95) stated as follows:

> "But if the tragic consequences to innocent victims were to become the standard by which appropriate sentences for such offences are determined, the courts would soon be reduced to choosing between either imposing the maximum legal term of imprisonment in all cases or embarking upon a comparative analysis of the seriousness of the consequences in individual cases. The first alternative would be an abdication of our responsibility and the second is unthinkable."

Now, the Crown and the defence, as you've probably gathered, have provided me with many cases in support of their positions. It is not my intention to go through each and every case to distinguish it from this or with this, as I've learned over all the years that I've been involved in this business that no two cases are ever the same. I have read all of these cases carefully. I am familiar with many of them. I've been involved in some of them. And I read them not just for the bottom line, numerically speaking, but also for the principles that they enunciate.

The Crown urged me to accept the *Doyle* and *Bailey* cases as a benchmark of 17 years parole ineligibility. When I reviewed the *Legere* case out of New Brunswick in which there was an 18 year parole ineligibility period, the *Mitchell* case, which was 21 years, and the *Muise* case, which was 20 years, I see cases with greater aggravating factors which brought them very close to first degree murder.

In *Mitchell* the accused was 22 and he inflicted cruel and sadistic sexual and physical abuse on his two year old stepson, causing that child's death. The court described his activities as torture over an extended period of time. As I've indicated, in *Mitchell* the sentence was 21 years of parole ineligibility.

In *Legere*, one of Canada's most notorious offenders seriously beat a couple in a country store in New Brunswick and caused the male's death by strangulation by means of a shirt tied around his neck. That was 18 years parole ineligibility.

In *Muise* the accused was involved in the death of three persons in a Sydney River McDonald's restaurant and he pled guilty and received 20 years.

Johnson resulted in 21 years and involved the death of a mother and a child, and the background has been very clearly canvassed by Mr. Taylor, who I know was involved in that case.

In *Francis* the facts were especially violent and the accused had a long history of violence and crime, and also in that case the jury made a recommendation of 25 years.

Now, the latest authority from our Court of Appeal is *R. v. Hawkins* which was a disturbing murder out of Sydney. The trial judge set parole ineligibility at 20 years and the Court of Appeal reset it at 15 years. Beveridge J.A. commented as follows at paragraph 95 of the *Hawkins* appellate decision, and I quote:

> "The facts speak of a brutal and callous murder of a vulnerable victim in his own home by an offender driven by the scourge of addiction to a corrosive drug. Most murders are brutal and callous. As recognized by many cases, the imposition of a sentence of life imprisonment without parole eligibility for at least 10 years already carries with it a significant element of denunciation and general deterrence. However, here the appellant recognized at trial and on appeal that some additional period beyond the automatic minimum 10 years was appropriate and suggested 15 years. I agree that, in light of the circumstances of this offence, some increase in the period of parole ineligibility is warranted. In my opinion, the acceptable range of sentence in these circumstances is between 12 and 15 years. I would accept the suggestion of the appellant and set it at 15 years."

I conclude that there were more aggravating factors in that particular case than the case at bar.

Now, *Cross* is somewhat akin to this case. It involved a stabbing during a domestic dispute. There was a history of domestic violence and addictions. Hood J. accepted a joint recommendation of 12 years parole ineligibility. Mr. Cross had no previous criminal record.

MacMurrer is a decision of the PEI Court of Appeal and McMahon J. commented on the facts at page 3:

> "The respondent did not murder his wife on a sudden impulse. He had been talking about it for a long time. He borrowed the rifle he used on October 4th. On October 26th he telephoned her workplace and tricked the only other person there was at the time into leaving. Once his wife was alone, the respondent went in and confronted her with the rifle, then at point blank range he fired not one, not two, but three bullets into her head. Each shot required a separate bolt action. Obviously,

the respondent wanted to make sure he killed her. Parole ineligibility was set at 12 years."

Sodhi out of the Ontario Court of Appeal set parole ineligibility at 14 years. Mr. Sodhi was convicted of murdering his wife and dumping her body at the side of the road. There was significant post-offence conduct, as was the case here. Justice Moldhaver commented at paragraph 131:

> "The appellant's attempt to cover up his crime and his persistent efforts to create suspicion that someone else had committed it were despicable and cowardly. This conduct amounted to a serious aggravating feature and, in and of itself, warranted a significant increase in the period of parole ineligibility. Combining that with the domestic nature of the crime and the brutality associated with it, I cannot say that the trial judge erred in imposing the sentence that he did."

Randhawa out of the Alberta Court of Appeal set parole ineligibility at 15 years. The attack was described as the grotesque culmination of at least 15 years of hostility between the deceased and the appellant. It involved several blows to the head with an axe. McClung J.A. offered the following at page 5 of *Randhawa*, and I quote:

> "In respect of the character of the appellant, the nature of the offence and the circumstances surrounding its commission, we find that, apart from his age and work record and lack of a criminal related record, there is little in the nature of mitigating circumstances, and indeed it is fair to say in summary that this man, now 51 years of age, acted as an overbearing bully and carried out a senseless, brutal slaying of his defenceless wife in her own home and in the presence of their daughter. Further, the evidence is that the daughter escaped from his grasp of her hair, down

the basement, where he had dragged both mother and daughter. Indeed, it may properly be inferred that, but for her escape, she may have suffered the same fate as her mother under her father's rage."

I have chosen to follow our court's decision in *R. v. Hawkins*. It is a current review of principles set by the highest court in this province. While *Hawkins* did not include a spouse, the victim was disadvantaged and challenged, and these were factors that were exploited and violently exploited by Mr. Hawkins. Mr. Hawkins went to trial and there was significant after-the-fact, post-offence conduct.

In light of these authorities which I have reviewed and applying the principles that have been provided to me and the submissions that have been made to me, I have determined that the appropriate range of parole ineligibility is between 12 and 15 years, so I sentence Mr. MacRae to life imprisonment with parole ineligibility set at 15 years.

Paula's case was supposed to set a precedent in our province and in our country so that perpetrators of violence would come to realize that the justice system was finally taking domestic and intimate partner violence seriously. The evidence was indisputable. He confessed.

In my humble, yet well-informed opinion, the decision made by Justice Kevin Coady to accept a lesser plea of second-degree murder with the possibility of parole after just fifteen years failed Paula and all women and girls impacted by men's violence. It failed all of the officers involved, and it failed a system that, at the time, seemed intent on changing for the better.

For 1,891 days from the time he killed my sister until he was convicted in court, Jason lived freely. He had the ability to do whatever he wanted, and he continued to feel the sun on his face and his daughter's hand in his.

Paula did none of that and never will.

The possibility of parole after fifteen years suggests that is all Paula's life was worth. I can't help but wonder if the decision considered:

- The cost of the investigation
- The toll it took on the police officers, and members of all the other agencies involved
- The message a verdict like this sends to the public; to the school children Paula taught and who will undoubtedly follow this case for the rest of their lives
- The precedent it sets for other cases in Nova Scotia, in Canada and elsewhere

We asked for an appeal, but that was denied by the Crown Prosecution. Apparently, no one likes to call out a judge for a bad decision. At last, it was time to close this chapter. It was time to start healing and it was time to be thankful for all the people who cared, who supported us, who loved us.

It was time to forget Jason MacRae ever existed.

Chapter 12

Lessons Because of Love

"A teacher affects eternity; she can never tell where her influence stops." —Henry Brooks

    I will confess, this effort, this work at lobbying, was transformative. It changed me in ways that were only possible because who I was before Paula's murder ceased to exist. I didn't know how I could ever go back to being someone with rose-coloured glasses. Someone who said hi to strangers. Someone who thought people were genuinely good. With the conviction of Paula's murderer, many, including some family, have asked why I continue to share her story. Now that justice has been realized, some feel I should try and put it all behind me and move on. I know some of these comments come out of genuine concern, fearing it may be too emotional and upsetting for me to continue. More than anyone, I wish I could say that my work was done.
    Throughout my effort of seeking justice for Paula and advocating for systemic-level changes, it has been my observation that the people who are in control and have the power to change things for women in this province have no face, no specific title, no budget line item, and no trauma-informed "to do" list. Without a doubt, there are good people working in this system—knights in shining armour—who are committed to finding the truth and seeking justice day-to-day, every day, in their jobs.
    When it comes to that *one person in charge*, the person who has one mandate, and one mandate only—to do something about

the prevalence of violence against women—they remain nameless. Under the scrutiny that comes from someone like myself, my sister, and many of our supporters asking who is in charge still results in lots of bureaucratic finger-pointing, usually at another department or another minister. We have many leaders in this little province, many of whom are distracted by their too-full portfolios. Many of these leaders have time-sensitive, competing priorities, usually focused around a four-year election—ahem, I mean, accountability cycles. Between the time of Paula's murder and the time of conviction, there were three different premiers and two different political parties in charge, all of which had their own agendas and to-do lists. Finding who murdered Paula didn't seem to be on any of those lists.

My advocacy may have started out focused on justice for Paula, but as the rose-coloured glasses shattered on my face, I learned that violence against women and girls isn't a priority for any one person. There have been many landmark reports written since Paula's murder:

- *Reclaiming Power and Place*, the final report of the National Inquiry into Missing and Murdered Indigenous Women and Girls, June 2019
- *The National Action Plan to End Gender-Based Violence,* April 2021
- *Turning the Tide Together*, the final report of the Mass Casualty Commission, March 2023
- *The Nova Scotia Equity and Anti-Racism Strategy*, July 2023
- *The Report of the Inquiry into the Deaths of the Desmond Family,* January 2024)

All have caused a stir, all have received temporary air time, and all have inspired promises of change.

In an effort to get long overdue attention, resources, and funding needed to make real change, the prevalence of violence against women and girls has recently been framed using a medical model. With Covid-19 still fresh in our collective memory, declaring violence against women and girls an epidemic in our society feels like a good strategy. I understand the theory behind this declaration, and I really, really want to believe it will work. But in my experience, in the almost twenty years that I have advocated, pleaded, begged, and bullied for change in how victims of violence and their families are treated, there is only one thing that seemed to work. There is just one lesson that I can share, that I believe was the reason we got a conviction 1,891 days after the crime was committed:

We made it personal. For everyone.

We made phone calls. We showed up, in person. We kept Paula's name in the news. We kept her story alive. We called it murder, not homicide. We didn't sugar-coat or shy away from difficult conversations. We ignored closed doors and unanswered phone calls.

So for those of you who are still wondering why I can't let *"this"* go . . .

Because *"this"* is about the *murder* of my sister Paula. It is also about the murder of someone else's mother, someone else's daughter. It is about the collective, yet deeply personal loss caused by continued, senseless violence against women and girls within a system run by busy, nameless, faceless government employees who get to go home at night and receive a paycheque every two weeks, regardless of what's left on their to-do list.

Until my own voice joins Paula's, I will continue to show up, I will continue to be present and make it very, very, uncomfortably personal, until the system and the people who work in it take this very, very personally.

Prior to 2011 my presentations, letter writing, and advocating was personal, and I sought justice for Paula and our family. Since that time, I am compelled to honour Paula's passion and her legacy as a teacher. I am not a teacher, but I do have lessons to share, and in a way it is how Paula continues to teach. All of the events we attended are special and important, and I never know who in the audience will be inspired or impacted or how. The following are a few events that I hold especially close to my heart.

February 11th, 2013 - Presented at the Launch of Paula's Silent Witness event, *An Evening to Remember*

Silent Witness Nova Scotia (SWNS) is a not-for-profit organization whose mission is to honour women who have lost their lives to intimate partner violence and are forever silenced. The organization gives voice to these women by raising awareness in Nova Scotia about intimate partner violence and domestic homicide. It involves families and communities in a proactive response to ending intimate partner violence, and pledging to continue doing this work until such a time that there is no longer a need for an organization of this kind.

Part of the work of Silent Witness Nova Scotia involves an exhibit of silhouettes. Each silhouette represents a woman in Nova Scotia who has been killed by her intimate partner. The exhibit, as a whole or in part, travels across Nova Scotia to educate and create awareness about intimate partner violence and domestic homicide. The six-foot-tall deep-red replicas honouring the women they represent are displayed in police stations, schools, training sessions, and businesses throughout Nova Scotia.

Paula's silhouette was created in the fall of 2012. My husband Alain traced the template on a sheet of plywood. As he cut the piece of wood the silhouette somehow "became" Paula for me; I cannot explain how—it just did. I cried deeply as the memory of how my sweet baby sister died resurfaced in my mind and heart, as if it was December 27th, 2005, all over again. I cannot explain how or why seeing Paula's silhouette standing there caused the return of all the hurt and pain, but it did.

Alain cutting out Paula's silhouette

After she was sanded and primed, I took her on a road trip to Pugwash NS. October road trips were not uncommon for Paula, as she was part of a special group of women who each year enjoyed a girls-only weekend retreat.

2012 was our 18th year of getting together with friends who had become family. Lana and I had decided years before that, if we ever had the chance to make a silhouette of Paula, it would be these women, our beautiful sisters, who would put the first coat of red paint on the silhouette. The girls had no idea Paula was joining us as a silhouette, and although it was a very emotional afternoon, we put on Paula's old painting smocks, our Sisters in Spirit pins, and shared in this very special time. With each brushstroke we all privately reflected on our memories with Paula, and through laughter and tears, celebrated her beautiful life and contribution to each of us. The Sisters in Spirit pins are part of a fundraiser that the United Church Women (UCW) in Truro does to raise awareness and money for their community.

After Pugwash, Paula's silhouette travelled to our home, where she stood in our kitchen, a very natural place to find a Gallant, and Paula in particular. It wasn't unusual for me to jump out of my skin when I walked into the dark kitchen forgetting that she was standing there! I admit, I grew attached to what this silhouette represented. There were days I wanted to throw a funky hat on her head or wrap a sweater around her bare shoulders to keep her warm. But when her Silent Witness Shield was placed on her chest, it somehow took the vulnerability away. It was like the silhouette of Paula's image was complete.

On the evening of Monday the 11th, Silent Witness Nova Scotia hosted an event, *An Evening to Remember* where Paula's silhouette was honoured for her role as a family member, friend, school teacher, and colleague.

Silent Witness gives Paula a vivid, physical presence, uniting her voice with that of others to influence change. Paula stood shoulder to shoulder with Linda, Bernice, and Marie. She is ready to stand with other silhouettes, and those yet to be created, to remind everyone that murder and violence against women is personal.

I fundamentally believe that until the general public sees a visual of how many lives have been lost to intimate partner violence, and how many more are at risk, change will be very slow. These women murdered by their intimate partners become a statistic, their stories too soon forgotten.

Paula's Silent Witness Silhouette

Silent Witness and the silhouettes, armed with their shields, remind us daily how special, how loved, and how important these women are, and that we need to end these senseless and horrific deaths. One day I would like to see every silhouette and shield encased in a display cabinet and housed in the Nova Scotia Supreme Court, as a reminder to all those decision makers that their one job is to honour and preserve the legacy of women who have been impacted by violence.

June 29th, 2015 - Paula Gallant Memorial Award

On June 29th, 2015, seventeen of Paula's Grade 3 students from her 2005 class at BLT Elementary School graduated from high School. Oh, how Paula would have celebrated these students! Our family worked with the school to create the Paula Gallant Memorial Award to honour Paula's legacy and to capture her spirit by supporting two students from this class. Anna and Emily presented the awards to the students as they walked across the stage at graduation. Our hearts filled with pride and love, knowing Paula was with them every step of the way. We felt privileged to be able to recognize these remarkable students and enclosed a special letter with some photos from their Grade 3 year as a keepsake for each student. As the last class Paula taught, these students will forever hold a special place in our hearts. As one parent wrote: *I hope somewhere she is smiling down on what she started and what I get to celebrate today.* As part of her curriculum, Paula spoke about the "Four Elements," which included the following quote: *The life I touch for good or ill will touch another life and that, in turn, another, until who knows when the trembling stops or in what far place my touch will be felt.*

Without a doubt, Paula continues to touch lives, twenty years later.

October 14th, 2016 – Presentation at the 7th Annual Shine the Light Campaign in London, ON

Shine the Light, London, ON

October 14th is Mom's birthday, so it felt very fitting to also be celebrating Paula when I was asked to share her story and participate in the media launch of the Shine the Light Campaign in London, Ontario. Paula and abuse survivor Mary Meadows, were honoured.

Initiated in London, Ontario by the London Abused Women's Centre, the goals of the Shine the Light on Woman Abuse campaign are to raise awareness of woman abuse by turning cities and regions across Ontario purple for the month of November; to stand in solidarity with abused women and support them in understanding that any shame and/or blame they may feel does not belong to them but to their abuser; and to raise the profile of the community agencies that can provide abused women with hope and help as they attempt to live their lives free from violence and abuse.

Paula and Mary were featured on buses, billboards, and in video productions which were broadcasted during the opening game of the NBL London Lightning basketball team. On November 1st, 2016, Paula was placed on the Tree of Hope in Victoria Park near Angel Street in London. It is a tree that remembers and honours all women abuse survivors and murdered women. During this campaign they launched a new Shine the Light Flag that was hoisted on more than thirty properties throughout the city of London. Mary and I helped raise the first of thirty flags on the flagpole in the parking lot of the London Abused Women's Centre.

November 15th, 2016 - Attended the Shine the Light Campaign at Parliament Hill

Anna and Emily at Shine the Light

Lana, Emily, Anna, and I traveled to Ottawa to attend a special reception at Parliament Hill, honoring women who have been murdered or abused, with a focus on Paula, Mary, and the 2016 Shine the Light on Woman Abuse Campaign. We had a great day at Parliament Hill, and it was amazing to be part of such a monumental event. It was the first time since its construction in 1916 that the

Peace Tower was illuminated in purple to raise awareness of men's violence against women.

During the visit we toured Parliament, met with the Speaker of the House Honourable Geoff Regan, explored the library, and participated in a reception held near the House of Commons and Senate chambers (Centre Block of the Parliament buildings). My nieces were deeply moved by the significance of the occasion, and their presence as young girls left a lasting impression on everyone there.

November 27th, 2021 - Placement of Paula's Bench on the St. Margaret's Bay Rails to Trails

For several years the Mothers' Union of the Anglican Parish of French Village held outdoor vigils during the 16 Days of Activism Against Gender-Based Violence. Our family has participated in these events to help raise awareness and to honour all the women and girls in Nova Scotia who have lost their lives to men's violence. In 2020, I worked with the St. Margaret's Bay Rails to Trails Association and Silent Witness Nova Scotia on the placement and dedication of a vivid purple bench on the trail in Paula's memory. The bench is a place of peace and reflection, and many feel Paula's presence when they come to visit. Purple is a symbol of courage, survival, and honour, and has come to symbolize the fight to end violence against women. This bench is part of Barb's Bench Project within Silent Witness Nova Scotia.

Paula's Purple Bench

December 6th, 2019 - The National Day of Remembrance and Action on Violence Against Women.

I had the honour of attending a ceremony at Pictou High Academy and shared Paula's story to raise awareness about prevalent men's violence against women and girls in our society and the impact it has on so many levels. I know Paula was happy I was sharing her story in Pictou County, as she always enjoyed spending time there with her dear friends. Not to mention the fact that *Miss Gallant's Favourite Season* was printed by Advocate Printing in Pictou. With such a deeply personal connection, it was also special having Ange McKay attend the ceremony as one of the five honour guards in attendance. Ange was a very special friend of Paula's and has provided our family with unconditional support and love since Paula's death.

At this event we had three Silent Witness Silhouettes (Paula, Linda Boudreau, and Honey Wright), our Remembrance Tree honouring the sixty-two women who have been killed by their intimate partner in Nova Scotia since 1989, and a red dress honouring all the murdered and missing Indigenous women and girls. Students were chosen to participate in the candle lighting ceremony and there was participation from Tearmann House and the Interagency on Family Violence. The school principal also shared her personal and heartbreaking story of losing her first cousin to intimate partner violence. I felt like Paula was there with me, in a place she loved–a school–continuing her role as an educator, empowering students with knowledge and skills to foster a new violence-free culture for all women and girls . . . It was a purposeful day!

> "One day you will tell your story of
> how you overcome what you are going
> through, and it will become someone
> else's survival guide." —Brene Brown

The following list represents additional presentations I gave and events we attended to advocate for Paula, and for all women and girls who have been impacted by men's violence. Although there is no detail supporting the list below, they are all significant and support the third goal we were working to achieve.

- 2007, June 27 - *Attended the Community Paula Gallant Memorial Walk*
- 2007, February 21 - *Attended the Mayor's Roundtable on Violence Forum*

- o 2008, February 15 - *Presented at The Metro Interagency on Family Violence Conference, "Ending Violence Against Women: Men Standing Up"*
- o 2008, October 3 - *Presented to Department of Justice, Victim Services*
- o 2009, May 18 - *Presented to the Cape Breton Interagency on Family Violence*
- o 2009, June 18 and various other dates - *Launch of* Miss Gallant's Favourite Season, *with proceeds supporting NS Transition House Art Therapy Program for Women Affected by Violence.*
- o 2009 - *Presented to St. Mary's University 4th-year criminology students*
- o 2009, October 31 - *Presented at the Canadian Congress on Criminal Justice*
- o 2009, April - *Published National Victims of Crime Resource Guide called* How One Victim of Murder Chose to be a Survivor
- o 2010, February 11 - *Presented at the Family Violence Prevention Week event*
- o 2010, May 18 - *Presented to the Cape Breton Interagency on Family Violence*
- o 2011, April 16 - *Presented to Halifax Victims Services, "Understanding the Impact of Homicide"*
- o 2011, February 17 - *Attended "Breakfast with the Guys: A Conversation with Dr. Jackson Katz"*
- o 2012, August 19 - *Presented at an Awareness Launch in support of Patricia (Patty) Kucerovsky*
- o 2012, *May 18 - Presented to the Cape Breton Interagency on Family Violence*
- o 2012, July 28 - *Presented at the Cape Breton "Take Back the Night" event*
- o 2014, May 13 - *Presented at the Cape Breton Interagency on Family Violence Annual General Meeting*
- o 2013, December 5 - *Presented to the First United Church Women Group in Truro*
- o 2015, January 31 - *Presented to the Salvation Army*

- 2015, June 25 - *Presented at Autumn House Annual General Meeting*
- 2015, November 21 - *Presented at the "Broken Relationships" event sponsored by the Anglican Mothers' Union*
- 2015, November 26 - *Presented at the Power, Gender & Language Perpetuating Violence Against Women Conference hosted by Autumn House*
- 2015, October 1 - *Presented to the Nova Scotia Public Prosecution Services*
- 2018, May - *Presented to Bell Service Management Team in Atlantic Canada*
- 2019, December 6 - *Presented to Pictou Academy High School*
- Ongoing attendance at the December 6th National Day of Remembrance and Action on Violence Against Women
- Ongoing attendance and presented at the Mothers' Union Gender-Based Violence Walk during the 16 Days of Activism
- Ongoing attendance at the Annual Paula Gallant Memorial Elementary Basketball Tournament, coordinated by the Glace Bay High School girls basketball team and Coach Kathy Donovan
- 2024, February 21 - *Presented to the Nova Scotia Insurance Women's Association*
- 2024, March 7 - *Presented at the International Women's Day Summit Hosted by Leeside Society and Be The Peace Institute*

Chapter 13

The Greatest of These Is Love

Helen Keller, in all her wisdom and empathy, once wrote, "What we have once enjoyed deeply, we can never lose. All that we love deeply becomes part of us," and this has proven true over and over again in the last nineteen years.

In death, Paula has become part of my core in a way that she might not have done had she been allowed to live. Instead of being *just* my sister, her legacy has and continues to inspire my own growth and transform me into someone so much more than I was before. I found depth, patience, and appreciation that I didn't have before. I know she has done the same for my family and for complete strangers, who told me so after each presentation and talk I have given. By demanding change that would have impacted our journey and will hopefully improve the journey for other murder victims, Paula's legacy as a teacher has had a ripple effect across the globe. Paula's life is and was so much more than how her life ended. The way her life ended was because of someone else's actions; it had nothing to do with her own choices, or the light she brought into every room she entered. My hope with this last chapter is that you can meet Paula, and she can teach you one more lesson.

Paula, like other murder victims, is so much more than a tragic headline. They are not statistics, and they are not nameless. In fact, they are someone's favourite sister, someone's favourite aunt, they are someone's favourite teacher, or someone's mom.

On our website that we launched in 2007, called *Come Meet Paula*, we honoured her life and legacy. I know Paul Kenny is getting a chuckle as he watches me from above, combing through old files on my laptop, CDs, and fourteen binders to find hard copies of information for this chapter and the book in general. Without further ado, please come meet Paula and see that how a person's life ends often has nothing to do with who they were.

Come Meet Paula - As a Daughter

Obviously, Mom and Dad have passed and are not here to provide their reflections on what Paula was like as a daughter. But for reasons that go beyond serendipity, Paula wrote the following journal entry, about what it was like growing up as one of the 7 Coady Street sisters. This brief entry offers some insights to Paula's sense of whimsy and appreciation for life.

I have so many thoughts to record but which are the most memorable? I know I always felt loved beyond a shadow of a doubt—even when I ripped their oil painting aiming Bamm Bamm Rubble from The Flintstones at Lana's head. I know I was respected, not only as a kid, but when Mom and I became best friends after Dad died. I know they loved each other, by the way they talked to each other and presented a united front to us on major issues.

What I remember most of all is the feeling of peace that was felt upon walking into 7 Coady Street. All the family and friends who visited were welcomed with open arms, a beer, tea and treats, whatever the occasion called for.

We were so lucky to have been born into such an amazing family and to have our memories in our hearts forever. They'll carry us through the rest of our lives and help us handle whatever life brings us.

> My Story - by Paula
>
> I have so many thoughts to record – which are the most memorable? I know I always felt loved beyond a shadow of a doubt – even when I ripped their oil painting throwing Bun Bun at Lara's head. I know I was respected not only as a kid but as Mom and I became best friends after Dad died. I know they loved each other by the way they talked to each other & presented a united front to us on major issues. What I remember most of all is the feeling of peace that was felt upon walking into 7 Coady Street. All the family and friends who visited were welcomed with open arms, a beer, tea + treats, whatever the occasion called for. We were so lucky to have been born into such an amazing family and to have our memories in our hearts forever. They'll carry us through the rest of our lives and help us handle whatever life brings us.
>
> Paula ☺

Paula's Journal Entry

There is so much I remember about Mom and Dad that it is impossible to record it all. Instead, I decided to record excerpts, and remember everyone's memories are different and unique as we all draw out what's important to us.

- Going to sleep while Hockey Night in Canada was playing
- Dancing with Mom in the kitchen
- Dad singing "I love my truck, my pretty little truck"
- Mom's kiss goodnight that always tasted like lipstick
- Driving to PEI—always driving past Pictou to go through New Brunswick
- Hanging out on the front step listening to the adults talk over tea and coffee
- So many wonderful Christmas Eves and Days—especially the one where we got up very early because Dad got called into work at the garage, our last Christmas as a whole family

We were so blessed with parents who would and did do anything for us. We were safe, cared for and given the best start in life.
Memories that will always be in our hearts.

As an artist Paula was just beginning to come into her own. Not only did she teach art, but she also committed to being a lifelong learner of the arts. Below is Paula's foray into mixed media, accompanied by some insightful and beautiful prose.

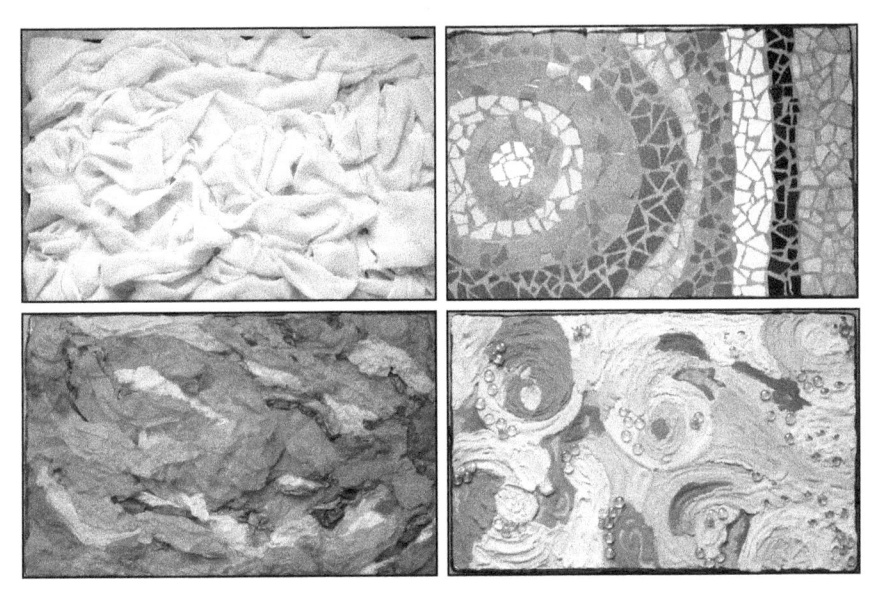

Paula's Art – 4 Images Air Earth Water and Fire

The Four Elements—Earth, Air, Water and Fire—are thought of as the building blocks of the universe. They influence our lives on a daily basis, with or without our knowledge or permission. This is much like the upbringing by our parents. Who or what we become relates back to the people who brought us into this world. Whether it's been a positive or negative influence, it is hard to deny it exists.

My parents have been the building blocks of who I am today. I was very blessed to be loved, cared for and protected by such strong people. The more I learned and discovered about the four elements, the easier it was to see the connection between their personalities and how it related to these elements.

The first, Earth—my dad to me was my earth. Nourishing and giving form to what I have become. As a family, we could always count on him to provide life's necessities to make sure we were taken care of. It is said that people who are born with common sense, dependability and practicality are closely associated with the earth's sign. I have so many vivid memories of this with him. He was the guy people called if they needed help . . . whether it was getting a car fixed, a fence mended, or a garage built.

He also is the Wind (Air) to me. This sign is associated with intelligence. Dad always used to say no one could take an education away from you. Even though he himself only completed up to Grade 4, he was an avid reader and whatever his interests were, he would read to find out more and more about it.

After my oldest sister started to play basketball, he read all about it . . . even though he never dribbled a basketball in his life. He eventually became the coach of the St. Anne's Jr. High girl's team.

I remember the two of us reading the same novel of my sister's, who was three years older than me. After we finished I was quite indignant when I realized he was going to quiz me on it . . . I was indignant until I realized I didn't know the answers. He made me re-read it and told me reading was too important to be taken lightly or breeze through it. This is a life lesson I still try to remember when tackling any new book, new concept, or new task.

My mom is a true surprise, as she is the opposite of Water and Fire. Just like she was opposites in her looks—petite in size, and what her personality was actually like. She represented Water to me because it is the essence of emotion. She taught me to express my feelings, whatever they might be, because there may not be a tomorrow to pull them all out. My mother cried easily over everything and anything . . . but at the same time loved to laugh and be silly and have a great time.

She felt our pain, which they say most mothers can, and as I got older, I could see in her face that she didn't want us to endure any type of hardship. The time I came running into the house with fake blood smeared all over my face was not such a great idea! Only after my mom turned white and almost fainted did I realize the error of my not-so-funny joke. It was the same look on her face when they wheeled me into surgery after having my jaw broken. Luckily that one wasn't my doing, so I couldn't get in trouble.

Then there is Fire, which represents the epitome of strength. After my dad got sick, she endured seven months of watching him suffer through a coma, while trying to maintain a sense of calm over three girls. She did all the things she hadn't had to take care of during their 25 years of marriage . . . and did them without a word of complaint. Then when Dad passed away, she did all she could do to maintain a sense of normalcy in our family.

Even though her heart was broken, and everything she knew had been ripped away, I can still remember the day I came home from school and saw her standing in the front yard, stringing the Christmas lights on this little bush, trying to make our first Christmas as four instead of five somewhat like it used to be. It hadn't even been a month since our dad passed away. I cannot imagine the strength and courage it must have taken to do that simple task.

Earth, Air, Water, Fire . . . the four elements. This is what they mean to me, and how they influenced my life . . . What do they mean to you?

In Paula's own words, you can feel the love she had for Lana, myself, and our parents. The incredible bond we shared by growing up in such a caring, wondrous and supportive home was the well from which Paula loved, tended and taught all who entered her life. What follows are notes and letters written to us, describing the impact of all the love that Paula gave out so freely, and without condition.

Come Meet Paula - As a Friend

> *"I've learned that people will forget what you said, people will forget what you did, but people will never forget how you made them feel."* —Maya Angelou

Written by Elena

Paula's sense of humour and sharp wit was captivating, her playful nature was infectious, and it didn't take long for people to be drawn to her. However, it was her big heart and inner strength that kept people close. Because of her ability to listen and her practical and encouraging advice, Paula quickly became a confidant to many. To be her friend meant you always had someone in your corner, someone loyal and fiercely supportive.

Paula was the first person you would call when you had good news because you were certain she would share in your excitement. Within seconds she was at your side, taking over the planning of the celebration. She was also the first person you would want to talk to when you had bad news to share. Paula was a natural in knowing when to just listen, when to give you words of encouragement and when to help you see the humour or lighter side of the situation.

Being a true friend is a full-time job and Paula took on this role with every fibre of her being. Her friendship and the example she set has had a lasting effect on all who were fortunate enough to call her "friend." This is evident in the way her friends have rallied together during this tragedy.

One of Paula's greatest legacies is the number of friends who continue to gather together in support of her family and of each other, and most importantly, to celebrate her life and remember how she made them feel.

Written by Ange

I have such a terrible memory of things that, at the time, were "just another night out," or "just another road trip/day with friends." That is why I have so many pictures and keep a journal. Ange Maclean usually reminds me of all the things that happened—whether she is making them up or they really happened, I'm never really quite sure. Do you guys have all of Paula's pictures? I always give people copies of mine and she has lots. If you don't have them, I will make copies for you. We had so many fun times, so many laughs. I miss talking to her so much.

I have really good memories of when Paula came to visit me in Kelowna, BC in 2001. I was sooooo excited for her to come. As our relationship went, I was usually trying to talk her into coming/going somewhere and she was trying to put the brakes on it (me) to some extent. But, she was coming and as part of our activities, I booked a hotel in Vancouver. We drove the three-and-a-half hours from Kelowna to Vancouver for our excursion.

At the hotel, we lay out on the roof—it was sunny and warm, I loaned her a T-shirt as she had none, it being March and all. It was beautiful. I have photos.

So, we went up to Grouse Mountain on the Gondola to see what we could see. It was very pretty and snowing lightly, which we decided to partake in. As we sat on the sleigh eagerly awaiting our ride, we were suddenly treated to the lulling sound of a diesel engine Bobcat lacing into the quiet, serene mountain air. As the Bobcat loudly towed off our little sleigh, I realized that my question of "How do they get the horses up here anyway?" would not go unanswered. As we thundered across the mountain top, amid skiers, etc., we laughed hysterically at the ridiculousness of it. Later, we went skating on the pond up there—neither of us had been on skates in a while. We had a great lunch and descended back down on the Gondola.

That night in Gastown we had a great Italian dinner with a very good-looking waiter—neither was wasted on us, despite the red wine. We then made our way to Richard's on Richards where we delightfully discovered it was '80s night! We had a blast observing the craziness of the big-city people and dancing to all our favourites, especially New Moon on Monday, which always brings me back there. We had so much fun and such a great visit.

Thanks, Lynn, for sending her out.

Written by Tammy

At first, I thought this was going to be difficult. Since I only saw Paula a few times a year, I fondly remember every time we were together, and every memory is special. So it was difficult to choose just one. Paula was so happy, funny and witty—it was my kind of humour, and I loved it and looked forward to seeing her every time. But after I thought about it, it wasn't difficult to pick one specific moment at all—it was actually quite simple. I just went with the first image that comes to my mind every time I think of Paula.

Anna was just a month old, and everyone was coming to my house for supper. I'll never forget Paula when she walked into my door that day with Anna in her car seat. I know every mother loves her child, but I remember thinking, "I have never seen a mother look so proud and happy!" Paula was glowing. And with the light beaming in from the window behind her, she looked like an angel. That is how I'll always remember Paula.

I just had the funniest thought, and I couldn't help but chuckle out loud. I was imagining Paula reading this, and some of the funny comments that would be coming out of her mouth. I can just hear her saying, "Yeah, Tammy—I was glowing. It was sleep deprivation and I was exhausted. Or maybe you were still drunk from the night before" . . . or something like that! She had a sense of humour that I loved. That is the kind of person Paula was, and how she is remembered. Happy, funny and beautiful.

Written by Nancy

I met Paula in 1988—her best friend from high school, Coralee Almon, was roommates with my best friend from high school, Suzy Jordan. There were lots and lots of parties at Dal that year and over the next few years, and Paula made lots of treks from the teachers college to Halifax and finally moved there!

It's funny because I have so many great memories of Paula and I find it hard to narrow it down to just one. Until 1995, I don't think we even lived in the same city but it didn't matter—Paula was a kindred spirit. Even after we became close friends, we still only talked once in a while but we always picked up right where we left off. My sister says these kinds of friends are called "forever friends"— people you don't see every day, or even that regularly, but ones you always know will be there for you and will make you happy.

Anyway, back to the story . . . I think the one I will write about shows what kind of person Paula was. I have lots of funny, even wild, stories but those are better shared over a glass of wine, and she would agree with that! I have so many things in my house that remind me of Paula: the sink she picked out for my kitchen, the "hand-me-up" clothes she gave me, etc. But I have this one teapot/cup that is my favourite.

One day, many moons ago, Paula was at my house for a visit. I offered to make her a cup of tea. I then put the tea bags in two teacups and added the hot water. Paula was horrified . . . that is not how you make tea! You need to make it in a pot! True to form, about a week later she showed up at my house with a tiny teapot and cup set that she bought for me so I could make it properly. Even now it makes me laugh and I love my little teapot and think of her every time I make myself my single cup of tea—never in a cup, always in a pot!

My memories of Paula:

- *Dressing up as Dalmatians for Halloween and being mistaken for a herd of cows*
- *Going on a big road trip to Toronto to see the Eagles and skipping the opening act to go shopping because we never heard of her before—Sheryl Crow*
- *Secretly trying to get Lynn's stereo cover fixed because Paula had a party at her house while she was away, and somebody broke it*
- *Driving to Dunvegan to go camping on July 1st weekend with all the windows down because Jimmy had been diving in the harbour (for work) and smelled really bad*
- *Camping in Dunvegan in sub-zero weather*
- *Going to Mass at the Cathedral on Sunday nights because that's when the cute boys went*
- *Paula visiting New Glasgow and bar hopping, then returning home having lost her Visa card. After I called every place she had been, she opened her purse, and guess what she found?*
- *Biff, her little black car*

- Carpooling together when I was subbing in Halifax
- Dragging her to Brandy's
- Meeting up in Halifax on conference days that are too many to count

Written by Dawn

My relationship with Paula was very unique. We were cousins who had a long-distance friendship: she lived in Nova Scotia and I lived in Ontario. As children (our dads being brothers), we would spend time together on our annual trip down East. As adults it was whatever time we could spend together we tried to squeeze in. Whether it be at an airport for a couple of hours, an overnighter or a couple of days, Paula and I would try our hardest to spend some time together. Many late nights and early mornings!

My fondest memory of Paula is when she agreed to be a bridesmaid at my wedding 12 years ago. She was such a great support and joy to be around, and it has only been since we lost her that I actually know how much it meant to her. She had such a maturity about her and inspired me with her positive outlook on life. I will never forget how she embraced me and my family. We miss her dearly and hold a special place in our hearts for her!

Written by Lori

Paula, my cousin, used to come to Toronto occasionally for courses or as a layover on vacation. Paula would always make sure there was time to visit my sister and have dinner with all of us.

One night, in about 2002, at one of these dinners, Paula ended up drawing pictures with my niece, who was about four years old at the time. As we all know, at that age when children are enjoying themselves, they do not want to stop. And so it went: Paula would draw a picture, Grace would love it and demand another, for at least an hour. By this time, if it was me, I would have already told my niece I needed a break and that we would continue later, but not Paula. She kept going, not annoyed or bored or wanting to hang out with the adults. She gave her full attention to this little girl as if she was the only person in the world.

I loved Paula, but that night I came to admire Paula. I miss her.

Written by Lynn Mac

This little anecdote took place when Paula would have been perhaps 15 years of age. While babysitting, she decided to make a cake, so she put the cake in the oven and set the oven but nothing happened. One hour later she removed her cake, but it had not baked. What to do?? My husband, Alan, and her dad, Paul, happened to come home just shortly thereafter, and Paula proceeded to tell them the oven was broken. Well, the two Mr. Fix Its decided they would take the oven apart—why bother paying the repairman? When I arrived home, perhaps another hour later, I walked in the back door to see knobs, nuts, bolts, screws, nails and an instruction manual all randomly placed around the floor. I asked what was going on and Paula explained that the oven was broken, so Alan and Paul were fixing it. Long story short, when Alan and Paul had finished their little repair job, there were a few "leftover" pieces on the floor. I asked Paul why they had all of these extra parts lying about, and he told me "Ah, you don't need them anyway." We all had quite the little chuckle over that but it seems the problem was not with the mechanics of the oven, it was all in the timer. Paula had set the clock on the time, hence the reason the oven would not work.

Ever the teacher, quite often while babysitting at our house (and it was a lot as Lynn and Lana can attest), Paula would engage the kids in crafts. It was nothing new to have a story hanging on my refrigerator which reflected the theme for the day. Her main resource was the Sears catalogue. She and my daughter Andrea would sit for hours and cut figures from the catalogue, each figure representing a member of the family or a character from the story they were portraying. The problem arose each time I wanted to order something from the catalogue: I would have to go back through the various stories and match the cut-out area from the catalogue with the shape on the storyboard.

When Andrea was just a little girl, Paula used to tell her that Dianne had pills to keep you small. Andrea called Dianne one day to ask her if she would give her the pills to keep her small. Paula was thoroughly entertained by this.

I remember snippets of Paula . . . Paula giving her green ballet suit to my daughter Andrea (the suit that Paula is so proudly wearing in the picture on her website photo gallery) and teaching her how to do ballet. Andrea was old enough to dress herself at this point (or at least she thought she was) and every other morning began with the green ballet suit... I remember Paula coming here on various Sunday afternoons to take the kids to the movies (she got a ticket during one of the drives as the car still had winter tires—God love her, she was so concerned when she came home that day. And we were equally as upset because we had caused her the upset... I remember her tying knots in Andrea's hair with strips of cloth to make curls (Paula would always chuckle the next day for the curls never stayed)... I have pictures of the kids that Paula took during afternoon trips to Wentworth Park to feed the ducks. I remember summer days when Paula would stand for hours and squirt the hose at the multitudes who seemed to congregate in our yard... I remember drives to Tasty Treat for ice cream, and calling Paula the day I got my microwave (wow, we were both excited). She came down immediately and we took it from the box to ooh and ahh over it—we couldn't do anything else with it, however, as it weighed a tonne... But one of the things I remember most about Paula, and which will forever be ingrained in my memory and heart, is the little girl with freckles and the wide beaming smile who grew into a beautiful and loving young mother whose outward beauty was only surpassed by her beauty within.

Written by Brenda

I don't think I have one specific story about Paula. Growing up we were a constant in each other's lives. Our parents spent a lot of time together, so we were at each other's birthday parties, family events, Christmas celebrations and weekend sleepovers. I remember spending much time on Coady Street playing with Paula and her friends who lived nearby. I even enjoyed when I would get some of her hand-me-down clothes. She was two-and-a-half years older than me, so I looked up to her.

It's always sad to me how life's circumstances and geography cause people to grow apart. The last time I saw Paula in person was at my brother Dan's wedding in August 2003. We spent most of that evening together laughing, dancing and catching up on each other's lives. It was like time had stood still and we were back on Coady Street again. Someone even came up to us who knew me but didn't know Paula and asked if we were related; he thought we resembled each other. We were both so tickled by this because I don't think any of our relatives would say we look alike. Since that time, we had kept in touch via email. I enjoyed receiving updates and pictures of her and Anna.

She is sadly missed.

Written by Stephen, 6 Coady St., and read at A Toast to Paula at the Awareness Launch in Glace Bay on December 5th, 2007

Everyone in attendance here this evening has experienced times of separation from a good friend. After a reunion with a friend who you haven't seen in a long time, you sometimes come away thinking, "Wow! Our conversation picked up like we had been speaking yesterday." This was always the case with Paula and me. She was genuine. She really wanted to know what you were up to, and she was truly interested. You could always count on easy conversation and a friendly face.

In Timberlea tonight, just like we heard here this evening at the Savoy, a lot of the stories focus on the fact that Paula was a fabulous educator who left an indelible mark on her students and colleagues. When I remember Paula, however, I remember the girl across the street. One of several kids who were blessed to grow up in one of the best neighbourhoods in the world.

She was one of the umpteen kids Barry Martin could fit into a green Suburban and head off to the beach with on a summer day. In our neighbourhood, Paula could play dress up with all of the girls . . . and just as easily flatten all the boys in a "friendly" game of basketball. I remember as young children playing "Paula's Charms," a game that involved Paula and other girls chasing the boys and trying to kiss them on the cheek. We must have been very young at the time because the other boys and I all tried to run away.

Paula and I were in the same grade throughout school, and I was honoured to be her Grand March partner upon graduation. Thinking back to our school days, the thing that stands out for me the most had very little to do with school itself. Almost every school day for 13 years, Paula was the last person I said, "See ya!" to, on the way home. We would all leave St. Anne's or St. Mike's as a huge mass, and then groups would separate as each intersection was passed. Coady Street kids would make their way up the street and some of my best of friends would branch off into each house. More often than not, however, it would be Paula and me at that last fork in the road home between houses #6 and #7. Most of the walks home were quite happy, some were just ordinary, but there were some sad ones as well. No matter the type of day, though, you could always count on easy conversation and a friendly face.

Paula left us far too early, but she has left an extraordinary imprint on all who knew her. There is an old Irish saying: "Death leaves a heartache no one can heal, but love leaves a memory no one can steal."

Tonight, we remember Paula on her birthday, as an inspirational friend, daughter, sister, teacher, and mother. I'm sure she's in Heaven now, greeting everyone with easy conversation and a friendly face.

At this time, I ask you all to raise a glass, and share a birthday toast for Paula. Happy Birthday, Paula!

Written and published by Shannon McKarney, an acquaintance from Nova Scotia Teacher's College

Yesterday afternoon, I was putting my cranky, overtired baby down for a nap. Her normal and very necessary nap earlier in the day had been interrupted about 20 minutes in by a barking dog, causing her to stir, then to stand straight up in her crib and grunt, demanding to know what the heck is going on out there and why isn't she involved, don't you people know anything about entertaining babies? Unfortunately, once that stage of fully awake-ness happens, the chances of her going back to sleep and finishing that nap are pretty much zero. No point in fighting it.

We got up. Had squishy pasta and stringy cheese and banana and milk for lunch, most of which ended up on the floor thanks to her new game where she chucks the food at lightning speed from her tray then points at it on the floor and then looks at us with wide eyes and palms upturned as if to say, I have no idea how that got there! IT'S A MYSTERY! After lunch, we wandered down to the beach where we spent an hour carefully selecting and washing stones, moving them from one brightly coloured plastic beach toy to another. We waded into the water, so warm after this glorious summer, and she finally learned how to kick her legs and make big splashes with her feet, with squeals and smiles of pure baby joy. After a while, baby getting sleepy, we plodded back up to the house and peeled her out of her bathing suit and swim diaper and watched her streak bare-butt through the house, laughing like a maniac, before getting wrestled into a diaper and clothes and a *sleep sack for a sip of milk and the completion of that much-needed nap. The overtiredness and routine-breaking meant she wasn't going to go to sleep on her own, so I did what I always do when necessary (and what I always want to do even when it's not): I lay down on the bed in the darkened room, baby snuggled in the crook of my shoulder, her hand on my chest, and held her bottle as she drowsed off to sleep. I pressed my cheek against her silky, messy hair as it tickled my nose and listened to her slowly slurp her milk as I quietly inhaled the sweet smell of sunscreen and sand and milk and sun and baby. These moments are precious, because I know that soon enough she won't be interested in being cuddled to sleep; she'll be on the phone or texting her friends till the wee hours, while I yell empty threats up the stairs about groundings or iPhone 9 seizure or whatever else I can think of that might just possibly get her teenage ass to listen to me. Right now, she's wee and I'm the mama and there's nothing more perfect, more soul-filling than moments like this. But yesterday . . . yesterday it was more precious. I stayed a little longer, breathed a little more deeply, squeezed just a little bit harder as I tried to keep my tears from rolling onto her hair as she fell asleep. Because all I could think of is how Paula never got to cuddle her sunscreen-scented baby to sleep on an August afternoon. Paula died on a cold December day, a week before her baby's first birthday, the joy of that moment and every moment henceforth denied to her. The details are well documented elsewhere; let it suffice to say she shouldn't have died, that someone took her life from her, that it was the wrongest of wrongs. I hadn't seen Paula for many years, but she wasn't a person you'd forget: she was bright, witty, always laughing, and always sharp. The loss of such a beautiful soul makes me cry and ache every time I think of it. And while I weep for her sisters, who were everything to her; and for her family, who she loved; and for her friends, who miss her every single day; and for her students, both the ones she was able to teach and touch and reach as well as the ones she should have been teaching for years to come; while I weep for all of them, it's for her baby I weep most of all. I have tried, but I truly can't bear to think about what a child just shy of her first birthday does when her mother suddenly disappears from her life, when her dynamic is jarringly, permanently altered. I also cannot bear to think about the fact that the person charged yesterday with that baby's mother's murder is also the person who's been looking into* her eyes as he put her to bed for the last four-and-a-half years. The thought makes me shaky, jittery, off-balance. And those are maybe the politest words I can use. That baby's world has been permanently altered once more, with her father's arrest and absence from her life; once more, the fundamentals of her life have been shifted. After this much time she's no longer a baby, but a child, a child who must have more questions than anyone around her feels able to answer. She shouldn't have to ask these questions. She should, instead, be shopping for school supplies with her mother before they go to the beach and play with stones and splash in the water before coming home for a sip of milk and a nap and a cuddle filled with the smell of sunscreen and sand and beloved child. All these moments, stolen from them both. Justice, however delayed, may finally be coming to the family of Paula Gallant. With that, I desperately hope they can finally achieve some semblance of peace. But most of all, I hope that Paula's daughter can now somehow be given a life as close to the life she should have had with her adoring mother by her side—a life filled with laughter and hugs and art and friends and family and love.

Love, most of all.

Come Meet Paula - As a Teacher

> "One looks back with appreciation to the brilliant teachers, but with gratitude to those who touched our human feelings. The curriculum is so much necessary raw material, but warmth is the vital element . . . for the soul of the child." —Carl Jung

Student Tribute to Paula

Written by Joanne, friend and classmate at Nova Scotia Teacher's College

Because of her compassion, Paula was an exceptional communicator. She cared about adults and children as well. Being passionate about the students whose lies she touched, she often spoke with caring and kindness of the gifts each brought to her classroom. When faced with challenging situations, a discussion of methods and ways to meet these challenges quickly ensued. In many ways, Paula could transcend age and roles when interacting with her students for she had the uncanny ability to work with them on their level. When dealing with parents, she did so with great empathy, her focus remaining centred on collaboration between parent, teacher and student. Paula communicated with her fellow educators because she truly thought many caring minds could make the impossible seem possible.

To her classroom each day she brought knowledge and she revelled in the fact that every day garnered her more knowledge to be shared and incorporated within the teaching paradigm. From her students, Paula learned of life and love. To her, knowledge was much more than academics; it was about life and touching each student and adult she encountered. Paula valued sharing, fellowship and professionalism among teachers. I remember conversations we shared about challenges in our classrooms. To help source out a solution to my challenge and as a show of support, Paula would appear at my door with books and papers.

Ms. Gallant was always interested. She was interested in reaching individuals and meeting them from where they came; she was interested in working to reach new heights both for herself and those she taught, and she was interested in making a difference. She believed that in working with children she could make a difference. To ensure her students learned, Paula connected with her fellow teachers by building positive, supportive relationships which allowed for professional conversations. Paula built bridges and climbed mountains to ensure her students learned. She worked tirelessly to ask questions, read books and search for better and more effective methods of meeting the needs of her students.

I respect Paula and all she did in her short, full life, and Paula respected each and every person she met. She respected what they brought to her emotionally, socially and academically. Paula cared deeply about doing what was right and in meeting the many challenges with which she was faced each day. She worked tirelessly to discover what made each child special and to build on those special qualities. It was the child before her that was important.

A word I now use to describe an educator is Paula. She epitomized education and all it should be in today's world. She was a teacher, but her true focus was on learning. Success, to her, was measured by the learning which occurred in each person as they communicated, shared knowledge, expressed interest and respected each other.

Written by Richelle, friend, colleague and classmate at the Nova Scotia College of Art and Design

It was a moment of fight or flight, as Paula and I stood on the doorstep of NSCAD University in the spring of 2004. We stood motionless with a "you go first" look in our eyes, until Paula assertively huffed "Come on! We only need a B to get our money back."

That was the moment that Paula made the decision to fight this thing and not only intrigued but terrified us. We walked, hand in hand, into one of the most prestigious art colleges in North America with nothing but guts and friendship on our side.

We were the same two middle-aged women who spent all morning trying to choose outfits that looked NSCAD-ish, trying to pull anything mismatched and Bohemian-looking out of our closets, wringing it in our nervous hands to get the subtle "indifferent" look of a real artist. Needless to say, this was extremely challenging for two Gap girls, who didn't own a pair of jeans that weren't made in some sweatshop within the last two seasons.

Having felt the need to get into the teacher certificate program, before we really knew what we were in for, Paula and I thought we would just slide in, get our required B's, to ensure financial reimbursement, all the while wowing our Type-A friends with our newfound level of "deep." Little did we know that this voyage would turn out to be the most gruelling, emotionally draining, life-altering journey we would be fortunate enough to experience.

Paula successfully completed a number of theory art studio courses. She pushed herself as a conceptual artist, explored a variety of mediums, and refined her techniques. From dabbling with paint in the old art room at BLT, under Andrea Malone's tutelage, to creating 30-hour sculptural pieces that would be shown amongst her peers at NSCAD, Paula made the leap from being a "teacher of art" to an "artist who teaches."

Paula's commitment to family and her personal history proved to be an underlying theme in all that she created. Reflecting upon and documenting life experiences through her art was a driving force behind Paula's work. Her work was always done with her daughter Anna in mind, communicating her love and legacy to her. Longevity was forever at the forefront of Paula's mind. As much pleasure as it gave Paula in its creation, how grateful we are that she discovered such means to communicate her story.

"A child her wayward pencil drew
On margins of her book;
Garlands of flower, dancing elves,
Bud, butterfly, and brook,

> Lessons undone, and plum forgot,
> Seeking with hand and heart
> The teacher whom she learned to love
> Before she knew t'was Art"
> —Louisa May Alcott

Some people look at a child's canvas and see splotches of colour. Paula looked at a child's canvas and saw possibility. A yellow circle was more than that, it was a sunburst of colour to bring happiness to the day; a blue line represented the rippling of water as it crashed against the rocks. Paula saw talent waiting to be nurtured.

Written by her Childhood Friend, Susanne - 23 Hillside Ave.
A Teacher's Insight

I knew Paula all my life. Some of my earliest memories were of her and I playing Barbies together as most young girls do. She would come to my house with her little blue suitcase full of meticulously maintained doll clothes and her Barbies with their hair well-groomed and set in braids, and wait patiently while I pulled my Barbie from under the bed, hair askew and knotted, then help me give the doll a haircut so it once again looked presentable. Patience . . . Understanding . . . Tolerance . . . virtues she demonstrated that would later help her in her chosen career.

Then there were the days spent re-creating "it", or "it-it", our code of course for our two favourite shows, Dukes of Hazard and Fame. Fame was our ultimate favourite, and we'd sing and dance for hours, with our record player, Paula as Coco and me playing Doris. I think this speaks to the professional she became – a teacher dedicated to teaching through the Arts. Creativity . . . Drama . . . Flair . . . again, traits necessary for an effective teacher.

As she grew up, Paula stayed active in dance and art – skills she would have to be the creator that she was.

I wasn't at all surprised when Paula chose teaching as her career. She spoke passionately about the philosophy of education, the methods courses that were so important and continued to add a spark of creativity so vital to the profession. A teacher was born. I didn't have the opportunity to work directly with Paula, but that didn't stop me from getting a very clear picture of the professional she became.

When we did come together, discussions about learners, funny stories, successful students and a clear passion for work, was obvious. Aside from the influences in childhood, the creative opportunities available to her from home, the course work at school and the passion shown at work, I can stand here tonight and easily reflect on the empathetic, passionate and professional teacher that was Paula.

You see, after her horrific murder, my Mom helped Lynn one day in Paula's classroom. Not knowing who to bestow with some of her precious materials, to my utter joy, Lynn and Mom filled a tub with resources from Paula's classroom, resources that to another teacher, spoke volumes about who she was in the classroom. I was elated to become the recipient of many Math and Language Arts resources, books that motivate, correct and allow for so much creativity amongst the students. I was able to share these within my school and teachers use them frequently. Then I pulled out posters, decorations and notepads. All of these spoke to enhancing the classroom, making it a colourful, fun, cooperative place to be. The most beloved and telling thing to me though were the stamps and stamp pads that now take pride of place on my desk. Every theme, occasion, character and motivational thought you can think of, are represented. Here was a teacher who thought so much of her students that she had multitudes of simple yet effective items to motivate and strengthen their school experience. A dedicated professional, who showed with simple tools her dedication, empathy, strength and passion. Now, I only have to look at them to stay motivated, inspired and committed, just as Paula was.

Presented by Paula's vice principal at the opening of Paula's Place

It is with honour and sincere pleasure that I share these words about our greatly missed colleague and teacher, Paula Gallant.

I would like to share some excerpts from two appraisals I had the privilege to give of Ms. Gallant. I believe these comments capture the essence of her performance as a classroom teacher and shed light on her many attributes as an effective educator.

I quote, "Paula's overt personality and great sense of humour enable her to establish a positive classroom environment in which curiosity is engaged, performance is challenged and rewarded, and students are taught to think.

"It is apparent that Paula utilizes programs and support resources to develop and enhance creative, imaginative and effective learning. There is a classroom climate in which students feel safe and trusted to speak their thoughts, to risk putting into words free of criticism and ridicule.

"An important message is conveyed through the words of Helen Keller who stated, 'I believe that the welfare of each is bound up in the welfare of all.' Ms. Gallant strives through an integrated, interdisciplinary approach of teaching to create a team in which teacher and students are partners who understand and care for each other as a community of learners."

Additional feedback from Paula's school administrators on her performance as an educator

It is said it is a combination of many fine characteristics, utilized together, that create a good teacher. However, good teachers, also, keep up on knowledge and research that can be used to improve their classrooms. Ms. Gallant possesses worthy attributes such as empathy, enthusiasm, and confidence, as well as a sense of mission. Her strong feelings about the importance of education drive her to enhance her own skills as she is currently completing a course at NSCAD and has sought the support of the school's math mentor to hone skills related to the instruction of mathematics. Paula uses all the resources she can get her hands on and collects knowledge so that her classroom runs smoothly and effectively. Perhaps one of the most important characteristics of a good teacher is organization. Organization is crucial to classroom management. Paula provides the structure needed to make students comfortable and at the same time minimize downtime. Students are aware of the exact consequences of their actions and behave accordingly. Her strength in this area has been offered, as well, to the school's discipline team.

Paula organized a walking group, recycling team, created an after-hours art program for her students, was on a number of school committees and was a member of the Fabulous Five Lunch Club. This was one of her favourite times as a teacher . . . five primary teachers who taught their students off "campus" as the BLT Elementary School had run out of room. No administrators on site and they were a cohesive team all working in union with the same teaching philosophies and lunch club passion!

Paula was a vocal advocate for her kids in need. In her classroom there was no use of erasers, as it was okay to colour outside the lines. She reached kids through non-traditional means, using art as one of her biggest avenues to engage students. Paula deeply committed to improving public school curriculum, and wildly passionate about art and ensuring it remained part of it. She became the person who professionally said what everybody was thinking and was afraid to say, particularly about the systematic cutting of the art curriculum in schools. So when they were going to a staff meeting, Paula would speak out. Sometimes that didn't win her any favours, but she didn't care because it was all about what was best for the children. As much as Paula respected the curriculum outcomes, she would deviate when necessary. A big part of the curriculum that she brought into the school was the love of art. Parents would regularly write her notes explaining that she reached children through art.

Written by Catherine, Miss Gallant's former student

Paula Gallant was an amazing teacher who taught her students so many things that have helped to create who we all are today. All her students can think back and remember all the jokes she used to play on her students and fellow colleagues, always giving everyone a little laugh. Paula was always there to listen and give advice when her students were feeling down, and if you ask any of Paula's former students, they would tell you how much she loved everyone, and how much they loved her.

Any teacher can teach the required curriculum, but it takes a special person to reach their students and teach them life lessons they will be thankful for, for the rest of their lives. Ms. Gallant taught her students respect, what is right and wrong, to love yourself and others, and to always be fair. Paula loved art and was an amazing artist who inspired her students with the art she created. She encouraged her students to express themselves through their own artwork, and even held after-school art classes to spend time teaching and creating art with the students at BLT. She taught us to see the beauty in everything, in every person, and every season.

Written by Samantha, Miss Gallant's former student

Paula was my teacher, my favourite teacher. I was just thinking about Paula yesterday when I overheard a stranger saying "clear as mud?" That was a phrase Paula would always say during our classes. I think about Paula often. I have found connections with her over many years. That may be a dragonfly landing on me, my desire to continue working with watercolour paints (I still remember tips she gave me back in elementary school). I remember her stories she told our class. One in particular that stands out to me is she was asked to paint a portrait using UV light in her own art class. She painted a self-portrait of herself with her pregnant belly, in a rocking chair. I remember seeing the beautiful

Paula's Classroom door at BLT School

portrait she painted (in different colours because the UV light distorted them). I listened and watched Paula intently. She was my role model; she felt like more than a teacher to me. When I think of Paula, I think of her peacefully sitting in a rocking chair with her beautiful big smile. I remember writing about Paula in my high school English class. My teacher came over and gave me a hug. She was close to Paula (Mrs. MacMillan-Turner). We shared memories with each other, and both have examples where we have felt her presence. She was a beautiful person. I will be thinking of Paula and her family today, and always.

Written by Jenna, Miss Gallant's former student

Miss Gallant was a great teacher and she loved life. Every Friday she gave us treats special if we were good. If we got 25 days in a row of incident free we got donuts.

Miss Gallant was a very good singer. She loved to sing in class a lot. Her famous song is jingle bell rock. Mrs. Gallant was a really good artist. She said we were good artists too. Miss Gallant was very beautifull. She had a daughter named Anna. On Halloween Anna was the great pumpkin. For Christmas Anna was the great gift. Miss Gallant taught us how to make candy dishes for our parents. She also had a dog named Cody. Cody is really cute. Miss Gallant was funny and forgettfull. She loved to play jokes on us. Miss Gallant was also very fun. I loved having Miss Gallant as a teacher.

THE END

Love, Jenna

Letter from a student

On September 14th, 2023, eighteen years after Paula's death, I woke up to this note in Facebook Messenger and my heart filled, once again, with so much pride and admiration for my sister Paula, who touched so many lives through her years as a teacher.

Written by Brandon, Miss Gallant's former student

My name is Brandon Boyd. I'm from Halifax, Nova Scotia. I used to be one of the students of the late Paula Gallant. She was a wonderful teacher, and a wonderful human being. When I was little and was going through the early stage of my autism, she taught me how to communicate by drawing. I still live in the same community of the school where she taught and every time I go on walks, I pass by and remember her. I have currently been working in the film industry because I'm very passionate about storytelling. I just want to reach out to you and other family members of the Gallant family to pay respects and share my story about how much of an inspiration she was in my life.

When Paula's Place opened in 2006 it was a reminder to everyone that Paula is still with us. Paula is watching over that art room and has witnessed all the talent that has been brought out in it and will be watching for all the future talent to blossom within Paula's Place. Paula's Place is a happy environment that holds so much of what Ms. Gallant loved. Students feel invited and comforted, just like students felt entering Room 104, and all the other classrooms Paula taught in.

Seeing Paula's signature P on a car warms my heart knowing that the community and so many around HRM are continuously showing their support and keeping the memory of Paula alive. Tonight is a huge step in spreading awareness of Paula's story and domestic violence, and giving these women back their voice.

Brandon's note highlights how he fulfilled his creative journey through resilience, perseverance, passion, and Paula's role in his life. This note and all the others demonstrate how through her love of teaching, compassion for her students, and belief that art in the classroom makes a difference in how children learn has allowed Paula's legacy as a teacher to live on. Even before she was a substitute teacher driving here, there and everywhere, and before she had her own classroom, there were big comfy armchairs and Paula took delight in teaching her nephews, Tim, Connor, and Dylan just about anything—reading, baking, and even basketball.

Paula was a magnet for the curious and gifted with a natural talent to meet students where they were. Forever remembered as a teacher, she continues to impact the lives of so many children in and out of her classroom. But there were very specific children who she longed to teach, that Paula had dreamt about teaching since she was a little girl, and those were her very own children.

Paula Reading to Dylan. Below Paula reading to Tim and Connor

Come Meet Paula - As a Muse

Lynn MacEachern, who was inspired to create Paula's P and is the author of many writings on Paula's website, is another Glace Bay family friend. Lynn is almost family, as her husband was a long-time friend of our dad's. Paula used to babysit her kids—Jeff, Andrea, and Grant—and as if that wasn't enough, Lynn's son Jeff married Alain's daughter Marci—see, almost family! I spent countless hours, night after night, on the phone with Lynn during my darkest, loneliest hours, as I didn't want to go to sleep, but the bond between Lynn and Paula was especially deep. In fact, Paula sent her last email to Lynn on December 23rd, 2005, where she shared her joy about being a mom and the excitement of buying a new house. Lynn has been so deeply involved in all aspects of our trauma and healing journey that she was inspired to use poetry to capture her own feelings. I will let Lynn use her own words to describe her collection:

During the brightest season of the year, my darkest hour was born . . . Dec. 27, 2005. That is when life as I saw it, was forever changed. My understanding of why bad things happen to good people became ever present. To help me work through the emotions of this tragedy, I put pen to paper. My words reflect sadness and grief as well as pain over the realization that Paula's heart was entrusted to someone who did not care for it.

I STILL CALL YOUR NAME
I don't see your face
I can't feel your pain
I don't hear your voice
But,
I
Still
Call
Your
Name

My Darkest Hour
During the brightest season of the year
My darkest hour was born;

A heart that once beat strong and happy
From my life, was forever torn.

Why did you have to leave, and
How can memories be so sweet;
Why did we not see the signs –
Life has become so incomplete.

How could we ever count the bitter tears
You shed on countless nights,
And who could measure the harshness of words
Spoken during the myriad of fights.

Tell me how I make sense
Of something I don't understand
Why you held this cold, dark secret; clasped,
In the safety of your trembling hand.

You wore your shame like a blanket of false pride,
While tears gathered in your heart

Silently,
Privately,
       You cried.

Without you here I now see how fragile life can be
And – even tho you've gone away,
Under cover of dark and in my heart,
I relive yesterday.

If Only Walls Could Talk

If only walls could talk,
the stories they would tell,
of a girl who bravely smiled each day
while living in such hell.

If windows all had voices
to whisper in our ear,
perhaps we would have noticed
a marriage filled with fear.

We might have stilled the monster
who lay in shadows dark
Waiting —
he pounced upon her defenseless and broken heart.

Naive.
Alone.
      Broken.

She saw him through blind eyes.
She couldn't believe he'd hurt her, nor
ever, make her cry.

With hands drawn cold & hard around her neck, he clasped.
Blind.
      Frozen in fear.
           She fought.

Her last breath she did gasp.

And as she did,
those dreams held close - which seemed so very right,
proved to be the greatest fight
of her precious, short-lived life.

How does he look in her child's face
and not see her mother's eyes?
How does he carry on, day-by-day
and not hear her final cries?

How does he hold his head so high
when walking down the street?
As the sun is slowly sinking

His undoing

    Was her feet.

Letting Go
While life is meant for living
It's hard to let go of the past,
Especially as I seek out those ever-elusive
Pieces *of you* – something that will last.

In the stillness of night I call your name,
With outstretched arms I reach;
But reality quickly comes crashing in -
Violent, rolling waves upon a beach.

Everything happens for a reason and,
Once upon a time life was gray,
But now I realize it is black and white
And that night moves into day.

Warmth is now a dream of you
Which usually comes to be,
During those unsuspecting times –
A solo dance with me.

Within My Memory, Caught
Just beneath the surface lies your memory - so wonderful, so
    soft.
Your beauty is now but a whisper that remains within the web
    of my memory,
caught.

Others have moved on, not stopping to see my sadness, my
    grief, my pain.
How I wish they saw you as I do when at night
you call my name.

I cry for you and for memories left undone - so much left to say.
I strain to hear you whisper even tho you have gone
so very far away.

I can't help but wonder what it's like in that place you now call home.
Do you see the movements of this lost drifter –
seeking you as I roam?

You brought so much to life dear friend;
eyes once sealed shut can now see the beauty you lived each day – but
nobody will ever know what you meant to me.

So now dear friend, sleep.
In love's embrace may you forever soar, happy and free.
And when you hear me whisper your name, know

That I am but a shadow of what I used to be.

At Night She Comes
He lured her in.
Deftly, methodically, he spun his thread.
He built rooms of deceit and fraud
Within his toxic web.

Oblivious. In love. Blind.
She fell for his devious game;
Now, all that remains is one child, smaller . . .
Smaller, yet the same.

From above at night, she now watches.
Eyes never deviating from her mark.
A great tiger . . . she waits
How he's grown to fear the dark.

Distant voice . . .
I hear you calling his name -

Does he hear your silent teardrops
As you unravel his deadly game?

And so now you sadly ask
"Is this someone else's dream"?
You can't believe you would fade away and . . .
I can't believe this nightmare was ever meant to be.

dark prince
in restless dreams he walks –
alone, years on end, who knows how long?
memories creep through his mind during the darkest hour of the night.
sleep deprived, the seeds are planted;
doubt . . . regret . . . fear.

be wary the memories of night,
watch not to call out - for the echoes will call back;
dare not to dream, dark prince
remain conscious - for she will come back to you

Harvest of Life
I see your pictures and am torn
Between feelings of happiness, thankfulness
and the pangs of grief and despair.

We have lost so much and yet gained -
For you lived loving life, loving you, loving all
Still you teach, and still we learn.

You sowed the seeds of living in 'now'
Do you not see us reap the fruits of our angst
As you smile upon the harvest of our life?

And my mind is now closed.
So many *I love you*'s left unsaid, memories never shared
For you aren't here anymore.

Come Meet Paula - As a Mom
Written by Lana Kenny

From the very first, precious moment that Paula found out she was pregnant in May 2004, she kept a special journal. Writing and reflecting allowed Paula to be present and savour every single day of her pregnancy, her birth experience and those amazing, early days and months with her darling baby Anna.

Paula told us about her pregnancy on May 20, 2004. Paula had known for a few weeks but wanted to ensure there were no complications in the early stages of her pregnancy. Paula beamed with pride and excitement when she announced her news and it didn't take long for a family pool to be created with the baby's weight, size and gender.

From day one, Paula was 110% dedicated to doing everything to support, protect and nourish her growing baby by eating well and exercising. Thankfully, Paula was healthy throughout her pregnancy and was able to spend many hours on walks and hikes with her dog Coady, by her side. Paula kept busy that summer preparing for her baby's arrival by getting the nursery ready, assembling furniture and washing and folding tiny outfits. We hosted a baby shower for her in November 2004 and from her family and friends she received many beautiful gifts, which Paula expertly used to decorate the nursery in an apple-red-and-tan theme.

When the time came, Lynn was by Paula's side during labour and birth, helping her as our mom would have had she still been alive. On January 6, 2005, "Anna Paul" was born at 3:05 a.m., weighing 7 lbs 9 oz and measuring 21 inches long. Anna was named after the two most important people in Paula's life—our mom, Dianne, and our dad, Paul, and it was a very fitting tribute as Anna turned out to be the last grandchild. Paul answered the phone, when Paula called to share her good news with us. With her fatigue and utter elation, Paula said Anna's first and second name rather fast, almost as if it was one name. So, for a split second, Paul thought Paula had called her daughter "An Apple." We still chuckle when we tell that story! As soon as we could, our families went to visit the newest addition to the Gallant family at the hospital. Paula dedicated her journal that day to Anna.

Paula and her sweet Anna by the window

You are absolutely perfect. It was the most amazing night of my life and my heart grew a hundred times with the instant love I felt for you. Anna, the second you were born, my life changed for the better. You are named after the two most important people in my life. I am so sad you will never get to meet them. I hope the stories I can tell you will do them justice. Meeting your dad allowed me to trust again. Now, meeting you has shown me the bond between mother and a child. No matter what the next one hundred years bring us, you can always count on me and Dad. I love you so much.

In these same journals, Paula often wrote how she promised Anna she would keep her safe, protected and happy throughout her life Anna was a colicky baby which made those first few weeks difficult, as sleep wasn't really possible. In the absence of our own mom, and with the Mom-type role that Lynn naturally adopted, we all agreed that she would be called Gramma. With that title bestowed, Lynn jumped into the role with glee, and would take Anna in those early days so Paula could get caught up on her rest. Having young families was just another reason, us, 7 Coady Street sisters spent a lot of time together, usually congregating at Lynn and Alain's house for supper and playtime amongst the cousins. There was nothing we sisters wouldn't do for each other before we became moms, *but this was especially true now that we all had children.* As older sisters tend to do, Lynn and I offered Paula a-l-o-t of advice—which Paula would graciously accept with a grain of salt, even if she didn't agree with it.

Like all first-time moms, Paula put a lot of love and attention into planning Anna's baptism, her first Easter outfit, attending church, and playdates with friends from college and neighbours who had babies close in age. Paula went back to work in September so she could set up her classroom, with plans to take the rest of her maternity leave in January. Paula took great care to arrange childcare during school hours and while she was enrolled at the Nova Scotia College of Art and Design doing her Visual Arts Certification for teachers. During the summer of 2005, Paula planned trips for Anna to meet family and friends. First, was a trip to Cape Breton, then to PEI, where both were celebrated and spoiled by our extended family. Paula was giddy preparing for Anna's first Halloween as a pumpkin, and of course, planning for her baby girl's first Christmas.

Grammie, Anna & Paula PEI

As my daughter Emily was born in May 2004, I was still on maternity leave when Anna was born, which meant Paula and I were fortunate to be able to spend a lot of time together in the early months. We were close as sister, but being new moms at the same time brought us even closer. I can easily remember the excitement and joy Paula felt about being a mom because I shared that sentiment with her nearly every day. We would take our children to Mom and Baby groups at the Tantallon Library, have picnics and take long walks. As new and busy moms we had many meals together, sometimes planned, and sometimes spontaneous if one of us couldn't face cooking that night. We ran errands and shopped together and sometimes for each other, just to get out of the house some days, even during snowstorms! We took our baby girls to visit Paula's school, where the students could meet "Miss Gallant's baby." There were also many long days spent at Lynn and Alain's pool that summer, just revelling in this special time in our lives and each other's company. As sisters who were also best friends, we talked about how wonderful it was that our little girls would grow up together and become best friends just like we did. We would daydream about the girls having sleepovers at each other's houses, going trick-or-treating together, and being completely spoiled by "Gramma" Lynn who only had boys and already couldn't resist buying matching outfits. The timing of Emily and Anna's births, made everyone feel so lucky.

Without a doubt, Paula loved seeing the "boys" spending time with baby Anna. Tim and Connor fed her and loved rocking her to sleep. Dylan would lovingly call her "Little Mouse Head" because she was so tiny. Emily, being eight whole months older, was fascinated by baby Anna and kept trying to pull Anna's soother out of her mouth. Of course, no one can forget how Paula's ever-present fur baby, Coady, was always around to watch over Anna when everyone was visiting.

Cousin Love, Emily, Tim, Dylan, Anna, Connor

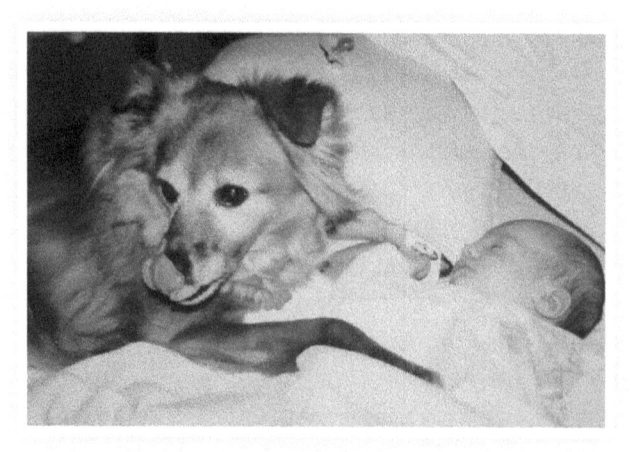

Coady watches over baby Anna

During Anna's first 11 months, Paula had taken hundreds of pictures and written so many short stories about what it was like being a mom and the silly antics Anna got up to. As they are written down, these memories can never be lost, and stand as a testament to how deliriously happy Paula was to be a mom and how she loved Anna with her whole being. As her family, we are ever so grateful for the journal and pictures that Paula captured of their life together.

Paula's writings have allowed Anna to learn how very much she was cherished through her mom's own words, and we hope she can feel Paula's unconditional love and acceptance through them. Anna has heard all about what a wonderful mom, sister, aunt, teacher and friend she was and the lasting impression Paula left on so many people. Through Paula's journals, Anna has discovered that Paula had two dreams for the future: being a good teacher and becoming a mom, which came true with her birth. Paula wanted Anna to be surrounded by the love of our family and to always be within the circle of care we have for each other. In October 2010, Anna came to live us. And just like Paula and I dreamed about, Anna and Emily grew up as sisters, with Dylan as their protective older brother. Never far away in thoughts or deeds, Lynn, Alain, Tim and Conner have been and continue to be a huge part of Anna's life, sharing in all our family celebrations. It was the happiest ending we could have ever hoped for in this senseless tragedy. The five cousins were united forever.

Emily, Tim, Dylan, Connor, Anna

While everyone misses Paula with their whole hearts, I especially miss having Paula to grow into motherhood with me, as our journeys were meant to run in parallel. We were all set to share the adventures of raising our girls to be best friends, and successful women, just as we, ourselves were. Naturally, Anna has grown in Paula's absence, every one of her "firsts" brought pride and joy to our whole family. For Lynn and me, a tiny sliver of what we hope is private grief, always followed these "firsts," as our sister's absence is felt so deeply with each one. Throughout Anna's life, we have always tried to maintain a circle of care and shroud of positivity as she navigates life without her beautiful mom. I can only ever hope we have succeeded.

The Kenny Family

Afterwards - Love Brings Peace

"She is somewhere in the sunlight strong, her tears are in the falling rain, she calls me in the wind's soft song and with the flowers she comes again." —Unknown

For many, many years, I questioned why my parents died so young. Why did they both die of a somewhat rare condition, just three years apart? I feel in my heart that I know now. I know both my parents had to go so they could be there waiting for Paula. Whatever is beyond this life, I realize now that Paula would need comfort from both Mom and Dad to get through how she left this place. This thought offers me comfort in the darkest of dark hours and a sense of peace that has allowed me to continue to breathe.

Paula's Headstone

Given the tragic way Paula's life ended and the needless delay in getting a conviction, we delayed having a graveside service and chose not to mark Paula's grave with a headstone until it was time for peace to prevail. On September 15th, 2012, we held a beautiful memorial service for Paula at the St. Margaret's of Scotland Cemetery in Glen Haven, Nova Scotia, followed by a reception at my family's home. During the service, Holly Chisholm performed an Alan Jackson song called *Sissy's Song*, and the words still echo in my mind.

> "She flew up to Heaven on the wings of angels By the clouds and stars and passed where no one sees And she walks with Jesus and her loved ones waiting And I know she's smiling saying Don't worry 'bout me"

Release of Doves

At the end of the service, Anna, Emily, and Dylan released white doves, followed by other doves released from baskets around Paula's headstone. These beautiful birds which symbolize hope, love, and peace circled overhead in the beautiful blue sky and Paula's presence was felt by all.

There were two very special moments that we will never forget. The first was when Anna saw a dragonfly pass by during the service, which brought tears to many as they represent resilience and transformation. The second was when Anna released her dove. This well-trained messenger bird ignored its natural instinct to take flight and instead lingered and walked back and forth between Anna and Paula's headstone. It was like the bird was delivering a message, that perhaps Paula wanted her presence to be known. The Smith family, who had released these amazing birds for years, had never experienced this before and saw this as a "sign." And we have seen many such signs since Paula's death—all messages of love, perseverance and peace.

Including the sign it was time to write this book.

Kairos, chance, and fate, all suggested it was time for me to write this book, especially since Anna is a young woman now, preparing to start her own story. Lana and I hope that with Paula's full, true story in print, Anna's life will never be overshadowed by the darkness and supposition of how her mother's life ended. Instead, she will be able to stand in her own unique and glorious light, knowing she comes from goodness, love, and joy.

My other hope is that this book will allow Paula's legacy to stand on its own, outside of any one person, and allow my sister's beautiful spirit to outlive the senselessness that ended her life. My wish is to ensure the lessons in advocacy and fairness are not forgotten and in some way can be a resource for others. Perhaps there is a small part of me which hopes that with this book I can pass along the torch of justice that I have carried for so long. If this book can be a place for Paula's irresistible zest for life to live on, to continue to inspire and to teach, well then, it will also be my gift to our family and friends.

Paula's life began with a tremendous amount—almost a surreal amount—of love amongst our family and our Coady Street clan. I wanted an ending to truly capture Paula's spirit, the boundless love she extended, and the love that enveloped us throughout this journey, all because of Paula's generous heart. Through Paula, we witnessed and continue to feel this profound truth—because she gave love so freely, we receive it abundantly.

To those who have lost someone to intimate partner violence, to those who are experiencing the same pain we did, I want to say: *With love, you have the power to persevere.* I want people to understand that they are not alone, and to seek help when needed.

I want to end with a tribute to who Paula was. Her legacy of love offers hope, even in the midst of sadness and grief. Through her, we find the strength to carry on, knowing that love is the most enduring legacy of all.

Paula proved, without a shadow of a doubt, that love conquers all.

About the Author

Lynn Gallant Blackburn

In December 2005, Paula Gallant, a 36-year-old mother and grade three teacher, was tragically murdered in Halifax. This devastating loss changed the course of Lynn's life. Inspired by Paula's life and legacy, Lynn is determined to find purpose in her sister's untimely death.

Lynn advocates for victims' rights, raises awareness about the impacts of violent crime, and actively works to end men's violence against women and girls. Through her personal experiences, she seeks to offer comfort and insight to other victims of domestic violence, reminding them they are not alone.

Milton Keynes UK
Ingram Content Group UK Ltd.
UKHW030937301124
451950UK00007B/94

9 781779 620705